THE EXPERIENCE ECONOMY

www.royalcollins.com

THE EXPERIENCE ECONOMY

Sun Yingxue

Books Beyond Boundaries
ROYAL COLLINS

The Experience Economy

By Sun Yingxue

First published in 2026 by Royal Collins Publishing Group Inc.
Groupe Publication Royal Collins Inc.
550-555 boul. René-Lévesque O Montréal (Québec) H2Z1B1 Canada

10 9 8 7 6 5 4 3 2 1

ISBN: 978-1-4878-1358-1

To find out more about our publications, please visit www.royalcollins.com.

Contents

Chapter III

TRANSFORMATION OF TRADITIONAL ENTERPRISES IN THE EXPERIENCE ECONOMY / 157

Chapter IV

SOCIAL DEVELOPMENT IN THE EXPERIENCE ECONOMY / 219

Preface

The river of human history has been flowing for millennia. Throughout this great journey, we have waged continuous struggles on two fronts. Confronted by the harsh and unforgiving forces of nature, humanity has overcome countless obstacles with courage and determination, forging a path of survival through innovation and ingenuity. In parallel, we have faced the profound mysteries of our own existence, delving into the enigma of birth, life, and meaning. Through bold exploration and deep introspection, we have sought answers to the most pressing questions of human existence.

As we stand on the threshold of a new era, it feels as though we are poised on a brilliant dividing line in history. Before continuing our march forward, we cannot help but pause and reflect. In the past five thousand years of struggle, humanity has largely solved the material challenges of survival. The focus of our efforts now must shift toward the progress of the human spirit, toward a new chapter in our development. The sages of the past have opened spiritual doors for us, but much of the energy dedicated to addressing our material needs has limited our ability to explore these spiritual treasures. Now, we finally find ourselves in a position to delve deeper into the wisdom left by our ancestors.

At this juncture, our attention turns inward, back to the very nature of humanity. As the most intelligent creatures on Earth, how do we engage with ourselves and the world around us? Where do our profound thoughts and emotions originate? How do our ideas and feelings evolve daily through these interactions? What makes each individual unique, and why, despite having solved the problem of material survival, do we still grapple with suffering and dissatisfaction? What, ultimately, is the key to human happiness? These are the central questions that will guide the progress of human society in the new era.

To answer these questions, we must begin by examining human itself. Much like blind men feeling different parts of an elephant, we take individual human experiences as the primary focus in studying mental life. By analyzing how emotions arise, we begin to uncover the greater mystery of human happiness. The experience is examined iteratively in terms of different levels of need, time, quantification, and speed of change. The elements that comprise happiness are then discussed.

In a manner analogous to how our predecessors studied the material world through mathematics, we endeavor to investigate the potential of mathematical methods for measuring human experience, with the aim of offering insights that are both thought-provoking and illuminating. In examining human socioeconomic activity, we re-examine the evolving nature of the fundamental economic elements from an experiential standpoint. The advent of new times necessitates the development of novel economic theories. As an increasing number of individuals prioritize quality of life over basic necessities such as food and clothing, experience is poised to emerge as a pivotal factor influencing economic activities. This shift will be accompanied by a comprehensive and structural transformation across the supply chain, the demand space, and the manner in which supply and demand interact. To ensure our social development aligns with this emerging trend, it is imperative to conduct extensive research, analysis, and the codification of rules and regulations.

In this book, the author presents a bold proposal for an analytical framework for the experience economy. The framework is then used to analyze and discuss a number of key issues, including the quantification of utility, the new characteristics of demand and supply, the characteristics and elements of the experience era, the changes in consumer surplus and producer surplus after being affected by the experience, and the changes in the mode of production in the experience era.

In light of the aforementioned, we anticipate a comprehensive examination of pivotal matters pertaining to social operations within the context of the experience economy. These include, but are not limited to, the following: the education issue, the issue of artificial intelligence (AI) emotionalization, the issue of enterprise reform and transformation, the issue of national culture experience, and the issue of virtual and real-world experience.

In addition, based on years of observation in the mobile internet industry, we present preliminary considerations and analyses on the specific experience performance, production process, and value assessment issues in specific industries.

This book presents an outline of the subject matter. In the course of composing this text, it has become increasingly evident that the experience economy is a vast and complex subject. Its advancement necessitates the collaborative efforts of experts and scholars from diverse disciplinary backgrounds, industries, and fields over an extended period.

The primary objective of this book is to courageously expose the subject matter and present a comprehensive overview of the most illuminating research methodologies for your consideration. It is my conviction that as human society continues to develop and progress, and as the profound wisdom of each individual gradually awakens, the future that will propel all of humanity to ultimate happiness and integration in the spiritual realm is imminent. The anticipation of that future is the fundamental motivation for my dedication to the study of the experience economy, and it is also the fundamental significance of my writing this book.

CHAPTER I

Experience

I. Definition of Experience

"Experience" (体验) in Chinese consists of two characters: 体 and 验. 体 refers to the body and is typically understood to encompass physical observation and personal experience. 验, as referenced in the *Shuowen Jiezi* (说文解字), is the name of a specific type of horse, and in the *Kangxi Dictionary · Hai Collection Part I · Radical Horse* (康熙字典 · 亥集上 · 马部), it primarily denotes confirmation, verification, examination, and inspection. Together, they make the word 体验, which is employed in conjunction with these concepts to signify the practical verification and examination through physical force and personal experience.

The term "experience" is frequently employed as a synonym for "feel," "sense," and "undergo." Yet it carries two distinctive connotations. The first is, similar to feeling and sensation, the perception and experience that occur through the interaction of the human body's senses with the outside world. Second, it denotes the process of testing and verifying ideas or perceptions through lived engagement.

In contemporary practice, the term experience is frequently employed in conjunction with the words "user" or "customer" to form phrases such as user experience or customer experience, which are utilized to summarize and describe the comprehensive perception that products and services evoke in users or customers. The distinction between user experience and customer experience lies in their respective focus. User experience is oriented toward the end user of a product or service, whereas customer experience is centered on the purchaser of the product or service. In either case, the emphasis remains on how people perceive and engage with a product or service firsthand.

The term "*experience*" should therefore be examined from two perspectives. The first is its affective dimension, referring to personal perception and feeling. The second is its evaluative dimension, referring to the testing and validation of ideas or phenomena.

II. Analysis of the Feeling Aspect of Experience

The human experience of feeling can be conceptualized as comprising two distinct levels: The first is the sensory level, which encompasses the direct contact and access to information, afforded by the human body and its sensory organs, with the external world. For the sake of convenience, this level may be referred to as the sensory level of feeling. It represents the primary and first-hand information that individuals obtain from their external environment. The second level is the emotional level, which encompasses the processing and analysis of information by the human brain, as well as the feelings that this information evokes.

All human senses originate from five primary sense organs: the eyes, ears, nose, tongue, and body (including the skin, muscles, bones, and other internal organs). The eyes are responsible for perceiving color, the ears for hearing sounds, the nose for detecting aromas, the tongue for tasting flavors, and the body for touch. In addition to these basic five senses, there is also the processing of thought through the brain, often referred to as consciousness. It is first necessary to observe how the senses function and the sequence of their various stages.

For instance, for the eye to perceive color, a number of conditions must be met for the eye to interact with the external environment and produce sensations:

(1) The material characteristics of the eye itself should be sound. In addition to perceiving light, the eye must also be capable of discerning color. A deficiency in either the light or color sense will result in corresponding alterations in the perception of light and color.
(2) In order to view the external scene, certain conditions must be met. First, the external light must meet the brightness requirements for viewing. Second, the scene must possess a visible range of light reflection characteristics. Third, the scene must be at a certain necessary distance from the eyes.
(3) The act of viewing is a conscious decision. This is reflected in two aspects: First, the eyes must be open. Second, the viewer must be aware of the act of viewing. If the viewer is in a state of daze or lost in thought, although the

eyes are open and the conditions for viewing are met, the viewer is unable to focus their attention and form an effective sense.

Once the fundamental prerequisites have been established, the viewer is able to engage in a state of focused observation. This viewing process may be conceptualized as a camera capturing an image of the external environment. The human eye enables the viewer to transform the visual fragment of the outside world into a sensory-acceptable image that can be processed by the brain. The objects and situations observed undergo a transformation as a result of the shift in the viewer's attention.

For instance, the viewer may direct their gaze to the entirety of the landscape outside the window, encompassing the verdant hills, trees, and lake. Alternatively, they may focus on a specific bird or flower situated in close proximity to the window. The eye is inherently reliable in its ability to reflect what it is capable of perceiving. Subsequently, the images captured by the eye are conveyed to the brain, where they serve as the foundation for further processing and organization. Once this material has been processed, the sensation of the scene is fully formed.

In this context, feeling is understood to be constituted by two elements: sense and perception. The sense is analogous to the photographic function of the eye, whereas the perception represents the subsequent processing of the content captured by the sense within the human brain. Once within the brain, the image is separated from the original object or scene. The lake continues to flow, the bird flies away, and the sun sets, yet the captured image is stored in the memory module of the human brain.

Upon the rapid capture of a scene by the eyes, the brain will immediately identify the initial image. It distinguishes and extracts the basic features of an object, such as color, shape, texture, among other characteristics, by matching and responding to them based on past experience. It then proceeds to recognize and extract the fundamental components of the visual scene, namely the mountain, lake, tree, bird, and sky. Simultaneously, the brain assesses the condition of these entities, determining whether the mountain is elevated or depressed, verdant or arid, and the extent of the lake, whether it is a narrow pond or an expansive body of water, and whether the sky is either clear or overcast.

Subsequent to these preliminary observations, the viewer can make some first judgments based on the lushness of the mountains, determining that the current season is spring or summer rather than fall or winter. Additionally, the viewer can ascertain the weather based on the sky. If the viewer's past experience and current emotions are involved, more complex feelings may result.

For example, a landscape reminiscent of one's childhood hometown may evoke a sense of nostalgia, while a cloudy and rainy day may evoke feelings of sadness. This kind of deeper feeling is typically referred to as empathy in the field of literary creation. Empathy is used to describe the emotional resonance caused by viewing objective scenery. This kind of emotion is pervasive in Tang and Song poems. For example, "Sorrow for national affair, flowers spill tears. / Regret for parting, birds feel soul stirring" and "Chirping of late-fall cicadas are melancholy. / In the evening, at the front is a roadside pavilion. / A bout of sudden shower has just stopped." These scenes evoke human emotions and poets portray them through the scenes.

The process of perception through different senses—hearing with the ears, smelling with the nose, tasting with the tongue, and touching with the body—is strikingly similar to seeing colors with the eyes. Each sense follows a comparable mechanism of sensation but differs in how the sensory organs interact with their respective objects.

A key distinction among the senses lies in the proximity required between the sensory organ and the object of perception. Smelling, tasting, and touching usually demand immediate, direct contact (as in the case of smelling, where scent molecules directly interact with the olfactory receptors). In contrast, seeing and hearing involve some degree of spatial separation, with perception varying depending on the distance.

Beyond the individual senses, our experience of the world is shaped by the harmonious interplay of all five senses. Over time, perceptions of the same environment may shift, influenced by changes in circumstances or the passage of time. Yet, at any given moment, our attention can only fully engage with one sense. Despite this, the human ability to rapidly shift focus among senses creates an impression of simultaneous multi-sensory perception over a span of time.

Take, for example, standing on a lawn at dusk. One might notice the gradual drop in temperature, the subtle shifts in the breeze, and the delightful aroma of meals being prepared as families light their stoves. In essence, the formation of sensations can be explored through four key dimensions or perspectives:

(1) The five senses (sight, hearing, smell, taste, and touch) as unique dimensions.
(2) Static and dynamic sensations. While static sensations, such as those evoked by photographs or paintings, are relatively rare, most sensory experiences in daily life are dynamic.
(3) The temporal dimension. Sensory experiences are deeply tied to the flow of time, encompassing the present moment while also connecting to memories

of the past or aspirations for the future. This temporal dimension not only shapes how we feel now but also links current sensations to emotional experiences across time. For example, the joy of eating a sweet cake might evoke fond memories of a childhood when one's mother baked cakes. Similarly, an aspiration to attend a prestigious university may present feelings about current academic performance, forging a connection between the present and the future.

(4) Shared vs. individual sensations. Sensory experiences can be classified into shared and individual sensations. Shared sensations are those rooted in the universal physical nature of the human body, leading to relatively consistent experiences across individuals. Boiling water feels hot, ice feels cold, loud sounds can irritate, and toxic substances often have unpleasant odors. Individual sensations, however, vary greatly from person to person. A red flower might be perceived as beautiful by some and unappealing by others. Similarly, the same symphony may inspire passion and excitement in one listener while leaving another feeling indifferent or even sleepy.

The "feeling" aspect of sensation, as commonly understood, refers to the various combinations of one or more of the five sensory dimensions mentioned earlier. These combinations, shaped by the immense variety of specific objects and experiences, are constantly evolving, producing an endless array of sensations. Does this mean that "feeling" is too elusive to comprehend or analyze? Not necessarily. In everyday life, when people speak of their experiences, they usually refer to specific individuals, objects, or events. This specificity, grounded in the tangible and unique characteristics of the subject, introduces a certain level of regularity, allowing sensations to be grasped and analyzed despite their inherent variability.

The "perception" aspect of sensation, however, calls for a more nuanced exploration. Typically, once sensory information enters the brain but before it prompts external actions, a series of cognitive processes take place. These processes fall under the realm of "perception." Sequentially, perception can be categorized into the following stages:

(1) Recognitional perception. The fundamental identification of "what" the object is.
(2) Discriminative perception. The evaluation of whether the object elicits a positive or negative feeling—judging it as good or bad.

(3) Analytical perception. A deeper, reflective stage where earlier judgments are reconsidered in light of past experiences. This involves confirming, refining, or overturning previous conclusions, often with varying degrees of complexity.
(4) Operational perception. The final stage is where a decision is made based on the analysis, influencing subsequent verbal and physical actions.

Of these stages, the initial recognition and the final operational phases involve relatively straightforward cognitive processes. The heart of perception, where the richest and most intricate human experiences unfold, lies in the discriminative and analytical phases. It is here that all emotions—dynamic and multifaceted—arise, making these phases the most profound and valuable areas for deeper study and understanding.

Let us delve into the stage of discriminative perception—the point at which we judge whether something is good or bad. This stage, which involves assessing the sensory "feeling" of an object, is grounded in certain criteria that already exist in a person's mind. These criteria are shaped by a combination of innate instincts and the cumulative influence of life experiences.

The innate aspect is instinctive and universal. From birth, humans exhibit a natural aversion to harmful or toxic substances, a reflexive resistance to anything detrimental to their well-being, and an inherent inclination to seek out people, objects, or situations that are beneficial. As individuals grow, their responses gradually evolve from instinct-driven reflexes to learned, more nuanced expressions, particularly as they develop language skills.

Once language emerges, children begin to learn the names of objects and gain the ability to articulate increasingly complex thoughts and emotions through both words and gestures. This linguistic capability allows them to more fully understand the guidance of adults, while simultaneously absorbing the subtle influences of the people and environment around them.

Studies in psychoanalysis have repeatedly shown that early life experiences leave a deep and lasting imprint, shaping cognitive patterns that influence a person's worldview and decision-making. Analyzing the family background and upbringing of psychiatric patients, for instance, often provides valuable insights into the root causes of their symptoms. In the same way, when exploring sensation and experience, an individual's past plays a pivotal role, forming a foundation for judgments and perceptions. These past experiences continue to grow and evolve with time; as long as life persists, this process of accumulation and transformation remains ongoing.

This phenomenon reflects a universal truth: Nearly all judgments are driven by underlying causes, whether consciously recognized or not. Since judgment is a subjective, deliberate action, it inevitably stems from some rationale. Some of these reasons are easily identifiable, others are shaped by ingrained cognitive habits from the past, and still others are deeply buried in the subconscious, beyond the reach of conscious thought. Regardless of their visibility, however, these reasons always exist.

Consider, for example, the experience of seeing a red rose. One might have positive, negative, or neutral reactions to it—sometimes even a combination of several emotions at once. Positive emotions might include feelings of beauty, romance, joy, or excitement. On the other hand, negative emotions could evoke sadness, ugliness, fear, or a sense of oppression. The reasons behind positive emotions might be rooted in a personal love for red flowers, cultivated over time, or in the pleasant memories associated with them (a fusion of personal preference and past experiences). In contrast, negative feelings could stem from personal dislike or negative experiences linked to red roses, such as emotional disappointments or physical pain from a rose's thorn. Once these feelings arise—whether positive, negative, or neutral—the mind naturally moves to the next phase: for things that evoke positive emotions, thoughts of liking, wanting, or desiring emerge; for those that evoke negative emotions, the mind may contemplate rejection, avoidance, or even discard. When something is desired, the result may be either fulfillment or disappointment. When the desire is fulfilled, the person feels satisfaction, and this satisfaction brings with it a subtle, subconscious expectation: That in the future, similar desires should be just as attainable. On the flip side, when desires go unfulfilled, the feeling of disappointment sets in. Initially, this manifests as sadness from not getting what was hoped for, but over time, this sadness can evolve.

If the feeling of disappointment is continuously reinforced in the mind, it may transform into a longing, and eventually, into a more intense desire. As this desire intensifies, it creates a sense of urgency within the person. Not only will they feel a more pressing need when encountering similar objects or experiences, but they may also feel a sense of envy toward those who have acquired what they long for. If left unchecked, this envy can deepen into jealousy, a mixture of admiration and resentment toward those who possess what they seek.

However, when the person who has obtained the desired object continues to effortlessly acquire more of what the other person cannot, particularly if this success seems effortless or unearned in the eyes of the latter, the disparity between the two becomes more glaring. This is when a subtle yet powerful shift occurs, and the difference between the two individuals gives rise to what is often called class disparity. For one individual, those who, like themselves, are unable to acquire the things they desire become part of their group or class, naturally fostering a sense of alliance. Conversely, those who easily obtain what the first person cannot, and those like them, form a separate, opposing group. This distinction, repeated over time, reinforces a sense of division, further entrenching the perceived gap between the two groups.

Negative emotions, much like positive ones, have the capacity to deepen and accumulate over time, gradually giving rise to complex layers of feelings. These new layers, though rooted in the initial reaction, evolve into something distinct from the original, simple emotion. For example, someone who dislikes red roses might develop an intense aversion if their room is deliberately filled with them against their will. This forced exposure could prompt them to secretly discard the roses or, over time, foster a growing resentment—even hatred—toward the person who placed them there. As these negative emotions intensify, the person might seek some form of retaliation. Whether the response directly relates to the roses or is triggered by an unrelated incident, such actions often serve as a release valve for the accumulated negativity.

Of course, the red rose scenario is relatively simple. In real life, emotional responses are far more intricate, shaped by a web of intertwined factors. These factors often work together to give rise to specific feelings and emotions. Yet, if we carefully untangle and analyze these influences one by one, we discover that even the most complex emotional experiences can be deconstructed and understood. Much like how proteins can be broken down into amino acids, amino acids into biomolecules, and biomolecules into atoms, emotions can be systematically examined at their core components.

To illustrate the interplay of emotional influences and outcomes, we can represent it with a mathematical equation:

$$y = f(X_{pos}, X_{neg}, X_{neu})$$

Here, X_{pos} denotes all factors contributing to positive emotions. X_{neg} represents all factors contributing to negative emotions. X_{neu} accounts for neutral factors that evoke no strong positive or negative feelings but remain as sensory perceptions (e.g., the sensation of boiling water being hot, which can be judged purely through physical sensation without emotional involvement). And y signifies the overall emotional outcome, reflecting the cumulative emotional state of the individual. This simple model frames emotional responses as a function of influencing factors. When $y > 0$, the overall emotion is positive; when $y < 0$, it is negative; and when $y = 0$, the emotional state is neutral, indicating that the stimulus elicits no significant emotional reaction and is perceived with indifference.

The emotional experiences of life are dynamic, continuously shaped by growth, accumulation, and transformation. For instance, as a child grows, their perception of the world evolves, leading to shifts in their emotional responses. Over time, attitudes toward the same object or experience typically follow one of three trajectories:

(1) Gradual evolution
- Like → Really like → Especially like
- Dislike → Really dislike → Especially dislike

(2) Consistent reinforcement
- Like → Like → Like
- Dislike → Dislike → Dislike
- Neutral → Neutral → Neutral

(3) Complete reversal
- Like → Neutral → Dislike
- Dislike → Neutral → Like
- Like → Dislike → Neutral
- Dislike → Like → Neutral
- Neutral → Dislike → Like
- Neutral → Like → Dislike

Naturally, as time passes and various circumstances unfold, the emotional transitions we've described are not the only possibilities. There could be more or fewer shifts in emotional states, depending on the context. We've outlined three general types of emotional transitions: The first is when emotions intensify over time, the second is when emotions remain consistent, and the third is when attitudes undergo significant changes, even reversing entirely.

Thus, it becomes clear that the factors influencing X_{pos}, X_{neg}, and X_{neu} are not fixed, but rather evolve with the passage of time. If we consider $a_1, a_2, \ldots, a_n, \ldots, a_{+\infty}$ as the factors gradually influencing positive emotions over time, $b_1, b_2, \ldots, b_n, \ldots, b_{+\infty}$ as the factors shaping negative emotions, and $c_1, c_2, \ldots, c_n, \ldots, c_{+\infty}$ as those that generate neutral emotions, we can represent this dynamic process with the following equations:

$$X_{pos} = f_{pos}(a_1, a_2, \ldots, a_n, \ldots, a_{+\infty})$$

$$X_{neg} = f_{neg}(b_1, b_2, \ldots, b_n, \ldots, b_{+\infty})$$
$$X_{neu} = f_{neu}(c_1, c_2, \ldots, c_n, \ldots, c_{+\infty})$$

It is crucial to understand that the sequences $a_1, a_2, \ldots, a_n, \ldots, a_{+\infty}$ evolve progressively over time. For instance, if a_1 arises at time t_1 and a_2 at time t_2, the influence of a_1 persists at t_2 (represented by a value that could be positive, negative, or neutral). At t_2, the cumulative influential factors would be a_1 and a_2. This pattern continues with subsequent factors. A similar process applies to the sequences $b_1, b_2, \ldots, b_n, \ldots, b_{+\infty}$ and $c_1, c_2, \ldots, c_n, \ldots, c_{+\infty}$.

Another important consideration is whether $a_1, a_2, \ldots, a_n, \ldots, a_{+\infty}$ are mutually independent. Let's consider a scenario involving A, whose influences include Friends B and C, Parents P_1 and P_2, and Relatives D_1, D_2, and D_3.

We can hypothesize the following:

(1) Friend B's opinion affects A as a_1.
(2) Friend C's opinion affects A as b_1.
(3) Parent P_1's opinion affects A as a_2.
(4) Parent P_2's opinion affects A as c_1.
(5) Relative D_1's opinion affects A as a_3.
(6) Relative D_2's opinion affects A as b_2.
(7) Relative D_3's opinion affects A as b_3.

If Friend B and Friend C know each other and share a close bond, their opinions might influence one another. For instance, if B persuades C to adopt their viewpoint, then C's influence on A may shift to align with b_1. Similarly, among parents or relatives, mutual communication and interactions could lead to correlated opinions.

Moreover, as human thoughts and emotions are dynamic, the influence of these individuals on A at any given moment reflects a composite (B, C, D, P, etc.) of their own evolving thoughts and feelings. Thus, the total impact on A can be expressed as

$$\begin{aligned} y_A &= f(X_{pos}, X_{neg}, X_{neu}) = f(f_{pos}, f_{neg}, f_{neu}) \\ &= f(y_B, y_C, y_D, y_P, \ldots, y_n, \varphi_1, \varphi_2, \ldots, \varphi_n) \end{aligned}$$

Here, $\varphi_1, \varphi_2, \ldots, \varphi_n$ represent non-human influencing factors. While these elements evolve over time, they do not necessarily change with every passing moment. It's worth noting this distinction.

At first glance, it may seem that a person's emotional state is subject to an overwhelming number of influences, making it exceedingly difficult to analyze or predict. This complexity is indeed a primary challenge in understanding emotions.

However, is the situation truly as daunting as it appears? Can we conclude that emotions are entirely erratic and beyond comprehension? Focusing on key individuals and pivotal events can bring clarity to this analysis, allowing us to identify significant patterns amid the seeming chaos.

For example, A's emotional response to an object X over their lifetime might initially appear as a random, erratic curve.

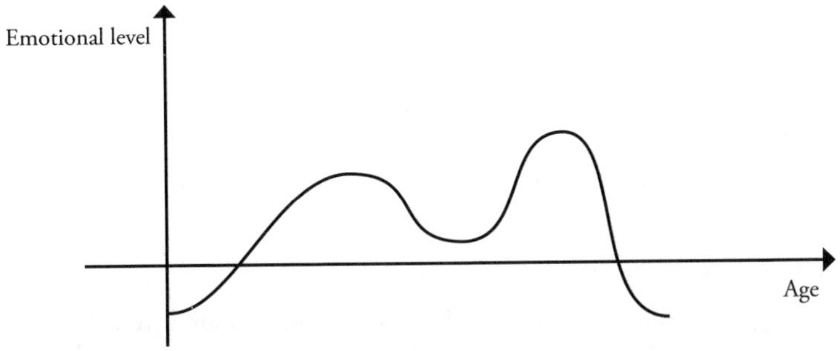

Figure 1-1

From figure 1-1, we can observe peaks, troughs, and significant fluctuations in A's emotional responses. These key moments typically correspond to significant life events. For example, although A may encounter numerous individuals, only a small group usually leaves a lasting impact—parents, teachers, spouses, children, or individuals with special meaning, such as a relative or idol. To be more specific, the primary influences shaping A's attitude toward a particular matter, such as object X, might be limited to just one relative and one teacher. Remarkably, the perspectives of these two people could account for over 80% of A's overall attitude toward X.

In traditional, isolated villages, social connections often follow concentric circles radiating outward: immediate family → extended family → the outside world. However, in today's highly connected world, thanks to advanced communication networks, the most influential figures in a person's life might not be those physically nearby. For instance, while parents usually play a major role, in cases like children of migrant workers, a distant celebrity or online influencer may have the most profound impact.

As communication technologies continue to evolve, the factors shaping an individual's beliefs and attitudes become increasingly complex and harder to pinpoint. Despite this complexity, there will always be a finite number of people or events that significantly influence an individual's outlook on a specific matter.

It's also essential to consider that some events exert influence at a collective level. Historical examples, such as peasant revolts, demonstrate how large-scale group movements propagate shared ideologies to individuals.

An additional factor worth noting is the intensity of emotions that an event evokes in A's mind, which is shaped by the interplay of two key elements: the significance of the individual conveying the idea to A and the scope of the idea's influence on A.

In essence, A's perception of any given matter can be understood along two dimensions: the overall nature of the perception—whether it is positive, negative, or neutral; and the intensity of the perception. Both dimensions are fluid and constantly evolving in response to external influences and internal shifts in thought. This dynamic nature of emotions is what contributes to the diversity of human experiences and the richness of personal growth.

In the discussion above, we touched on how individuals interact with the external world through their senses and cognitive processes. Beyond the objective sensory impressions derived from external stimuli, emotions play a pivotal role in shaping one's overall perception of an object or event.

Let us now return to the core and delve into another intrinsic characteristic of an individual, along with the emotional complexities that stem from it.

Humans acquire initial sensory information through their five senses. This information is then processed, analyzed, and evaluated through thought, leading to judgments that guide their actions and responses. But what powers this entire cognitive machinery? What compels us to pursue what we love and reject what we dislike? How do these desires fuel subsequent emotional fluctuations and contribute to the evolution of our experiences?

From the moment of birth, a human being's first cognitive realization is an awareness of the self. Through seeing with their eyes, hearing with their ears, and experiencing the world around them, they begin to perceive the existence of an external reality distinct from themselves. This realization establishes the sense of "self" in contrast to the "other." They become aware that this "self" experiences hunger, cold, and discomfort, as well as joy and warmth when treated kindly or pain and distress when faced with hostility. They recognize themselves as unique, independent beings—different from everything else they see, hear, or interact with. Whether feeling joy or pain, the external world remains indifferent, further solidifying their understanding of the existence of "I."

This sense of "I" gathers information through the body's senses and processes it in the brain. Signals such as hunger, warmth, cold, comfort, and discomfort are interpreted as personal feelings and experiences. From the earliest stages of life, the instinct for survival ensures that even a newborn can sense and respond to external conditions that either support or threaten their existence. This foundational self-awareness is the origin of all sensations a person will experience throughout their lifetime.

With the emergence of self-awareness comes the recognition of others. The self's sense of well-being naturally gives rise to an evaluation of how others treat "me." When sensory inputs favor what feels good—where "good" refers to a pleasurable sensation rather than an objective benefit (e.g., a spoiled child may feel "good" when indulged in unlimited sweets but "bad" when denied, even though restraint may promote health)—the self tends to feel joy and happiness. Conversely, when inputs lean toward the negative, the self may develop a sense of crisis, leading to feelings of disgust, hatred, or anger.

Emotions significantly influence perception, often distorting it and preventing a purely objective understanding of reality. Each person unavoidably views the world through the lens of their own biases, shaped by emotions and past experiences. These biases create limitations in cognition. Breaking free from such limitations requires tremendous effort. Only by actively working to empty oneself of preconceived notions, emotional attachments, and ingrained prejudices can one begin to approach true understanding.

The concept of the "seven emotions and six desires" has been interpreted in numerous ways throughout history. Generally speaking, the seven emotions encompass joy, anger, sorrow, fear, love, hatred, and desire, with some interpretations also including worry, longing, grief, surprise, and fright. Meanwhile, the six desires are often understood in two ways: One interpretation focuses on the five senses—sight, hearing, smell, taste, and touch—along with the mind, while another refers to basic physiological desires such as hunger, sexual desire, emotional longing, possessiveness, the thirst for knowledge, and the desire for excellence. These varying interpretations each carry their own insights. Here, we will briefly explore two particularly representative emotions—fear and surprise—alongside the more straightforward emotions of joy, anger, sorrow, and happiness.

Fear, on the surface, appears to be a psychological response to an unknown danger. In reality, it can be divided into two categories: fear that threatens one's life and fear that does not. The first type is a physiological reaction, such as the fear of heights when standing at the edge of a cliff, or the primal fear one might feel before engaging in extreme sports like bungee jumping, skydiving, or diving. This kind of fear arises from an awareness that these actions carry a significant risk to one's life, especially if they have never been experienced before. This fear persists for as long as the possibility of danger remains unknown, disrupting the person's thoughts. However, overcoming such fears often brings with it a sense of heroic pride or accomplishment to whoever tries to do so, offering a stark contrast to the initial feelings of dread.

The second type of fear is one that poses no direct physical threat, but still triggers fear due to other reasons. For example, many people experience nervousness or anxiety when speaking in public, a fear that has even affected some of history's greatest figures. In these situations, the fear does not stem from the threat of physical harm, but rather from the concern that one might say something inappropriate or encounter an embarrassing moment on stage, leading the audience to mock or oppose them. The true fear lies in the potential rejection and disapproval from the group. Furthermore, when the person imagines that this rejection could extend to their social circle, they fear being ostracized by the entire community. In such moments, they become acutely sensitive to every subtle reaction from the audience, and the experience can feel as though they are not facing fellow human beings, but rather a group of lions—watching with intensity, ready to tear them apart.

Beyond the fear of public speaking, the anxiety encountered when pursuing someone romantically also arises from the fear of rejection and the worry of being ridiculed. Therefore, even when there is no direct threat to one's safety, much of the fear experienced by individuals stems from the desire to avoid being rejected or cast aside by others. This form of fear can trigger a range of unusual reactions: persistent insomnia, sweating without realizing it, hesitation to act, envy and jealousy toward those who are brave enough to take risks, as well as self-loathing and feelings of inferiority. What ultimately drives a person to take that first step is often the desire for success, coupled with the fantasy of being admired and respected by others upon achieving it. The intensity of this fantasy will determine whether the person chooses to step forward and embrace the challenge. Ultimately, fear is a response born from a protective instinct toward the self.

The emotion of surprise originates from the discrepancy between reality and one's expectations. People naturally form predictions about events based on past experiences, and when the actual outcome deviates from these expectations, the degree of surprise is directly proportional to the magnitude of the difference.

For instance, a woman unaware of a man's affections may feel astonished when she suddenly receives an extravagant gift from him as a declaration of love. A seasoned investor might be deeply shocked when a "black swan" event disrupts their long-held understanding of market patterns. Similarly, a devoted housewife who has invested significant time and effort into preparing an elaborate meal might feel profoundly surprised if her husband dismisses her efforts entirely.

When surprise is positive, it manifests as delight; when negative, it becomes shock or dismay. In many household conflicts, a husband may feel perplexed because his response does not align with his wife's expectations. His failure to recognize the underlying issue often escalates into a cascade of seemingly irrational emotions, fueling a cycle of disputes. Upon deeper reflection, it becomes clear that surprise often stems from an individual's expectations. People constantly compare reality to their preconceived notions. When the two align, everything feels normal; when they diverge, surprise arises. These expectations, however, are shaped by personal experiences. Thus, surprise is not a random phenomenon but a reflection of an individual's inner world, mirroring their past and revealing their deep-rooted sense of self-preservation.

As individuals grow, their self-awareness strengthens, leading to the development of self-esteem and self-love. When left unchecked, these traits may expand into arrogance or conceit. Nearly all human emotions are rooted in one's self-perception. Situations that make "me" feel respected, admired, appreciated, accepted, or cared for evoke positive emotions. Conversely, situations that make "me" feel rejected, excluded, criticized, or mistreated lead to negative emotions. One of the most significant sources of human emotion—possessiveness—is also tied to the desire to affirm the self through ownership. When desires remain unfulfilled, individuals may experience negative emotions, as these unmet goals highlight a perceived sense of inadequacy.

In essence, human emotions are fundamentally connected to an individual's self-awareness. They arise from the interplay between external information received through the senses and the internal self-concept.

III. Analysis of the Verification Aspect of Experience

The concept of "verification" in human experience can be divided into two fundamental types: real experiences and virtual experiences.

Real experiences refer to sensations obtained through the interaction of one's physical senses with the external environment. These experiences are characterized by input originating from the outside world. It's important to note that the "external world" in this context includes not only the tangible natural realm (the material world) but also virtual realities created through electronic devices. These devices simulate external input, providing sensory experiences that feel real.

Virtual experiences, on the other hand, arise solely from mental activity during the period of experience, without any external input. These encompass daydreams, fantasies, and imaginations. It's crucial to emphasize that the distinction between real and virtual experiences is purely descriptive, without any inherent value judgment. To maintain clarity in subsequent discussions, real experiences will be referred to as material experiences, while virtual experiences will be termed mental experiences.

In daily life, material and mental experiences coexist, evolve together, and complement one another. Both have their own focus, purpose, process, and outcomes.

Material experiences are rooted in the interaction with the physical world, which includes humans, natural landscapes, animals, and plants. The purpose of material experiences often extends beyond mere appreciation of beauty to include observing, exploring, and understanding the underlying laws of nature and society. A significant aim is the accumulation of knowledge and skills crucial for survival.

Laws and patterns validated through repeated observation are considered accurate and preserved, while disproven notions are discarded. For example, studying plant and animal growth patterns informs agriculture and animal husbandry; investigating geological formations reveals climate patterns and mineral deposits; understanding human relationships fosters cooperation, enabling individuals and communities to achieve shared goals.

The process of material experience requires sensory organs to actively acquire external information—light, color, sound, texture, or temperature—and interpret it. This makes material experiences inherently empirical.

Despite their empirical nature, the outcomes of material experiences may not always perfectly reflect reality. For example, dim lighting may lead someone to mistake a rope for a snake or a shadow of a tool for that of a person. The physical state of sensory organs can distort the accuracy of sensory input. For example, blurred vision or color distortion may occur when the eyes are strained, and a cold may impair one's hearing or sense of smell. Nevertheless, material experiences can gradually approach greater accuracy through repeated verification under varying conditions. This iterative process makes material experiences the foundational raw material for human experience.

Mental experiences are the products of material experiences, transformed and elevated within the realm of the mind. For instance, when we see an apple with our eyes, we perceive the apple itself. However, the mental experience of that apple could take many forms. It might be the apple we see with our eyes, or it could be the iconic Apple Inc. founded by Steve Jobs and its products, or the apple that famously fell on Isaac Newton's head, or even the forbidden fruit that Eve had in the Garden of Eden.

Beyond the fundamental cognitive materials shaped by past experiences, human thought has the unique ability to freely arrange, combine, extend, and imagine these elements, creating experiences that transcend anything the physical world has known. Consider the works of great artists—paintings, symphonies, musicals, myths, and novels. These are all products of mental experiences. These works are often called "divine works" or the "will of the gods" because they diverge so drastically from the raw materials of the material world. People are often compelled to believe that a force or process beyond the material realm has shaped the artist's mind to create such masterpieces.

In the spiritual realm, experiences drawn from the material world undergo reconfigurations that transcend the limitations of time and space—blending, reshaping, and transforming. It's akin to the hazy, dizzying perception one has when intoxicated, where everything seems fluid and shifting. Similarly, those who experience mental transformation may feel as if these altered experiences are just as real as those in the material world, as though they've entered another dimension. In that dimension, one can fully unleash their imagination and creativity, reconstructing a world entirely of their own making. Some of these worlds are shared with others through artistic expressions like plays, musicals, or literature, making them visible to the outside world. But there are countless other mental worlds constantly unfolding in each person's mind, far beyond what the senses can perceive. Each individual harbors their own private world inside their mind, and like the material world, it is ever-evolving.

When someone inadvertently stumbles into another's inner world, it can feel like the discovery of a profound secret, as if they've witnessed a divine revelation. The stark contrast between these worlds can provoke the emotion of surprise, as it reveals something both extraordinary and otherworldly. Ultimately, what we witness in human interactions is, at its core, the collision of different worlds. As quantum mechanics shows us, particles only reveal their position upon collision, and until that moment, they exist in a state of uncertainty. In the same way, everything we "see" or "hear" in the material world—whether people, animals, plants, or objects—is merely a snapshot of a fleeting moment. In the next instant, that moment will be gone, and the world will have shifted.

Which world is vaster—the world of mental experiences or the world of material experiences? This question is akin to asking which of two infinities is greater. To draw a meaningful comparison, let us approach it from a different angle.

For any given individual, their mental experiences reside within their own unique spiritual world. While this world is infinitely flexible in the way its elements can be combined and arranged, it is ultimately limited by that person's own life experiences. Now, how vast is the external material world they encounter? First, the material world contains elements and laws that a person will never fully comprehend. Second, there are parts of the material world that they will never come across in their lifetime. Furthermore, within these unknown realms, some aspects belong to other human beings' or animals' mental worlds—either related or unrelated to their own.

When we attempt to encompass the totality of the mental worlds of all humans (or even all living beings in the universe), comparing it to the material world becomes a challenging task. Humanity may not have discovered all the laws of the material world, but the material world itself does not account for the mental creations that humans have produced—things that exist only in the realm of thought and imagination.

Moreover, the two worlds—material and mental—are in an eternal state of mutual influence. The material world becomes richer and more complex as it absorbs human creations, while human thought evolves and expands upon the new material conditions introduced into it. Imagine, for a moment, if all living beings lost their consciousness. What purpose would the operations of the material world serve? All human-made creations would fade away, and the natural world—mountains, rivers, the sun, the moon, and plants—would eventually decay, as dictated by the universe's natural laws. This forms the basis of idealism, which asserts that meaning and spirit precede material existence.

However, to claim that the world is entirely a creation of the mind overlooks an important issue. Many things existed before humans arrived, and much of the material world evolves independently of human thought. The debate between materialism and idealism is not the focus here, so we will set it aside for the moment.

The distinction between material and mental experiences within the verification aspect of experience provides a solid foundation for understanding the nature of experience itself. Experience is not merely about sensation; it also involves a verification dimension. For example, if someone hears that a Xiaomi phone offers great value-for-money, this is not yet a true experience. It's simply hearsay. In the mental realm, they might form an initial impression, but until they actually engage with the product themselves, they have not truly "experienced" it. The "experience" they've had is merely an impression formed through the sensory input of others' statements.

True experience requires the individual to interact directly with the object, combining both material verification (sensory input) and mental verification (thoughtful analysis). Over time, this experience may accumulate, with repeated exposure leading to a more developed understanding. From an initial sensory reaction, the individual gradually forms more stable thoughts and attitudes toward the object. This progression can be seen as the experience process, which we can divide into four stages: initial contact stage, repeated use stage, evaluation formation stage, and evaluation stabilization stage. As the object of experience evolves, updates, or improves over time, even past experiences will involve new engagements, leading to fresh encounters. Moreover, since the individual's own situation is constantly changing, their experience of the same object will differ depending on their environment, mood, or circumstances, resulting in significantly varied reactions each time. These varying experiences influence the overall evaluation of the object, which we call the experience level. It's important to clarify the relationship between experience level and sensory level.

The sensory level represents the immediate perceptions of a target object at any given moment as time progresses. It reflects the raw, real-time feelings experienced through the senses. On the other hand, the experience level goes beyond this, incorporating cognitive analysis and verification to form a more comprehensive evaluation. It is a synthesis of both sensory impressions and thoughtful reasoning.

For example, giving candy to a young girl might evoke a strong sense of delight, resulting in a high sensory level. However, if that same candy later leads to cavities and associated pain, the act of eating candy—though pleasurable at first—may ultimately receive a negative evaluation. As a result, the girl's experience level of candy would likely not be as high as her initial sensory enjoyment suggests.

This distinction shows that the experience level is generally more stable and rational compared to the sensory level, though it is equally important to acknowledge that experience is rooted in the continuous accumulation of sensory input. The two are deeply intertwined, shaping one another over time.

To draw an analogy, sensory level can be likened to emotion, while experience level corresponds to the combination of emotion and reason.

In commercial contexts, particularly in consumer behavior, the overall experience level—the fusion of emotional and rational evaluations—becomes the primary focus. When a consumer makes a purchasing decision, it is not driven solely by fleeting emotions or cold rationality but by their holistic judgment of the object.

Even in cases of impulsive purchases, there is often an underlying element of rational thinking. For instance, a consumer might justify their decision with thoughts like "I'll need this eventually, so buying it on sale now is a smart move." "This tool offers great value for the price." "The excitement this game item brings me right now is well worth the cost." The experience level therefore is the central focus of this book's exploration.

IV. Observing Individual Experiential Behavior

Let us return to the dynamics of human society and explore how individuals express experiential behaviors in their daily lives. While human existence inherently involves a constant flow of sensory input and output, resulting in a continuous state of experience, our primary focus is on experiences shaped by the fulfillment of human needs. This requires us to delve into the hierarchy of human needs in social life.

We propose categorizing these needs into three distinct levels: first, survival needs; second, happiness needs; third, self-actualization needs.

Survival needs represent the essential requirements for maintaining life and ensuring the continuation of human existence. These needs include nutritional needs—access to food and sustenance for survival; respiratory needs—the ability to breathe and sustain life; shelter needs—protection from cold and adverse environmental conditions; safety needs—security from natural disasters, human conflicts, and threats from wild animals; reproductive needs—the continuation of the species; and social needs—interactions necessary to sustain life and facilitate survival.

Happiness needs, while not critical to survival, significantly enhance the quality of life. These can be categorized into two types: needs for life enrichment and needs for personal pleasure. It's worth noting that enriching one's life does not necessarily increase personal pleasure, and heightened pleasure does not always lead to a more enriched life. Key happiness needs include respect needs—

living with dignity, free from discrimination or mistreatment; emotional needs—fostering relationships and nurturing the soul through love and connection; leisure needs—opportunities for relaxation and rejuvenation from work-related stress; entertainment needs—activities that make life more vibrant and enjoyable; quality and refinement needs—pursuing elegance and higher standards in basic living essentials; and self-improvement needs—opportunities for personal growth, learning, and development.

Self-actualization needs are defined by an individual's pursuit of meaning, purpose, and value in life, often manifesting as career or life aspirations. While these needs may appear similar across individuals, the underlying motivations often differ significantly. For example, the pursuit of power, wealth, or influence may stem from ego-centric needs—a desire to assert dominance and fulfill vanity; altruistic needs—a commitment to addressing societal issues and contributing to the greater good. This category can be broadly divided into two dimensions: self-focused needs and others-focused needs.

This categorization leads to a conceptual framework of a hierarchy of needs, as illustrated in figure 1-2.

Human behavior in society is fundamentally motivated by the desire to fulfill these various needs. Take, for instance, the act of exchange: An individual engages in trade to barter surplus goods they produce for items they cannot produce but require for survival. This process introduces challenges such as measuring value and facilitating transactions, ultimately spurring the development of trade systems and the invention of currency.

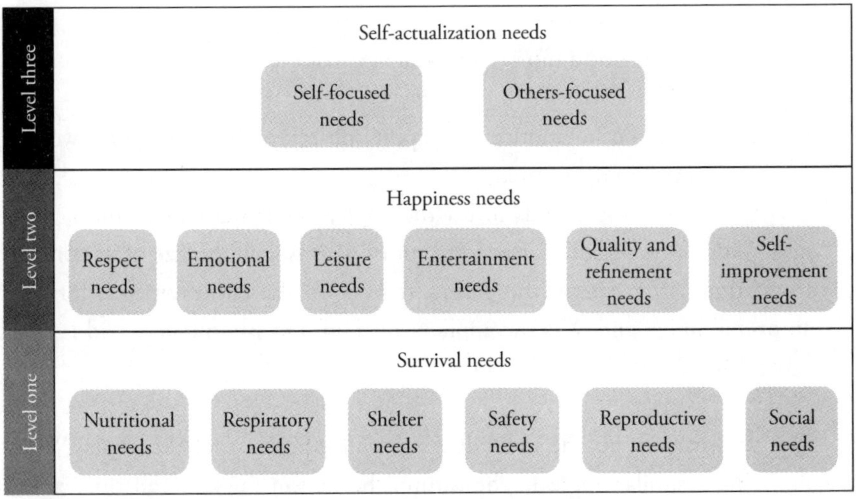

Figure 1-2 Hierarchy of needs

The things that fulfill human needs inherently possess use value, which is their fundamental reason for existence. While exchange value emerges during transactions, use value remains the cornerstone of their significance. Thus, the focus here is on the needs that drive human behavior.

In figure 1-2, the various levels of needs are not strictly separate; rather, they are interconnected and build progressively upon one another. Depending on an individual's circumstances, the specifics of each need evolve. Take nutritional needs as an example. At the most basic level, the primary goal is survival—consuming the minimum amount of food necessary to sustain life. Once survival is secured, individuals begin to pursue more refined aspects, such as nutritional balance, whether ingredients are organic, the healthiness of seasonings, cooking methods, flavor, aesthetic presentation, and even factors related to the dining experience, like the dining environment and quality of service.

As people's needs become more refined with improving living conditions, they evolve in complexity and diversity, often extending into what is known as the "long tail effect." When an individual, driven by a need, encounters something that could fulfill it, the experience begins to take shape. These are three steps of experience:

(1) Encounter. The first step of experience involves encountering the object.
(2) Usage. After contact, the individual engages in a process of use, which constitutes the second step.
(3) Evaluation. Finally, the individual evaluates their sensory impressions and synthesizes them into an experiential outcome.

For example, imagine a hungry individual encountering an apple:

(1) Encounter. The person notices the apple, observing its shape, size, weight, color, scent, and temperature.
(2) Usage. The person proceeds to eat the apple, evaluating its sweetness, firmness, juiciness, whether it's free from rot or worms, and the size of its core.
(3) Evaluation. After eating, the person reflects on the entire process, forming an overall judgment. Was the apple tasty? Did it satisfy hunger? Did it meet expectations?

This summary forms the individual's overall experience of the apple. When encountering a similar apple in the future, the person might recall this experience, form expectations, and validate these through repeated trials—this iterative process defines the essence of experience.

From this example, we can identify several key elements of the experience process:

(1) Need. An experience begins with a corresponding need. In this scenario, the need was hunger and the desire to eat. Needs can arise from internal cues (e.g., hunger triggered by the body) or external stimuli (e.g., seeing appetizing food). Here, the primary need driving the experience was hunger.
(2) Seeking fulfillment. The next step involves seeking to meet the need. This process varies in complexity and duration. The person may have wandered for hours in search of an apple tree. The person might have encountered apple trees on private property or seen food they couldn't afford. The person might have passed others eating apples without being able to get one themselves, or found apple trees but couldn't reach the fruit. Whether straightforward or challenging, long or short, this process of seeking fulfillment is a vital part of the experience, all until obtaining an apple. The fulfillment seeking in the aforementioned case is the active behavior of the person. In some cases, it is passive—such as Newton's famous experience of being struck by a falling apple. Regardless of how it occurs, this stage reflects the individual's pursuit of need fulfillment.
(3) Contact and sensory impressions. The third element involves direct contact and sensory impressions. This step may vary in duration. The individual might savor the apple over several hours or eat it quickly in a few minutes. They might eat while walking, save half for later, or share it with someone else.
(4) Experiential outcome. Finally, the experience culminates in a result: Having finished the apple, the individual reflects on the entire process and synthesizes their impressions into an overall evaluation. For example, they might evaluate the apple's taste, portability (e.g., its size and weight), and whether it met expectations. Did it have worms? Did the tree have more apples for future picking? Was the apple's appearance appealing? Could it serve as a benchmark for identifying good apples in the future? All these reflections collectively form the individual's experiential outcome.

Experience therefore can be broken down into six interconnected components: need, seeking to fulfill the need, contact and sensory impression, the experience process, reflection on the experience, and the experiential outcome. These components, however, do not always occur in a fixed sequential order.

At times, individuals may not even recognize their own needs (what they want) until they encounter something specific. For instance, upon encountering a particular object, one might exclaim, "Oh! This is exactly what I need!" or "This is just what I was looking for!" This raises a question akin to the "chicken-or-egg" dilemma: Which comes first—the need or the object that fulfills it?

In many cases, people initially perceive a need (e.g., feeling hungry or cold) and then seek ways to address it by finding food or clothing (or accommodation). This process aligns with conventional logic. However, there are instances where the object itself triggers a need—such as seeing appetizing food that suddenly evokes hunger.

In the digital age, many user needs are prompted by exposure to new products. Take, for example, a sleek, innovative iPhone. Its design and features may cause someone to think, "Everybody loves it!" In such cases, encountering the product generates a new desire. Social influence also plays a significant role in creating needs. For example, the thought "Everyone else has it, so I need it too" often drives behavior and decision-making.

Regardless of their sequence, these six components are always present in a complete experience. While some elements may be brief, occur passively, or unfold with time gaps, they remain integral to the process.

For products with complex functionalities, is it necessary to explore every feature to complete the experience? Not at all. The six components apply to any single function or feature that a user engages with. For example, if a product has multiple features but someone only uses function 1, their experience consists of engaging with that specific function. Even if the exploration of function 1 is incomplete, the partial interaction still constitutes an experience. As long as the individual has interacted with the product and gained meaningful impressions, an experience has taken place. We define an individual's complete engagement with a specific object within a given timeframe as an experience event.

Over time, as individuals engage more deeply with different functions or features of an object, their experience may expand to encompass all of its aspects. This progression is referred to as experience accumulation. Experience accumulation represents the totality of past interactions and impressions with an object. This comprehensive process enables individuals not only to evaluate the object's overall quality but also to comment on and analyze specific details and nuances with greater depth. Together, these insights contribute to the experience outcome.

So, what roles do sensory impressions and emotional responses of the feeling aspect of the experience mentioned earlier play in the experience process? They form the core of the experience, collectively referred to as the experience content. The verification aspect of the experience, on the other hand, represents the cognitive analysis and reasoning applied to the experience. The raw material from sensory and emotional inputs, combined with rational verification, results in a complete experience outcome.

From another perspective, each of the six components of the experience process comprises both sensory/emotional content and rational verification. While the six components describe the procedural framework of the experience, the outcome reflects the integration of emotional and cognitive insights into a cohesive conclusion.

The discussion above examines an individual's engagement with a single object. Next, we will explore how individuals simultaneously interact with multiple objects within the experience process.

The complexity of real-life experiences makes them inherently challenging to describe and analyze. In the ebb and flow of daily life, we are often immersed in a multitude of overlapping sensations, and most of the time, we neither consciously observe the process of these experiences nor reflect on how different stimuli influence each other.

As we go through our lives, multiple sensory organs are activated simultaneously, creating a rich and multifaceted influx of information. Yet, due to varying focus at different moments, we only absorb a limited portion of this sensory input. To illustrate this point, let's consider a simple, yet relatable scenario.

Imagine a person sitting in a cozy café: Their eyes take in the café's decor, the people walking by or engaged in conversation, the view through the window, and the flow of life happening outside. Their ears absorb the mellow, relaxing music in the background, along with snippets of nearby conversations. Their nose detects the rich aroma of freshly brewed coffee, the subtle fragrance of flowers on the table, the scent of meals being served, and the passing whiff of someone's perfume or cologne. Their tongue savors the complex flavor of their coffee—be it bitter, sweet, or acidic. Every so often, they pull out their phone, scrolling aimlessly, then sip their coffee, all while their thoughts wander to recent events or to family members far away.

This simple scene encapsulates a common, everyday experience. While the location, context, and sensory details may vary from person to person, we are all continuously immersed in such multi-sensory experiences. Often, people say that life is an experience, simply because, as we live, we are perpetually navigating the realms of sensation and thought. Yet, what tends to capture our attention the most are the experiences that occur at the boundaries.

Take temperature, for instance. Most people feel comfortable in a range of 15°C to 25°C—not "too hot" or "too cold." Of course, a fluctuation of 5°C on either side might still be tolerable for many, but when the temperature dips below 10°C or rises above 30°C, we begin to experience a distinct sensation of "cold" or "hot." These extreme boundaries of experience are where our sensory awareness sharpens, as we suddenly feel a marked difference. Under normal circumstances, each sensory dimension of the five senses corresponds to specific domains and recognition patterns—ranging from light to sound, smell, taste, and touch. Too much or too little light can distort our perception, leading to errors in what we see. Sounds outside of a certain range, whether too loud or too soft, may be uncomfortable or even inaudible. Each sense has an optimal range, and when stimuli fall outside these ranges, they either go unnoticed or become overwhelming.

The most striking and memorable experiences often occur at the edges of these sensory capabilities. These boundary moments typically provide intense stimulation and are the ones that leave a lasting impression. What makes boundary experiences even more remarkable is how they interact with our accumulated life experiences. For example, someone who has lived in tropical climates might find temperatures between 30°C and 40°C comfortable, while someone from a temperate region may feel uncomfortable at 35°C. The most vivid experiences are those that break away from what is considered ordinary or expected. It is precisely these "differences"—whether in sight, sound, taste, or touch—that trigger heightened sensory stimulation, leaving an indelible mark on our memory.

Let's return to the person sitting in the café. While countless people and things pass before their eyes, not everything captures their visual attention. They might gaze idly out the window for an extended period, only to suddenly notice someone with an eccentric outfit walking by. Their focus shifts entirely to this unusual figure, momentarily forgetting everything else around them. Later at home, they might eagerly recount the encounter to their family: "Today, I saw someone dressed so peculiarly—I think they might be an artist or an actor." This example highlights that, no matter how much sensory input we encounter simultaneously, we truly experience only the things that draw our attention.

However, our experiences aren't limited to what we consciously focus on—they also encompass what our subconscious registers. While this person observes the scene outside, their other senses don't shut down. If something unexpected happens—like a waiter spilling coffee on them—their attention will swiftly shift from the window to their immediate surroundings. This sudden disruption not only redirects their focus but may also affect their overall perception of the café experience.

In this way, a person's overall experience can be broken down into two components: the baseline, tolerable experience during normal conditions and the incremental experiences triggered by specific, notable moments. These incremental experiences can enhance or detract from the overall impression.

The baseline tolerable experience represents the general sense of satisfaction when no single aspect of the environment demands focused attention. For example, factors like the ambient temperature and humidity, lighting levels, seating comfort, table ergonomics, and the size or temperature of the coffee cup all contribute to this baseline. Most people have a range of tolerance for such elements, and as long as conditions fall within this range, evaluations tend to remain in the "acceptable" category. When completing satisfaction surveys, the majority of responses might fall within "average," "mostly satisfied," or "adequate," reflecting an experience that meets basic expectations but lacks any notable highs or lows. These baseline experiences don't typically evoke strong negative emotions. They sustain users' needs, helping to maintain loyalty, but they rarely generate glowing recommendations or rapid loss of customers.

Another category of issues exists at the threshold of "sudden shifts" and "experience boundaries." These are unique events capable of profoundly influencing user perceptions, often leading to significant changes or even reversals in the overall experience. Such events leave a lasting psychological impression and warrant special attention. Simply put, these impactful moments are defined by their ability to introduce noticeable "differences" or striking "distinctions."

Let us return once more to observe everyday life. Why, as people move past merely satisfying basic needs and strive to enhance their living standards, has the word "experience" gained such prominence—becoming not just a concept, but almost a cultural trend? Why is it that today, people proudly declare, "I'm not just buying a product, I'm buying an experience"? What exactly differentiates this "experience" from the same products or services of the past?

The answer lies in the essence of what this "experience" represents: the pursuit of something distinct. "Experience" is inherently personal, a reflection of individuality. It symbolizes a deeper human drive for self-reliance, self-liberation, and self-respect. When each individual comes to see themselves as a unique being, their aspirations shift from simply meeting basic needs—clothing, food, shelter, and transport—to desiring a lifestyle that reflects their own personal, unparalleled "experience." At its core, this is rooted in human self-awareness.

This shift has, however, brought about a fundamental change in production dynamics. In the past, the aim was to achieve a similar standard of living—everyone wore the same clothes, ate the same food, lived in the same kinds of homes. As long as basic survival was taken care of and life was an improvement over past struggles, people felt satisfied. But once these basic needs were met, a new sense of self-awareness emerged. People began to crave "clothing that stands apart from others," "food that feels unique," and "experiences that differ from the norm," ushering in an era of comparison and competition based on individuality.

If we revisit the demand hierarchy we discussed earlier (fig. 1-2), we see that all the needs in the second and third levels arise from this fundamental desire for "being different." We often hear people talk about "self-actualization" in modern life, but when we delve deeper into what this truly means, we find that beyond a drive for superiority or vanity, it's essentially the pursuit of uniqueness. The only distinction lies in the nature of that vanity. Some people seek differentiation to impress others, to seem exceptional or extraordinary; others pursue it to satisfy personal desires or to try things they never had the opportunity to before; some seek to make a lasting impact on the world during their short lives; and others seek difference with the goal of benefiting others, lifting them from hardship, or creating positive social change. These motivations are what shape a person's "worldview," "life philosophy," or "values."

Even when confronted with the same object or experience, people recognize that each individual brings their own unique perspective. Take, for example, a film: Every viewer interprets it differently, each with their own understanding and emotional response. The same historical event is analyzed in countless ways, with each person viewing it through the lens of their own experience. Even something as simple as a shared family faucet—each person uses it at different times, in different ways, and with varying degrees of frequency. This understanding of "difference" reveals that each person's needs, desires, and experiences are as diverse as they are.

With the continuous diversification of material goods and the rapid advancement of technology, what was once a barrier—technical limitations—is no longer a hindrance. Now, everyone has the opportunity to engage with a wide array of "different lives," and in doing so, life itself has become an "experience," and "different" lifestyles have become what people pursue.

As people's self-awareness and life needs have undergone profound changes, these shifts have also driven a dramatic transformation in the way suppliers approach production. In the past, a manufacturer of glass cups could easily produce according to a few standard sizes. However, today, with growing demand for "quality" and "differentiation," consumers seek not just glass cups, but also purple clay cups, ceramic cups, metal cups, jade cups, and more. Beyond material differences, people also desire an endless array of creative designs and unique shapes.

For manufacturers, however, production resources remain finite. Relying on a one-size-fits-all production model struggles to keep pace with the increasingly diverse needs of the market. In response, many manufacturers have developed new strategies: They offer standardized templates for mass production but also provide custom design services on top of these templates. In the past, scale economies limited the range of customization, and manufacturers would often set a minimum order quantity. Today, however, many individual customers are willing to pay a premium for products tailored to their personal tastes, prompting manufacturers to gradually embrace these bespoke services.

The additional price that customers are willing to pay reflects their valuation of a "personalized experience"—essentially, the value inherent in the experience itself. Our focus on the economic dimensions of experience stems from a desire to explore whether it is possible to make the value of these experiences more tangible, thereby enabling a deeper analysis of their impact on economic relationships.

V. Primary Dimensions of Experience Analysis in Human Society

The essence of experience is closely tied to human needs and the constant flow of sensations that individuals encounter in their daily lives. Political economy traditionally classifies the value of goods into use value and exchange value. Use value pertains to the inherent utility of a commodity and lacks the distinct characteristics of a tradable good. Economic relationships, in contrast, are established on the foundation of exchange value, which represents the concentrated embodiment of a commodity's intrinsic worth during the act of trade.

However, as the various facets of a commodity's value begin to diverge, exchange value may take on different meanings depending on the context. With advancements in living standards, new insights have emerged, revealing that every commodity possesses an additional dimension beyond its use value: experience value. This value dimension encapsulates the emotional and sensory experiences associated with a product. Exchange value, therefore, can be understood as the combined result of use value and experience value. Under certain conditions, both use value and experience value have the potential to transform into exchange value.

To illustrate, let us revisit the classic example from *Capital: A Critique of Political Economy*: 20 yards of linen = 1 coat. This equation holds because both commodities share an equivalent exchange value, which is determined by an underlying value-measuring scale. If all linen in the market is of uniform specification and all coats are of identical material and style, this measuring scale allows for a straightforward assessment of their exchange relationship.

Yet, when the ideal conditions are relaxed, complexities arise. Suppose the coats in the market vary in color, style, texture, or size. Individual preferences and economic capacities then come into play. A coat with a distinctive design might lead someone to trade 40 yards of linen for it, while a poorly made coat might only command 5 yards of linen. In such cases, the exchange value of some coats rises to 40 yards of linen, while for others, it falls to 5.

The situation becomes even more intricate if the linen itself varies in quality. The exchange relationship between the two commodities and the scale used to measure their value must also evolve, dynamically adapting to the demands of the market.

To navigate these complexities, we propose an expanded framework for analyzing commodity value. This framework divides value into three dimensions: basic use value, experience value, and exchange value. Consider the coat as an example. Its basic use value lies in providing warmth and covering the body. Attributes such as style, comfort, and uniqueness constitute its experience value. Meanwhile, exchange value is shaped by the combined influence of these two dimensions.

Mathematically, we can think of exchange value as a function of basic use value and experience value. In the past, when social productivity was low and products were largely homogeneous, experience value had minimal impact. People prioritized basic needs—eating enough food and staying warm—over aspirations for gourmet meals or fashionable attire. But as productivity surged, material abundance grew, and the demand for better, more diverse lifestyles increased, experience value began to take center stage. Today, it has even become the primary determinant of exchange value in many cases.

Remarkably, even when a product's use value is negligible or nonexistent, the presence of experience value can still confer significant exchange value. Decorative items and ornamental objects are prime examples of this phenomenon.

In recent years, driven by government policies promoting industrial innovation and fostering entrepreneurship, a wave of products and services championing "ultimate user experience" and "differentiated experiential services" has captured public attention, delivering impressive results.

For instance, Haidilao's exceptional service experience has revolutionized service quality across the catering industry. WeChat's seamless product experience has brought unprecedented focus to user experience design within the app industry. Brands like ROSEONLY, which specialize in creating unique emotional experiences, have emerged as standout examples. Similarly, Chinese smartphone brands like Xiaomi, catering to the exclusive needs of specific demographics, have repeatedly redefined success in the business world.

Across industries—be it retail, catering, hospitality, technology, or automotive—traditional companies are evolving to focus on differentiated brand experiences, while emerging businesses are homing in on the unique demands of niche markets. These enterprises emphasize the production of customized, personalized, and emotionally resonant products. Today, the concept of user experience has become a household term, with the quality of that experience increasingly shaping consumer decisions.

Given this landscape, when experience value begins to play a pivotal role in determining product value, influencing consumer choices, and shaping production processes, its analysis and integration into economic evaluations become not just relevant but essential.

Throughout human history, economic activities have consistently been intertwined with the fundamental principles of philosophy and political science. In philosophy, the world is often categorized into two realms: the material and the spiritual. The question of which realm is primary and how the two interact has been the foundation of countless schools of thought, fueling debates that have endured for millennia. At its core, this persistent discourse arises from the inseparable nature of material and spiritual dimensions—they are distinct yet deeply interconnected.

When this philosophical divide extends into the economic sphere, it transforms into the debate surrounding the relationship between the economic base and the superstructure. The development of societal productive forces naturally gives rise to corresponding production relations, which, in turn, influence and shape the trajectory of productive forces. Observing the grand arc of human history across both Eastern and Western civilizations, we see a progression from primitive societies to slave societies, feudal systems, and eventually to the modern eras of capitalism and socialism.

In the transition from primitive to feudal societies, the overall productive forces advanced gradually. However, this progress was punctuated by fluctuations driven by dynastic transitions and social upheavals. The Industrial Revolutions in the West marked transformative leaps in productivity, akin to tectonic shifts that create towering peaks and deep valleys in the earth's crust. Similarly, pivotal historical events acted as seismic forces, producing pronounced disparities in productivity levels among different societies and regions.

Each level of productivity aligns with specific forms of production relations, economic foundations, and superstructures. Additionally, cultural influences profoundly shape societal development, imparting distinctive regional and ethnic characteristics. Even within a single nation, differences in geography and ethnicity result in diverse societal expressions, enriching the fabric of human life and creating a vibrant mosaic of global cultures.

Consider Chinese society as an example. The customs and traditions across its regions and ethnic groups trace their origins to the Xia, Shang, and Zhou dynasties, took shape during the Spring and Autumn and Warring States periods, and evolved through more than 3,000 years of history. This evolution was marked by alternating periods of unification—such as during the Qin-Han, East Jin and West Jin, Sui-Tang, Yuan, Ming, and Qing dynasties—and fragmentation, including the Three Kingdoms, Northern and Southern Dynasties, Five Dynasties and Ten Kingdoms, and the Song-Yuan periods. This history gave rise to a political, economic, and cultural system that is simultaneously unified in its continuity and diverse in its regional and ethnic characteristics.

Chinese culture, deeply interconnected yet profoundly inclusive, has been shaped by indigenous philosophies like Daoism and Confucianism, complemented by the Hundred Schools of Thought. It also absorbed external influences such as Buddhism from India, Islamic thought from the Middle East, and Judeo-Christian ideas from the West. In modern times, Chinese society has seamlessly incorporated the influential Marxist philosophy from the West, allowing it to maintain its distinct independence from Western nations and cultures, while simultaneously fostering a deep and dynamic connection with global civilization.

When assimilating foreign philosophies, the Chinese critically evaluated and localized these ideas, blending them with their indigenous traditions. This approach preserved the core principles of the imported ideologies while infusing them with distinct Chinese characteristics, resulting in a synthesis that is both similar to and distinct from the original.

The state of productive forces and production relations in each era of Chinese history is closely intertwined with the prevailing cultural, political, and economic contexts. These differences manifest in every facet of life—food and cooking methods, clothing materials and designs, architectural materials and styles, and more. From the lifestyles of peasants to the preferences of the elite, each historical period offers a cross section of consumption habits, production practices, aesthetic tastes, and personal experiences.

This leads to a profound realization: Human experiences vary greatly across eras, regions, and environments. Indeed, it is no exaggeration to say that each individual possesses a unique philosophy, worldview, and way of experiencing life.

So, does the existence of these differences mean that human experience is entirely unpredictable and beyond comprehension? Not at all. Just as the history of human development unfolds according to discernible patterns, human experience itself follows a certain logic. The reason we emphasize these differences is to encourage attention to the complexities of human experience. Even when we attempt to identify some key principles through analysis, their application must always be context-specific. It is vital to ground our understanding in objective facts and respect for reality, lest we fall into the error of dogmatism.

With that said, let us now explore and analyze the fundamental phenomena and underlying patterns of human experience across five key dimensions.

i. Different Levels of Human Needs

For every individual, all their experiences in life collectively form their overall experience. As long as a person is alive, they are constantly engaged in an exchange of information with the outside world through their senses, leading to ongoing experiences. These experiences can broadly be categorized into two types: One addresses the basic survival needs, which in philosophical terms is referred to as the economic foundation, while the other caters to the spiritual or self-fulfillment needs, which are part of the superstructure.

As previously discussed, the first level of needs, survival needs, corresponds to the basic experiences tied to the economic foundation of life. The second level, happiness needs, and the third level, self-actualization needs, are associated with supplementary experiences, or the needs of the superstructure.

For first level survival needs, the characteristics of their experiences are as follows:

(1) Rigidity. These needs are essential for survival and cannot be compromised.

(2) Homogeneity. There is little variation between individuals in these basic needs.
(3) Priority of fulfillment. In times of scarcity, these needs must be prioritized.
(4) Low tolerance. When these needs are unmet, individuals exhibit low tolerance and are likely to experience strong negative emotions, with a higher likelihood of resistance or protest.

For second level happiness needs, the characteristics are as follows:

(1) Flexibility. These needs are less rigid and allow for significant variation.
(2) Differentiation. People's preferences for happiness can vary greatly.
(3) Elasticity in priority. Each person places different levels of importance on different aspects of happiness.
(4) High tolerance. When these needs are unmet, people generally have a higher tolerance and are less likely to engage in negative actions compared to survival needs.

For third level self-actualization needs, these typically emerge only after the second level needs have been partially satisfied. Even for individuals who are considered "born wise," self-actualization becomes a possibility only once their survival and happiness needs are addressed. The characteristics of these needs are as follows:

(1) Significant variation. People's self-actualization needs differ widely based on personal experiences, education, and upbringing.
(2) Non-essential. These needs are not compulsory but rather dependent on an individual's education and accomplishment.

Historically, first and second level needs have been universally present throughout different periods of human society, but the third level needs have tended to become more prominent during specific times of societal evolution. During periods of intense social upheaval, for example, class conflicts often push both egoism and altruism to the forefront, becoming key drivers of human behavior. In times of prosperity, both egoism and altruism thrive and after basic needs are met, higher-level self-actualization needs are given more attention and expressed in various forms throughout society.

In less extreme periods, third level needs still manifest in everybody, though in different forms and degrees. For some individuals, these needs may hold greater significance, but in broader societal terms, the focus on these needs is less pronounced except during extraordinary times.

ii. Time

Time and space constitute the fundamental dimensions of human existence. While space provides the environment in which human activities unfold, time is the underlying foundation that enables societal growth and transformation. In essence, time itself is development, and development is the cumulative result of constant, fleeting changes. Every entity in the world—whether mountains, rivers, trees, flowers, lightning, thunder, creatures, or even human societies—constantly undergoes change and evolution.

Time not only alters the external forms of objects but also reshapes the inner landscape of the human spirit. Take an individual as an example: from the embryo at conception to the infant in swaddling clothes, then through the innocent youth, the energetic young adult, the ambitious middle-aged, the seasoned elder, to the frail elderly. Each stage of life, each interaction with people and events, continuously impacts one's worldview, life philosophy, and values. Every experience at a given moment is shaped by the accumulation of all prior experiences and reflections. Since a person's physical and mental states are in perpetual flux, their response to the same object or event may differ depending on their age, condition, and context. Therefore, time becomes a pivotal factor in human experience, making it a crucial subject of analysis and reflection.

Today, the term sentiment is frequently used. As the word implies, sentiment refers to the emotions and thoughts evoked when a person encounters something familiar or nostalgic. Although the term itself does not inherently carry a temporal dimension, it is often used in daily conversation to describe feelings triggered by encountering objects or memories from the past. For instance, when a person far from home stumbles upon a childhood toy, a nostalgic food, or meets an old friend by chance, their heart stirs with a powerful sense of sentiment. This wave of emotion may transport them back to their childhood, evoking vivid memories of their hometown and triggering reflections on past experiences with friends. It can bring a smile to their face or tears to their eyes.

These kinds of experiences are deeply rooted in the passage of time. They are often emotional and have the potential to trigger irrational behaviors. Classical Chinese literature frequently speaks of this as "the sight stirs up one's feelings" or "sentiment evoked by objects," referring to the profound connection between personal memories and the physical world around us. The reason a particular scene elicits such emotions is not only due to its visual appeal or uniqueness but because it prompts the viewer to recall past memories. Emotion arises from recollection—from experiences lived long ago.

Thus, experience takes on a new feature—it possesses continuity and temporal depth. Past experiences can influence present and future encounters. But conversely, new experiences can reshape how we perceive and reinterpret past ones. This idea is encapsulated in the famous Chinese proverb, "When the old man from the frontier loses his horse, how can one know it is not a blessing." Laozi also said, "Misfortune may be the source of fortune, and fortune may lie hidden within misfortune." These sayings imply that what was once considered fortunate may, over time, lead to misfortune, thereby reversing or changing our perception of that past event.

For human societies, the evolution of thought and knowledge is built upon the continual reassessment and revision of previous understandings. On an individual level, a person's intellectual growth is grounded in practice, reflection, and an ongoing process of rethinking past experiences. Therefore, human experience is intrinsically tied to human development. It is a part of the constant, moment-by-moment evolution of the self, and just as personal development is continuous, so too is the transformation of experience.

Time represents a dynamic dimension of growth and evolution. While it signifies the process of change, it does not directly dictate the direction or magnitude of those changes in human experiences. Instead, time provides a framework for understanding and analyzing experiential evolution. By tracing the flow of time, we uncover patterns and pathways that help us grasp the laws governing human experience, and this is a feasible way to do so.

For individuals, life can be divided into distinct periods, each defined by unique behavioral patterns. By examining these phases, we can identify the fundamental inclinations, preferences, and attitudes that shape their experiences during each stage of life.

For groups with shared traits—such as clans, ethnicities, or nations—we can study their collective tendencies toward specific experiences at various points in time.

From a broader perspective, the experiences of humanity as a whole can be examined across historical epochs for common features and collective tendencies. For instance, before the invention of electric lighting, people relied on candles, matches, and kerosene lamps for illumination. Those unfamiliar with electricity initially approached electric lights with fear, imagining potential dangers like explosions. Over time, as electric lighting became commonplace, people embraced its benefits. These shifts in perception illustrate how technological advancements lead to significant changes in experience across different periods (early, middle, and late stages).

Similarly, the collective experiences of the feudal era, the Industrial Revolution, and the internet age differ dramatically. While basic survival needs remain consistent, the ways people perceive and interact with their environment evolve, resulting in distinct experiential patterns.

As society advances, so do aesthetic preferences. Certain eras value intricate designs, while others champion minimalism. Some prioritize functionality, while others embrace romanticism. There are periods when unique, nationalist expressions dominate, and others when multicultural fusion is celebrated. Despite these variations, all changes in aesthetics and tastes are deeply rooted in humanity's fundamental needs at different levels.

Periods of war and upheaval destabilize the material foundations of daily life. For those struggling to meet basic needs, simplicity and practicality often become the guiding principles of existence. With energy focused on survival, spiritual (superstructure) aspirations are often suppressed. And those noble souls, deprived of opportunities to fulfill their ambitions, found solace in expressing their pent-up frustrations through various creative and impactful avenues. For example, through poetry, literature, and art, poets and artists critiqued societal issues and imagined idealized, romantic worlds; warriors and reformists sought to manifest their ambitions through heroic acts, aiding the downtrodden, or engaging in political struggles to reshape society in alignment with their ideals.

For these individuals, the harsh realities of their time fostered a deep disdain for corruption and a yearning for an idealistic world. They cherished simplicity and pragmatism, yet their hearts were deeply immersed in the world of romanticism. They yearned for freedom and the liberation of their souls, yet found themselves unable to break free from the constraints that held them, thus finding poetry in "withered vines, old trees, and crows at dusk." Their sense of beauty was often drawn from austerity and solemnity. Encountering people or things that aligned with their values brought them solace and joy, while the decadence of affluent households was met with a mix of envy and scorn.

As for those born into wealth and aristocracy, their primary concern lies in preserving their material foundation and further accumulating riches, while indulging in a life of luxury and pleasure. Within this group, there are two distinct types: Those who, despite their wealth, remain indifferent to the suffering of others; and those who, with wealth in hand, possess a deep empathy for human suffering and strive to improve the lives of others. The latter are willing to part with some of their fortune, working diligently and standing side by side with other social classes to drive the collective advancement of society. For these diverse groups, their differing worldviews shape their perspectives, which in turn influence their experiences and attitudes toward the world around them.

In times of prosperity and peace, when material living standards have reached a certain threshold, the majority of people are no longer weighed down by the struggle for mere survival. They can instead pursue their deeper ideals with relative freedom. During such periods, people's expectations for the refinement, diversity, and complexity of their surroundings increase dramatically. They favor vibrant and colorful displays over the starkness of withered branches or crows. They indulge in luxurious comforts instead of simple living, and they seek intellectual height, which often gives rise to numerous philosophical and religious movements.

These times, marked by a profound tolerance for cultural diversity, often lead to the emergence of rich, multi-layered cultural expressions. Various cultures, mixing and colliding, create a spectacular, kaleidoscopic cultural landscape. In such an era, people are naturally drawn to pursue what is unique, seeking out newness and novelty at every turn. The rarer and more unusual something is, the more it attracts attention. However, the interests and passions of the time are often fleeting, with trends coming and going in rapid succession. What is in vogue today may be replaced by something fresh tomorrow. One moment, people may be enamored with intricate, ornate designs, only to shift toward the beauty of simplicity, then explore exotic foreign styles, before eventually returning to local traditions.

In such an age, the pursuit of ultimate experiences often equates to the pursuit of profound differentiation—being valued for what sets one apart, cherished for its rarity, and treasured because of its scarcity. This relentless desire for uniqueness fuels the creation of countless short-lived yet highly profitable niche industries. On the flip side, the rapid emergence of new trends and the equally swift obsolescence of old ones often have an element of chance. What becomes popular in one era may do so due to unforeseen circumstances.

Thus, when analyzing experience, it is crucial to first clarify the specific era, national development stage, social group, and life phase being discussed. Without establishing these foundational elements, an analysis of experience lacks the necessary historical and contextual grounding. After conducting independent analyses of different groups, cross-referencing and comparing experiences across various times, stages, and life phases becomes an essential component of a thorough study.

In the exploration of experience from a temporal perspective, one key issue demands consideration and attention: the accuracy of past memories, particularly when they are triggered by nostalgia or emotional reflection. Every individual recalls the past through their own unique lens, colored by what they perceive to be true, and often influenced by what they wish or need to remember. As a result, memories are rarely an exact match to the reality of past events, especially when it comes to key moments or personal biases. These deviations, especially in the context of significant events, can be particularly pronounced.

Experience analysis, however, primarily focuses on how past memories shape our emotional responses to present events. Therefore, the key subject of study is not the objective reality of past occurrences, but rather the way an individual recalls and interprets those events. In this context, a person's authentic feelings take precedence over the factual truth of the past. This distinction is what sets experience research apart from traditional scientific inquiry. While conventional research, including psychology, tends to prioritize objective facts and the quest for truth, experience analysis is concerned with the "truth of experience" itself—that is, the lived and felt realities of individuals.

iii. Quantification

The foundation for scientifically analyzing experience hinges on whether it can be quantified. If experience can be measured in some way, enabling a mathematical description and expression, then it becomes possible to describe and analyze experience not only as a tangible reality but also as a source of measurable value.

From a directional perspective, experience inherently carries both positive and negative qualities. As previously discussed, whether for individuals or groups, experience can be classified into "good" or "bad." If we categorize all "good" experiences as positive, and all "bad" experiences as negative, we can further label those experiences that evoke feelings but lack a distinct "good or bad" distinction as relatively neutral experiences. This gives us a rough, preliminary linear diagram of experience direction, as shown in figure 1-3.

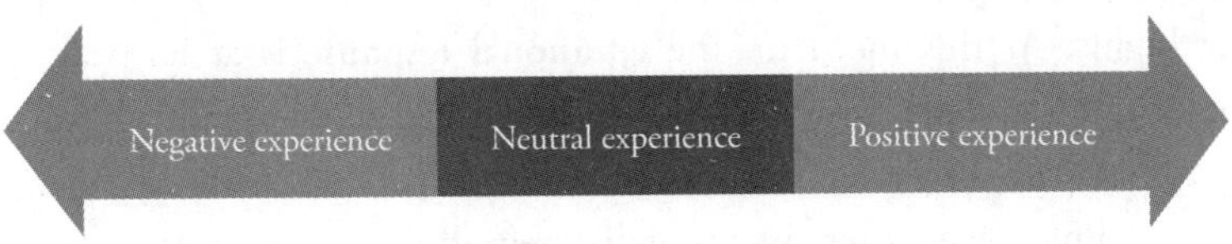

Figure 1-3 Direction of experience (conceptual)

Moreover, if we can pinpoint clues and quantify the varying degrees of experience, we can refine our understanding of experience levels and intensities. If we succeed in finding reliable units of measurement, we will be able to create a data axis for experience (fig. 1-4).

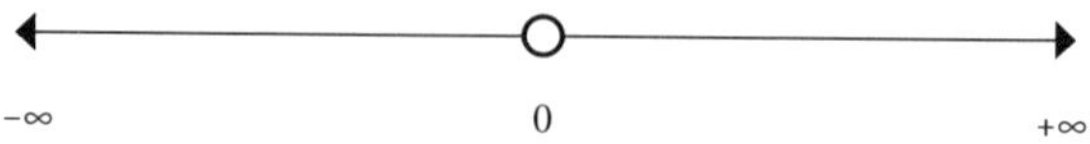

Figure 1-4 Direction of experience (numerical)

So, is it possible to develop a practical method to measure the intensity of experience? The answer is unequivocally yes, and this confidence stems from our daily observations. In everyday life, we all perceive that a person's feelings and emotions differ in intensity. Taking happiness for instance, we all experience small joys, such as the satisfaction of a minor success or the pleasure of an anticipated outcome; moderate happiness from friends or family sharing good news; hearty laughter from watching comedy or skits; great joy from unexpected surprises or momentous news that lasts for days; and, on rare occasions, extreme happiness so overwhelming it leads to a breakdown, much like the exaggerated joy portrayed in the story of Fan Jin, who was so overjoyed upon passing the imperial examination that he lost his sanity.

If we classify all experiences that generate positive feelings and emotional responses as positive experiences, it becomes clear that these emotional responses vary in degree. These positive experiences are directly correlated with the intensity of the emotions they evoke. Likewise, neutral and negative experiences follow a similar pattern. However, it's important to distinguish between experience and emotion—they are correlated, but not synonymous. While emotion is indeed a key element of experience, experience also includes the rational processes by which individuals reflect upon, refine, and elevate these emotions—what can be called "rational analysis."

For example, consider a visit to the cinema. During the screening, a viewer might be particularly impressed by the adjustable seats in terms of their material and angle, resulting in a very positive feeling, leading the viewer to rate the cinema highly. At this moment, the emotional response is at its peak, but as the movie ends and the viewer leaves the cinema, time will gradually cause this feeling to dissipate. However, the overall positive experience with the cinema may continue to linger even after the immediate emotional response fades. Although the intensity of the experience diminishes over time, it leaves an enduring impression on the viewer. This lasting experience can shape future decisions and behaviors. Furthermore, it may influence others through word-of-mouth, shaping their actions as well.

Therefore, compared to immediate emotional responses, the effects of experience tend to be more persistent over time and have a broader, more far-reaching impact.

It is essential to delve into the concept of experience extremes and the transition between positive and negative experiences, as these factors directly impact whether the measurement model for experience is linear, axis-based, or of another structure.

From an individual perspective, the experience of any specific thing—whether positive or negative—cannot extend to infinity in degree. Human physiology inherently limits the intensity of sensations to a specific range. Our sensory faculties have a finite capacity to receive external stimuli, and their conversion into neural signals, which generate feelings, is similarly constrained. Consequently, the sensory aspects of experience are necessarily bounded. While individuals may differ in their thresholds, the sensory capabilities of humanity as a biological species are ultimately finite.

Moreover, as previously discussed, even the same individual's experience of a particular thing can evolve over time due to changes in external conditions and personal growth. These changes may manifest as shifts in intensity within the same direction or as abrupt reversals between positive and negative experiences. For instance, consider a smartphone designed with sleek aesthetics, intuitive functionality, and broad appeal, leading to a high degree of positive experience for its users. If news suddenly breaks that the manufacturer compromised safety by using substandard materials—resulting in severe hazards, such as explosions—public perception may shift dramatically. In such cases, the same group of users could experience a sudden decline in positive sentiment or even a complete reversal to strong negative feelings. This reversal occurs because foundational needs, like safety, are more rigid and essential compared to secondary needs like comfort or appearance. Once a critical need is undermined, no amount of secondary satisfaction can offset the deficit.

In traditional Chinese culture, there is a saying: "When things reach an extreme, they inevitably reverse." This reflects the idea that when something reaches its peak, it already carries the seeds of its own decline, and under certain conditions, it may turn bad. Conversely, even in the depths of misfortune, there exists the potential for a turn of fortune. The earlier story that "when the old man from the frontier loses his horse, how can one know it is not a blessing?" embodies this same underlying principle.

In the realm of human emotions, similar dynamics can be observed. Phrases like "a mix of love and hate" or "the deeper the love, the stronger the hate" capture this interplay. The closer and more intimate a relationship, the more likely minor disagreements can escalate into intense negative emotions. In everyday life, we often see that something once adored can abruptly become detested, or conversely, things or individuals we once despised can transform into sources of great affection as our mindset evolves. Emotional intensity, shaped by cumulative experiences and reinforced perceptions, directly influences the degree of an individual's experience.

Figure 1-5 The *yin-yang* symbol

As the saying goes, quantitative change leads to qualitative change. When emotions accumulate to a critical level, they can undergo a fundamental shift, sometimes even reversing direction. This transformation is often illustrated in Chinese thought through the iconic *yin-yang* symbol (fig. 1-5).

The *yin-yang* symbol encapsulates the dynamic transformation between opposing forces: *yin* and *yang*. It demonstrates that *yin* contains *yang*, and *yang* contains *yin*, with both energies evolving sequentially and cyclically into one another. At its essence, the symbol captures the ebb and flow of these energies, emphasizing their shifting dominance and balance over time.

When describing experience levels, a dual-perspective approach is necessary due to the complex nature of experiences: The first is emotional aspects. Positive and negative feelings are treated as *yang* and *yin*, respectively. The second is rational vs. emotional components. When analyzing a person's experience of a specific event or object as a whole, the emotional and rational dimensions can also be viewed as another pair of opposing forces.

To understand the transition between positive and negative feelings, a simple categorization method can be applied. Positive and negative feelings are each rated on a scale from 0 to 9, as shown in table 1-1.

Table 1-1 Levels of emotional experience

Feeling direction	**Emotional levels**									
Positive feelings (*yang*)	0	1	2	3	4	5	6	7	8	9
Negative feelings (*yin*)	0	1	2	3	4	5	6	7	8	9

It's important to note that feelings are not discrete or isolated but part of a continuous spectrum. The integers from 0 to 9 serve only as reference markers.

A neutral state arises when the difference between positive and negative feeling levels is ≤ 1. However, neutrality can be further divided into stable and unstable neutrality. Stable neutrality occurs when both positive and negative feelings are ≤ 4. In this state, neither energy is dominant, resulting in mild emotional fluctuations and relative stability. As the intensity of positive and negative feelings increases beyond 4, their energies grow stronger, leading to fierce internal conflict. Although neither dominates, this results in a volatile state, akin to someone torn between deep love and intense resentment in a complex relationship. The *Book of Changes* · Kun *Hexagram* poetically describes such scenarios, "The dragons (*yang*) wars upon the wild (*yin*). Their blood flows in a chaos of dark and yellow." This metaphor signifies intense conflict and instability.

The relationship between positive and negative feelings can be expressed mathematically:

$$\text{Emotional level} = |\text{Positive feeling level}| - |\text{Negative feeling level}|$$

The highest possible emotional level is 9, representing absolute positivity, while the lowest is –9, representing absolute negativity. This spectrum is summarized in table 1-2.

Table 1-2 Emotional level scale

Emotional level																		
–9	–8	–7	–6	–5	–4	–3	–2	–1	0	1	2	3	4	5	6	7	8	9

Here, positive and negative feelings are analyzed separately rather than represented as a single overall value with positive or negative signs. This approach highlights the fact that one's overall emotional state toward the same object often formulate through the interplay of coexisting positive and negative emotions, a process that requires attention as well.

The fluctuations in positive and negative feelings are the underlying drivers of sudden shifts in overall emotional levels. Much like studying a biological macromolecule as a whole while also examining its atomic structure and chemical bonds, it is essential to explore the evolution and interaction of positive and negative feelings. These dynamics form the foundation for understanding changes in the overall emotional experience.

With this foundation, we can now examine the relationship between the rational and emotional components of experience. For simplicity, we assume that the influence of rational and emotional factors on experience levels is equal—that is, a 1-unit change in emotional intensity has the same impact on experience as a 1-unit change in rational judgment. The rational component, like the emotional one, can also be measured on a scale from –9 to 9, as shown in table 1-3.

Table 1-3 Comparative levels of emotional and rational evaluation

Emotional level																		
–9	–8	–7	–6	–5	–4	–3	–2	–1	0	1	2	3	4	5	6	7	8	9
Rational level																		
–9	–8	–7	–6	–5	–4	–3	–2	–1	0	1	2	3	4	5	6	7	8	9

Does this scale meet the practical requirements for evaluating experiences? Typically, the level of experience should reflect emotional evaluation processed through rational judgment. However, is this processing a straightforward linear addition or subtraction? Could it involve multiplicative or even exponential effects? For instance, if the emotional level is 2 and the rational level is –3, should the overall experience level be calculated as $2 + (-3) = -1$, $2 \times (-3) = -6$, or something else entirely? The outcome depends on the specific nature of the rational processing. To explore this, let us analyze a few representative scenarios:

(1) Case 1: positive emotion and positive rationality. For example, eating an apple feels sweet (positive emotion), and it's deemed healthy (positive rationality). The result is a delightful experience—the sweet apple is perceived as a positive experience overall.

(2) Case 2: positive emotion and negative rationality. For example, eating an apple feels sweet (positive emotion), but for someone with diabetes, the sugar intake is harmful, leading to a conflicting outcome: a positive feeling but an overall negative experience. However, the individual may still associate the apple with a positive experience if they purchase it for family members without diabetes. In this case, the positive experience stems not from the apple itself but from the joy and appreciation received from their family. For the family members without diabetes, the apple becomes a source of enjoyment. Meanwhile, the individual, though personally having a negative experience with eating the apple, finds positivity in the happiness it brings to their loved ones. This observation can be further refined into two specific scenarios: First, the emotion is positive, but rationality is negative, with the negative rationality outweighing the positive emotion. In such cases, the influence of rationality leads to an overall negative experience. Second, the emotion is positive, but rationality is negative, with the negative rationality being less significant than the positive emotion. Here, despite the negative rational influence, the overall experience remains positive. For instance, a person might know that consuming sugar is harmful to their health but find such joy in the act that they are willing to compromise their well-being to indulge in the pleasure of eating sugar.

(3) Case 3: negative emotion and positive rationality. For example, eating bitter gourd tastes unpleasant (negative emotion), but it's recognized as healthy (positive rationality). There are two results: First, rationality outweighs emotion—the experience is positive overall due to the stronger rational assessment; second, emotion outweighs rationality—the negative emotional response dominates, resulting in a negative overall experience.

(4) Case 4: negative emotion and negative rationality. For example, bitter almonds taste unpleasant (negative emotion) and are judged to be toxic (negative rationality). As a result, this is a wholly negative experience, with no mitigating factors.

The interaction between emotional and rational levels can generally be modeled using simple changes in scale values, effectively capturing many common scenarios in daily life. The experience level can be calculated as experience level = emotional level + rational level. The scale ranges from [−18, +18], where both emotional and rational levels are continuous variables within finite bounds. Consequently, the experience level can take on integer values, fractions, or even irrational numbers.

iv. Accumulation of Experiences and Their Rate of Change

In life, "emotion" is a theme that never fades. Before exploring the dynamics of experience accumulation, it is essential to address a closely related question: How emotions are formed. Human experiences of the external world arise from both sensory perception and rational judgment. Naturally, the patterns by which sensations occur and evolve significantly influence the development of experiences. Let us examine this through the journey of a human life.

From the moment a newborn enters the world, they begin to interact with their surroundings through their senses. For an infant, the first points of contact are their parents, close family members, and the immediate home environment. Under the loving care of their family, the child thrives. As they grow older, their interactions expand to include other children and their families. Over time, as their physical and mental capacities mature, their independence and critical thinking abilities also develop and deepen.

Gradually, they broaden their circle of interactions, encountering an ever-growing number of people and things, and witnessing the vast wonders of the world and the myriad expressions of humanity. During this exploration, some individuals enter their lives, becoming cherished friends or antagonists, while others remain fleeting acquaintances—brief encounters that end as quickly as they begin.

As they transition into old age, many of the people they once knew gradually fade away. Only those bound by familial ties and lifelong friends, forged through shared trials and profound connections, remain by their side. Finally, as they approach the end of their journey, they pass away quietly amid the grief of loved ones, returning to solitude once more.

Throughout such a lifetime, they inevitably meet countless individuals, but not every meeting results in a meaningful emotional connection. Even fewer relationships leave behind profound and lasting emotions. Upon reflection, the formation of relationships between individuals appears governed by two fundamental factors: the serendipity of encounters and the reinforcement and elevation of those connections through repeated interactions.

The serendipity of encounters determines whether individuals have the opportunity to meet and form an initial bond. Familiarity and understanding, however, depend on repeated reinforcement, which in turn shapes the development and depth of emotional connections.

For instance, it is often said that filial piety is the foundation of all virtues. For an individual, their parents hold the deepest bond of fate due to the gift of life itself. Society frequently measures a person's character and moral standing by their treatment of their parents. This is because the bond of blood relations, combined with the profound and selfless love between parents and children, is unparalleled. Parents typically dedicate themselves to their children with unwavering care and sacrifice, making parental love one of the most revered emotions in human life.

In reality, particularly during early stages of life, individuals live under the protection and guidance of their parents. Compared to other relationships, the parent-child connection is far more intimate due to constant interaction and proximity. Parents (or other caregivers) are the people a child encounters most frequently, their voices the most heard, their embrace the child's longest safe haven, their meals the primary source of nourishment, and the home they create the central living environment.

A person's initial way of life, habits, fundamental outlook on the world, and even their personality and preferences are largely a reflection of their upbringing and the influence of their parents. Children often bear profound imprints of their parents' behavior, even before forming their own self-awareness. Just as parents love their children deeply, children, particularly in the early stages of life, share an equally profound love for their parents. As parents age and require more care, the increased time spent together often strengthens this bond even further.

Thus, the essence of a deep relationship lies in frequent, intimate interactions and the shared life experiences that cultivate profound emotional connections.

Beyond the parent-child relationship, individuals encounter many people throughout their lives. Generally, all emotional bonds are rooted in sustained, meaningful interactions over a period—whether during one continuous phase or across multiple intervals.

For example, two individuals who initially do not know each other may begin exchanging messages or phone calls daily at a set time. Over several months, this routine could evolve into a habit. If suddenly interrupted, even if their relationship was previously insignificant, both may feel an unfamiliar sense of discomfort.

When these daily exchanges go beyond superficial communication to include emotional elements—such as sharing thoughts, experiences, and encouragement—a budding emotional connection begins to emerge. An unexpected disruption of this communication could spark curiosity and concern, prompting further interaction and potentially deepening the bond.

On this foundation, if the two individuals begin meeting in person with some regularity or attending activities together, their emotional connection will likely deepen further, provided there is no strong mutual aversion. The frequency, depth, and substance of their interactions directly contribute to the growth of their bond. Romantic relationships between men and women exemplify this dynamic.

While the specifics of real-life experiences vary widely, the underlying emotional process remains consistent. For instance, some couples establish deep connections through intense interactions over a short period; others, constrained by external factors, develop their bond more slowly over an extended timeline; some relationships blossom quickly due to an immediate positive impression, requiring fewer subsequent interactions to solidify; others start modestly, gradually evolving into deeper affection through repeated interactions.

Naturally, there are instances where repeated interactions between two individuals fail to cultivate a deep emotional bond. This often occurs when one party lacks genuine interest in the other, resulting in an unwillingness to foster deeper connections or even a deliberate reduction in the frequency and substance of communication.

Consistent interaction and dialogue undoubtedly enhance mutual understanding. However, this understanding encompasses both areas of alignment and areas of divergence. The degree to which these aspects align ultimately determines the nature of the emotional connection, the closeness of the relationship, and the depth of affection shared.

When mutual interests are aligned—such as shared career aspirations, similar lifestyle preferences, or agreement on significant issues—emotional resonance deepens, bringing the individuals closer together. Conversely, when interests conflict—such as differing life goals, contrasting views on effort and reward, or incompatible visions for the future—these discrepancies can create rifts that push them further apart.

As the connection between two individuals deepens and their understanding of each other grows to a certain degree, a sense of familiarity inevitably sets in. This familiarity often diminishes curiosity and novelty, and even minor changes in established routines can give rise to conflicts and misunderstandings. This phenomenon is universal, occurring in relationships with family members, close friends, romantic partners, and even business associates.

In parent-child relationships, such shifts are particularly evident during adolescence and menopause, periods marked by significant changes in attitudes, behaviors, and coordination. For romantic partners, this phase typically arises after the initial passion of courtship wanes, during the transition to a more stable but less exhilarating routine, as differences in habits and expectations become more apparent. Similarly, friendships and business partnerships often follow a trajectory where closeness peaks before gradually giving way to distance or detachment.

This principle also applies to people's relationships with objects. For example, when someone is hungry, a simple piece of bread may feel like a divine feast. However, once the hunger is satisfied, even the most exquisite cuisine can lose its appeal. To reignite interest, the individual must either experience hunger again or develop a renewed sense of anticipation for the food.

When a person's emotions toward someone or something are steadily building and intensifying, their progression often mirrors the principle of diminishing marginal effects observed in economics, and it applies equally to both positive and negative emotions. When someone dislikes another person, continuous exposure may lead to habituation, gradually dulling the intensity of the aversion. Unless new incidents repeatedly reinforce negative impressions, the initial hostility often subsides, eventually settling into a state of indifference—a phenomenon frequently described as "getting used to it." Because human experiences are intrinsically tied to emotions and perceptions, they tend to follow these same patterns.

An individual's experience of a person or object evolves over time, accumulating, changing, and developing through fleeting impressions and the frequency of interaction. The trajectory and depth of this evolution depend on the nature—positive or negative—and intensity of each interaction, as well as the frequency and timing of these encounters.

v. The Infinite Nature of Experience Content

Previously we have discussed the limitations of the degree of experience. Another crucial aspect warrants attention: the infinite nature of the content of experiences. Life is a dynamic tapestry of ever-changing phenomena—be it the impermanence of the natural world, the unpredictability of human relationships, or the complexities of social interactions. Living in a world that constantly evolves, our experiences, from childhood to adulthood, from personal ideas to social, ethnic, and national perceptions, are in perpetual flux. The infinite nature of experiential content manifests primarily in four key dimensions.

1. The Infinity of Experiential Objects

As human society progresses, our transformation into the world continually expands. Urbanization and rural development bring shifts in daily life and production tools, while advancements in science reshape our relationship with nature. The ways we connect and communicate, particularly in the information age, have undergone profound changes. These evolving conditions alter the objects and mediums of our interactions with the external world.

Scientific developments have widened our observational scope—from the macroscopic universe to the microscopic quantum and string theory dimensions. Our natural sensory limits are supplemented by technologies that allow us to perceive electromagnetic spectra, sound waves, and other previously imperceptible phenomena. Given the boundless nature of external realities in terms of scope and transformation, the objects of human experience are infinite in number and diversity.

2. The Infinity of Sensations

The emotional and sensory aspects of experiences are equally infinite, evident in two main ways. First, within the finite range of experiential intensity, each level can be infinitely subdivided. Second, as time passes and personal experiences evolve, even feelings toward the same object can shift, not only in degree but also in fundamental nature.

Human emotions possess considerable complexity, which arises from and evolves with the synthetic outcome of experiences and their derivatives. They transcend simplistic dichotomies like warmth or coldness, sweetness or bitterness, manifesting instead as a rich spectrum of sentiments such as love, nostalgia, resentment, hesitation, confusion, melancholy, jealousy, and more. These emotions often coexist, intertwine, and influence each other, creating unique and multifaceted emotional states. This inherent complexity underscores the infinite variability of human sensations.

3. The Infinity of Rational Analysis

In addition to emotions, experiences involve rational analysis and verification. Rationality is shaped by an individual's unique worldview, values, and methods of reasoning—products of their life experiences and subject to continual refinement over time.

Rational analysis is influenced by two factors: the completeness of information about a given object and the individual's perspective and approach to interpreting it. It encompasses logical connections and seemingly spontaneous "eureka" moments, which, while rooted in prior experiences, often appear as sudden bursts of creativity. Such moments of inspiration, whose existence should be acknowledged, frequently drive innovation and artistic creation, underscoring the infinite possibilities within rational analysis.

4. The Infinity of Interconnected Experiences

The previous discussion, which included a mathematical expression of how experiences are influenced by various factors, underscores the deeply interconnected nature of individuals' experiences with related phenomena. From the perspectives of people and objects, the following insights emerge: First, in social interactions, an individual's perception and understanding of a specific object are often significantly influenced by the opinions of others. Second, people's views on two related objects tend to influence and interact with one another. In the realm of retail and consumer behavior analysis, correlation analysis is frequently utilized, particularly when determining how products are arranged on supermarket shelves. These arrangements often rely on the relationships between items commonly purchased together. Similarly, in daily life, individuals frequently base their expectations for new products on their early experiences or impressions of similar items.

For instance, one who has had highly positive experiences with the first and second generations of iPhones is likely to hold high expectations for future iterations of Apple products. Similarly, fans deeply moved by Steven Spielberg's earlier films often anticipate his new works with great enthusiasm.

This inherent interconnectedness between objects, with their countless forms of relationships and varying degrees of closeness, underscores the infinite possibilities of such connections. Consequently, experiences associated with these objects naturally embody the same boundless potential.

vi. Summary

Through the discussions and analyses in this section, several key characteristics of experiences can be summarized as follows:

(1) Experiences are intrinsically linked to needs. Each category and level of need is associated with distinct experiential characteristics.
(2) Time is a critical determinant. The evolution of experiences is heavily influenced by the passage of time, making it essential to consider temporal attributes in any analysis.
(3) Experiences are dynamic. They evolve and change continuously over time.
(4) Life events shape experiences. The content of an individual's experiences is closely tied to their sequence of life events and personal growth over time.
(5) Experiences can be quantified. They exhibit directionality, have a finite intensity, and can vary continuously within those limits. Additionally, their levels can be infinitely subdivided for detailed analysis.

(6) Experiences are cumulative. They are shaped by immediate impressions during interactions, the frequency of those interactions, and the reinforcement of these impressions in memory. Both positive and negative experiences show diminishing marginal effects as they accumulate.
(7) Experiences are finite in intensity but infinite in scope. While the depth or intensity of experiences has limits, their content and diversity are boundless.

VI. General Methods for Quantitative Evaluation of Experiences

i. Categorization of Quantitative Methods for Evaluating Experiences

Understanding that experiences can be quantified and refined into varying degrees and levels, it becomes essential to identify appropriate methods for measuring an individual's experience with specific external stimuli. Based on the internet industry insights and practical applications, measurement methods can be categorized along several dimensions.

Experience evaluation can be divided into three stages, based on the timing of interaction between the subject (the individual experiencing) and the object (the stimulus of the experience):

(1) Pre-experience measurement. This involves assessing impressions and expectations formed before any direct interaction with the object. These impressions may stem from recommendations, advertisements, previous encounters with related or similar objects, or personal imagination based on prior knowledge and expectations.
(2) During-experience measurement. This evaluates the subject's perceptions and feelings during their interaction with the object. For experiences occurring over multiple interactions, this includes feedback from each encounter.
(3) Post-experience measurement. This measures the overall impressions and reflections formed after the interaction is complete. For multi-phase experiences, it encompasses evaluations after each individual encounter and a final summary assessment once all interactions are concluded.

Measurement methods can also be classified based on how subjects express or demonstrate their experience:

(1) Opinion and attitude measurement. Through interviews, questionnaires, or similar tools, this method captures subjective feelings as expressed by the

individual. This approach is advantageous for exploring authentic emotions and deeper motivations but is influenced by the subject's ability to articulate their experience, and psychological barriers or biases, which can lead to incomplete, distorted, or inaccurate responses.

(2) Physiological metrics measurement. This objective method uses specialized tools to monitor physiological responses such as heart rate, blood flow, brain activity, facial expressions, and reflexes. These indicators are scientifically analyzed to infer emotional states and translate them into measurable experience levels. However, two main challenges arise: difficulty in accurately correlating physiological indicators with subjective psychological experience, and the influence of extraneous factors (e.g., health or environmental conditions) on physiological states, potentially affecting reliability.

(3) Behavioral response measurement. It refers to methods that assess the level of experience based on a series of physical actions exhibited by the subject. Examples include evaluating body coordination during the use of fitness equipment, analyzing finger tap patterns and frequencies on touchscreen devices, tracking purchase behavior rates, and observing recommendations made to others. Behavioral response measurement, as a method that focuses solely on assessing actions directly related to the experience object, is particularly valued for its ability to leverage comprehensive data sets; deliver objective and reliable results; and provide insights with clear, actionable value. However, while it can capture and analyze behavioral motivations in certain contexts, there are limitations: They focus on observable actions and often fail to reveal the underlying motivations; and they require significant investments in data collection systems, instrumentation, and ongoing optimization, which incurs notable resource costs.

It is particularly noteworthy that, within behavioral response measurement, a distinctive method for acquiring and assessing information involves capturing and analyzing public interactions with specific products. This includes tracking search keywords, reviews, opinions, ratings, and shared content. By applying keyword analysis techniques, this approach transforms public sentiment about a product's experiential value into measurable data, commonly known as public opinion monitoring.

Opinions and attitudes toward a commodity, expressed naturally in unstructured interactions, can provide an authentic and valuable supplement to the information often missing from structured interviews, where environmental constraints or personal reservations may limit disclosure. Moreover, public opinion monitoring excels in its capacity for automation, broad scope, and integration with big data and cloud platforms, enabling efficient computation and automated reporting. These features make it particularly attractive within the internet industry. However, this method has limitations. For instance, individuals with specific motives may manipulate reviews or ratings, hiring others to fabricate feedback and skew public perception. Despite such risks, this method is especially valuable for analyzing public attitudes that require large sample sizes, often yielding insights that reflect macro-level trends and patterns.

Measurement methods can also be categorized based on sample size, yielding six primary types: qualitative small-sample measurement, qualitative large-sample measurement, qualitative full-sample measurement, quantitative small-sample measurement, quantitative large-sample measurement, and quantitative full-sample measurement. The sample size is directly tied to the measurement method and its objectives.

(1) Small-sample measurement. This is typically employed for in-depth interviews or observational studies requiring detailed analysis of each participant. Such measurement is often limited by time and resources provided to participants as incentives. However, a small sample size does not necessarily mean incomplete information. According to Nielsen's classic usability testing theory, as few as 6–8 participants can uncover over 80% of usability issues. In practice, 10–12 participants with appropriate demographic representation are generally sufficient to yield reliable and persuasive results.
(2) Large-sample measurement. This does not necessarily involve full samples but instead focuses on representative samples with sufficient demographic diversity to address specific objectives. Large sample sizes vary depending on the context and may range from hundreds to tens of thousands. Researchers typically design standardized surveys distributed via online or offline channels to gather feedback effectively.
(3) Full-sample measurement. This approach involves monitoring every individual product through embedded data points or sensors throughout its life cycle—from production to usage and eventual disposal. And the product management system gathers comprehensive data by meticulously tracking and monitoring every product, enabling detailed analysis based on this complete data set. Full-sample measurement requires upfront investment in data platform development and the integration of monitoring devices (e.g., sensors or data points) during manufacturing. Additionally, ongoing updates to

both hardware and software systems are necessary to maintain and enhance monitoring capabilities over time.

When conducting quantitative evaluations of user experience, the appropriate method can be selected based on predefined dimensions, as illustrated in the sample template provided in table 1-4. This systematic approach ensures clarity throughout the measurement process.

Table 1-4 Experience evaluation measurement (template)

Name	(Enter the name of the product or item being measured)
Objective	(Describe the purpose or goal of the measurement)
Category	☐ Physical product ☐ Service product ☐ Electronic virtual product ☐ Smart hardware product ☐ Other
By experience phase	☐ Pre-experience ☐ Mid-experience ☐ Post-experience
By operation method	☐ Opinion/Attitude ☐ Physiological indicators ☐ Behavioral response
By qualitative/ quantitative	☐ Qualitative ☐ Quantitative
By sample size	☐ Small sample (≤ 30) ☐ Large sample (> 30) ☐ Full sample
Sample size	(Specify the exact sample size)
Sample attribute distribution	**Gender**: ☐ Male ☐ Female **Age**: ☐ Below 14 ☐ 14–35 ☐ 36–45 ☐ 45–60 ☐ Above 60 **Monthly income**: ☐ Below RMB 5,000 ☐ RMB 5,000–10,000 ☐ RMB 10,000–20,000 ☐ Above RMB 20,000 **Region**: Province: City/County: District:
Output format	☐ Data charts ☐ Analytical report ☐ Market strategy recommendations ☐ Other

ii. Example of Quantitative Experience Evaluation

To demonstrate the methods described earlier, let's take the example of evaluating a specific item—a water cup. The evaluation process comprises six primary stages: defining evaluation indicators, planning and allocating resources, executing the plan, collecting and analyzing data, producing evaluation results, and applying the findings. In this example, we will focus exclusively on opinion and attitude measurement during the experience phase.

The evaluation consists of three interconnected components:

(1) The object-specific indicator table is designed to align with the characteristics of the object and the evaluation objectives. It balances practicality and operational simplicity of implementation, with scoring systems that can vary based on specific needs, such as 100-point, 10-point, 7-point, or 5-point scales.
(2) The experience level measurement table is a standardized tool that reflects the overall experience level of the object. It allows for horizontal comparisons across different objects. An example of such a scale is the previously mentioned range of [−18, +18].
(3) The conversion relationship table serves as a link between the object-specific indicator table and the experience level measurement table. It facilitates the transformation of diverse metrics into a unified, comparable experience measurement scale.

The object-specific indicator table should be tailored to the specific measurement objectives. For instance, when evaluating an individual's experience with a particular water cup (the measurement object), and assuming the individual has no prior expectations of the product, the objective would focus on assessing the participant's actual usage experience—specifically, their real-time interaction with the product.

Key evaluation dimensions for the water cup include basic size and weight; aesthetic appeal; handling comfort; safety features—anti-scald, anti-slip, and durability; additional preferences—unique features or material preferences. If the water cup serves a specific purpose, specialized indicators should be established to evaluate its performance. However, for simplicity, this example assumes the cup is intended for regular, everyday use.

Based on the analysis above, we can develop a simple experience measurement table (table 1-5) and assign appropriate weights, scoring criteria, and evaluation methods tailored to the actual context.

Table 1-5 Experience measurement table (template)

No.	Primary indicator	Secondary indicator	Weight	Description	Score
1	Size & Weight (5%)	Length/Width/Height	2.5%	Optimal size and weight, avoiding extremes	
2		Weight	2.5%		
3	Aesthetic appeal (25%)	Material	10%	The aesthetic appeal of the appearance resulting from material combinations (e.g., reflective or refractive effects)	
4		Colors	8%	The attractiveness of the colors	
5		Shape	7%	The aesthetic appeal of the shape and design	
6	Handling comfort (30%)	Short-term comfort	18%	Comfort level within five minutes of holding time	
7		Long-term comfort	6%	Comfort level for holding time greater than five minutes and less than two hours	
8		Heat retention	6%	The heat retention effectiveness	
9	Safety features (40%)	Anti-scald	15%	Anti-scalding mechanism design	
10		Anti-slip	15%	Anti-slip mechanism design	
11		Durability	10%	The hardness and flexibility of the material, and its ability to withstand heavy pressure and collision	
12	Additional preferences (0–20 points)	Special preferences	Bonus points	Unique user preferences	
	Total		100%		

The most commonly used scoring method is the rating scale, such as a 10-point scale. Each metric is assigned a score ranging from 0 to 10, creating 11 levels in total. Test participants are invited to use the water cup and rate each metric individually based on their experience. For some specific products or features, the evaluation process may include task-based experiences. Participants complete designated tasks, and evaluators not only gather scores but also observe and record participants' performance, noting any challenges or difficulties encountered. This helps identify negative experience issues. Additionally, observing participants' facial expressions and emotional reactions during the process provides insights into positive feedback.

After defining the evaluation metrics, scoring methods, and standards, the next step is to organize the assessment. This involves determining the number of participants (along with their demographic attributes), arranging suitable venues, and preparing necessary documents and tools, such as recording devices. If incentives like small gifts or transportation reimbursements are offered, these resources should be secured in advance.

Once all preparations are complete, the quantifiable experience evaluation can proceed. Data is collected and analyzed, culminating in the creation of a comprehensive report. The findings from this report can then be utilized in various ways—providing insights to experience object (commodity) designers for optimization, or serving as a reference for the quality control team to assess and improve performance.

iii. Universal Experience Evaluation Model for Different Types of Items

In the evaluation process described earlier, the most crucial factor influencing the final results is the formulation of a quantifiable experience evaluation model. When developing such a model, the following two approaches can serve as useful references:

First, pleasure evaluation model. This model assesses the experience level of a target item by considering a comprehensive range of sensory and emotional dimensions, typically including the following:

(1) Sensory pleasure. Incorporates perceptions from sight, sound, smell, taste, and touch.
(2) Behavioral comfort. Evaluates ease of use and intuitiveness of operation.
(3) Temporal aspects. Includes nostalgic value from past experiences and anticipation for future use.

(4) Emotional value-add. Considers elements such as satisfying vanity, showcasing personal value, and enhancing dignity.
(5) Rational judgments. Focuses on logical factors like value-for-money assessments.

When designing this model, it is essential to allocate appropriate weights to the number of experience dimensions considered and the intensity of experience within each dimension. Generally, the more dimensions a target item satisfies and the higher the experience level within those dimensions, the greater its overall evaluation score will be. Conversely, failing to meet these criteria will result in a lower evaluation score. Table 1-6 offers an example of this type of model for reference.

Based on table 1-6, once the number of dimensions and their respective scores are determined, the next step involves converting these scores into a comprehensive evaluation. By assigning appropriate weights to both the dimension count and individual scores, a final experience level score for the evaluated item can be calculated.

Second, experience hierarchy model for various needs. This model aligns experience evaluation with distinct levels of human needs, typically categorized into the following:

(1) Level one, survival needs, includes nutritional needs, respiratory needs, shelter needs, safety needs, reproductive needs, and social needs.
(2) Level two, happiness needs, includes respect needs, emotional needs, leisure needs, entertainment needs, quality and refinement needs, and self-improvement needs.
(3) Level three, self-actualization needs, includes ego-centric needs and altruistic needs.

Table 1-7 illustrates a sample model of this type. It provides a framework for assessing a typical restaurant's experience level. The evaluation covers the following dimensions:

(1) Nutritional needs: how delicious the food is.
(2) Safety needs: the quality and safety of the food, as well as the adequacy of safety measures like fire and explosion prevention in the restaurant environment.

Table 1-6 Pleasure evaluation model (template)

		Dimension count		Pleasure score											
				Low				Medium			High				Score
		Counted	Number	0	1	2	3	4	5	6	7	8	9	10	
Sensory pleasure	Sight	Yes	1												8
	Sound	Yes	1												5
	Smell	No	0												0
	Taste	No	0												0
	Touch	Yes	1												6
Behavioral comfort	Ease of use	Yes	1												6
	Intuitiveness of operation	Yes	1												7
Temporal aspects	Nostalgic value from past experiences	Yes	1												5
	Anticipation for future use	No	0												0
Emotional value-add	Vanity	Yes	1												7
	Dignity	Yes	1												6
	Personality	No	0												0
	Emotional bonding	No	0												0
Rational judgments	Value-for-money	Yes	1												6
Total			9												56

Table 1-7 Experience hierarchy model for various needs (template)

		Dimension count		Pleasure score											
				Low (basic)				Medium (proper enjoyment)			High (enjoyment)				Score
		Counted	Number	0	1	2	3	4	5	6	7	8	9	10	
Level one: survival needs	Nutritional needs	Yes	1												8
	Respiratory needs	No	0												0
	Shelter needs	No	0												0
	Safety needs	Yes	1												9
	Reproductive needs	No	0												0
	Social needs	No	0												0
Level two: happiness needs	Respect needs	Yes	1												7
	Emotional needs	No	0												0
	Leisure needs	Yes	1												6
	Entertainment needs	No	0												0
	Quality and refinement needs	Yes	1												8
	Self-improvement needs	No	0												0
Level three: self-actualization needs	Ego-centric needs	No	0												0
	Altruistic needs	No	0												0
Total			5												38

(3) Respect needs: the level of politeness and respect shown by the staff toward customers.
(4) Leisure needs: how relaxing and comfortable the restaurant's decor makes the environment feel.
(5) Quality and refinement needs: the overall sense of satisfaction and enjoyment provided by the restaurant.

Using this framework, the number of dimensions and their respective scores are calculated. These scores are then converted into weighted values to derive the restaurant's overall experience level.

iv. Transforming Quantitative Evaluation Results into a Standardized Scale

After evaluating individual perceptions of an object's experience level using the aforementioned methods and tools, standardization is necessary. This is due to variations in evaluation content and scoring methods across different objects. A straightforward method is to map the scores directly onto a standardized experience level scale, such as the [−18, +18] range. However, practical complexities often necessitate further adjustments and refinements.

There are two levels of the conversion of the evaluation results: First, individual-level conversion. Each participant's evaluation results are converted into a score that reflects their personal experience level with the object. Second, aggregate-level analysis and conversion. Results from all participants are statistically analyzed to produce an overall experience level score for the object.

The example provided focuses on a relatively simple case: measuring mid-experience attitudes and perceptions. However, to achieve a more comprehensive understanding of participants' experience levels, it is essential to evaluate all phases of interaction with the product—pre-experience, mid-experience, and post-experience—ensuring each phase is thoroughly assessed and assigned appropriate weighting. For physiological indicators, psychological research methods and tools are typically utilized for measurement and evaluation. These results are then translated into insights on emotions and attitudes using established psychological models. For behavioral response indicators, data collection is often achieved through embedded tracking points or sensor-based observations. Advanced big data technologies are employed to analyze this information, transforming the findings into actionable insights about participants' perception levels.

CHAPTER II

Analyzing the Economic Characteristics of Experience

Economic activities, fundamentally defined by the exchange of goods and the evaluation of value, represent the processes of resource allocation in human society. Goods become commodities within economic activities due to their exchange value, circulating through markets via economic transactions.

Does "experience" influence economic activities? If it does, in what forms and through what mechanisms does it manifest? To what extent does this influence affect economic outcomes? What economic patterns emerge as the nature of experiences evolves? Does "experience" hold measurable value? Can its value be effectively quantified? These questions form the foundation for our exploration of the role of experience in economics. This chapter seeks to provide a focused analysis of these questions.

I. Manifestation and Role of Experience in Economic Activities

Let us begin with the most fundamental unit of economic activity: the commodity. Using a water cup, a common household item, as an example, we can explore how human experiences intertwine with such an object. Based on the analysis of varying levels of human needs from chapter I, the demand for a water cup can be classified into three distinct tiers:

(1) Level one: survival needs. At the most basic level, a water cup fulfills its primary purpose of storing and holding water, meeting essential hydration requirements. To address safety concerns, the cup's design should feature

smooth, rounded shapes to avoid sharp edges. Additionally, materials with insulating properties should be used to protect users from extreme temperatures, preventing potential injuries caused by excessive heat or cold.

(2) Level two: happiness needs. Moving beyond utility, the water cup becomes an object of personal enjoyment and comfort. A visually appealing design satisfies aesthetic preferences, while unique or personalized styles cater to individuality and vanity. Customization—such as tailoring the cup to fit the user's hand size and usage habits—enhances comfort during use. Special materials can be employed to regulate the temperature of specific beverages. Additionally, cups adorned with meaningful inscriptions or creative designs can serve as tools for emotional expression, fostering deeper connections between individuals.

(3) Level three: self-actualization needs. At the highest level, the water cup transcends its physical form to become a medium for fulfilling personal aspirations and contributing to the happiness of others. Examples include designing specialized cups to meet the needs of specific user groups, donating surplus cups to underserved communities, or using the cup as a canvas for artistic expression or a symbol of personal ideals.

Research reveals that even an everyday product like a water cup can meet a remarkably diverse range of needs. In periods of relatively low economic development, people's primary concerns centered on basic necessities—having access to water and simple water cups for drinking. To meet this fundamental need, water cups were produced with a focus on uniformity, standardization, and mass production. As economic conditions improved, the demand for water cups evolved beyond their basic function of storing and drinking water, expanding into more diverse and sophisticated needs. On the one hand, manufacturers, having accumulated sufficient capital, gained the capability to pursue differentiated production through innovative design, research, development, and procurement. This newfound flexibility in labor costs and capital resources paved the way for creative experimentation. On the other hand, higher-income levels and increased purchasing power enabled consumers to prioritize personal preferences and seek products tailored to their unique requirements. The more advanced the economic development, the stronger the production capacity, the higher the income levels, and the greater the diversity in consumer demand.

From the perspective of commodity value, the diverse demands surrounding a water cup can, under certain conditions, transform into its exchange value. The exchange value of a commodity is inherently tied to the variety of needs it fulfills, and this diversification contributes to the water cup's varying forms in the market. Different materials and designs of water cups cater to distinct consumer demands, resulting in varying willingness to pay among consumers (the demand side). Simultaneously, producers (the supply side) face varying production costs and value assessments for these variations, ultimately leading to a diverse market pricing structure. These varied demands generate corresponding value expressions, creating a vast space for value transformation. Compared to the traditional, singular function of a water cup as a basic drinking vessel, this transformation introduces a new market value dimension.

To analyze this, let's define V_b as the basic exchange value of a water cup as a drinking tool, V_d as the exchange value arising from other demands beyond its basic utility, and V as the total exchange value of the water cup. This relationship can be expressed as

$$V = V_b + V_d$$

Thus, the exchange value of a water cup comprises two components: its basic exchange value and the exchange value derived from additional demands. Together, these components determine the total value and market price of the water cup.

Experience plays a critical role in shaping demand. Demand arises from experience, which reflects the perception of needs on a sensory level. Whether a demand is fulfilled, and to what extent, is assessed through experience. Experience serves as the foundation for evaluating demand satisfaction and acts as a driving force for generating new demands. In economic analysis, experience can be seen as an alternative representation of demand. The value generated by demand corresponds to the value formed by experience within economic activities. Demand itself cannot directly manifest in the market or form an exchange; it must be realized through commodities that satisfy the demand. Since a commodity's experience serves as the standard for assessing demand satisfaction, the value space created by demand is reflected in the value space measured by experience. Substituting V_d with V_{ux} (the exchange value of user experience), we can rewrite the formula as

$$V = V_b + V_{ux}$$

This equation redefines a commodity's exchange value as the sum of its basic exchange value and its experiential value. From this foundational value relationship, we observe that when $V_b = 0$ or approaches 0, the total value of the commodity (V) approximates its experiential value (V_{ux}). For example, consider artistic water cups or collectible water cups valued for their materials, craftsmanship, or historical significance. Here, consumers' primary demand lies not in the cup's practical utility but in its experiential value. Consequently, the value—and even the price—of these water cups is predominantly determined by their experiential value. Conversely, when $V_{ux} = 0$ or is relatively insignificant, the total value of the commodity (V) primarily depends on V_b, reflecting its utility as a vessel for holding and drinking water. The values and proportions of V_b and V_{ux} constitute the structure of a commodity's value. When one component decreases, if the total exchange value of the commodity remains constant, it implies an increase in the other component. Conversely, when the total exchange value changes, it indicates that at least one of these components has undergone a transformation.

The diverse array of water cup styles and designs in the market highlights the genuine diversity in consumer demands. The existence of specialty goods such as art pieces, collectibles, and luxury items further illustrates that water cups—and other commodities—possess values beyond their basic utility. Similarly, diverse consumer demands and specialized trading markets are widespread and thriving across a wide range of goods. This universality of experiential value underscores its critical role in economic exchanges, making it an essential element in the study and analysis of economic activities.

As China's economy continues to grow rapidly and living standards steadily improve, experiential value is becoming an increasingly significant factor in the national economy. It is only when living standards and economic capacity reach a certain threshold that this topic garners widespread attention and becomes a vital subject for scholarly research and discussion. The key question is: How does experiential value influence and function within the national economy? This can be explored from two perspectives: the supply side and the demand side.

i. The Role of Experience on the Supply Side

The supply side of economic activities centers on production and the expansion of reproduction. The primary goal of production is to establish clear objectives. Once these objectives are defined, enterprises allocate resources, organize production processes, and work toward meeting their targets. Revenue generated from product sales exceeding production costs provides profits, part of which is reinvested to enhance and expand production, drive product innovation, and achieve higher production objectives.

Historically, when products, namely, production goals were relatively homogeneous (i.e., differentiation was minimal), production resources were standardized, and labor productivity differences were negligible, suppliers' income primarily depended on the amount of labor time workers invested. However, with increasingly diverse production goals, varied resources, and distinct production processes and methods, the contributions of production stages and processes have undergone profound changes.

Consider the example of water cup production, comparing three different companies: Company A focuses on manufacturing standardized ceramic cups for government and state-owned enterprises. Company B specializes in producing stainless steel thermos cups in various specifications and designs. Company C offers personalized water cup customization, providing ten material options and twenty design styles, with the flexibility to modify existing designs to suit customer preferences. Each company's production goals dictate distinct production methods and resource allocations. Assume they have the same initial investment.

Company A focuses on standardized production, maintaining a uniform approach to raw materials, processes, equipment, and labor tasks. With minimal investment in product design, there is limited scope for optimization or adjustment. Even if inventory accumulates, the standardized nature of their products ensures they remain sellable over time. By employing a stable workforce and relying on consistent production equipment, the company achieves steady output, which is adjusted according to customer orders. Reinvestment in production is simple for Company A: Increasing output requires proportional additions of labor and standardized equipment. Due to the uniformity of its products, pricing remains consistent. If Company A secures long-term, stable clients, its revenue primarily depends on labor time—more input results in higher output and revenue. However, its heavy reliance on a fixed customer base makes it vulnerable to market shifts. A loss of key clients could pose significant risks, as the company has limited flexibility to adapt to changing market conditions.

Company B operates with greater complexity compared to Company A. It dynamically adjusts the production of various thermos cup styles and specifications based on market performance, and allocate corresponding production resources accordingly. The product lines of each different-styled thermos cup may require unique production setups, tools, and labor allocations. The diverse range of products allows for differentiated pricing strategies, creating flexibility in revenue even at similar sales volumes, compared to Company A. This flexibility stems from product differentiation and the added experiential value (V_{ux}) they offer. On the other hand, when expanding production, Company B's growth is not solely tied to increasing labor hours. Significant value is derived from optimizing product designs, refining production molds, streamlining processes, and adopting advanced automated tools. As the use of automation increases, the value generated from design improvements and process efficiencies outweighs the value from extended labor hours. In this context, its revenue is influenced not only by the extended working hours of its employees but also by factors such as dynamic pricing adjustments, strategic optimization of non-cost reinvestments, productivity enhancements during production processes, and effective cost reductions. Company B exhibits a higher degree of market sensitivity and flexibility to adapt to changes. It invests resources in R&D to create products aligned with market trends while keeping an eye on competitors' innovations. Unlike Company A, it does not rely exclusively on specific clients and is better positioned to adjust its strategies to capture new growth opportunities.

In the past three decades, Company C's production model has gained prominence and attention, driven by the rise of personalized consumer demands, greater purchasing power among older generations, and an explosion of diverse market needs. Homogeneous water cup products are no longer sufficient, and the variety of products on the market has experienced explosive growth. Water cups are now segmented by factors such as age group, usage scenarios, material, and design. For instance, even within the niche of baby thermos cups with straws, there are numerous choices in straw material and hardness. For office, home, and conference use, an extensive selection of materials and styles is available. In response to this surge in demand for diversity, companies like Company C have adopted partially or fully customized production models. To balance efficiency and costs, the company provides basic design templates for water cups, allowing customers to request personalized modifications, such as adding insulation pads, matching spoons, or specialized lids. Pricing for such customized products is determined individually. Production begins only after client confirmation and deposit payment. Beyond the intrinsic value of the product, prices include the value of personalized design services, offering significant pricing flexibility and often reaching the upper limits of what customers are willing to pay. Experiential value (V_{ux}) plays a pivotal role in these scenarios. In terms of cost, this made-to-order production model enables precise resource allocation, reducing idle inventory and waste. This approach generally results in superior cost management compared to the traditional produce-first, sell-later models. Company C's revenue growth is driven by higher pricing for customized products and its ability to effectively control costs through flexibility and efficient resource allocation.

As per this analysis, it becomes evident that as production gradually shifts from standardization to personalization, the contribution of V_{ux}—the value derived from user experiences—becomes a vital new source of profit for businesses. During production, technological advancements have accelerated this shift, where automated machinery increasingly replaces, or even entirely substitutes, manual labor. This transition propels human labor from predominantly physical tasks toward cognitive and intellectual work. The fundamental distinction between cognitive and physical labor lies in productivity. Unlike physical labor, which heavily depends on time investment and repetitive skill proficiency, cognitive labor draws on a combination of expertise, creativity, efficiency, time management, and adeptness with tools. As societal divisions of labor grow more specialized and undergo structural transformations, workers in repetitive, monotonous roles tend to transition in two distinct directions: Toward advanced roles—workers with higher education move into specialized technical positions or managerial roles, and toward service roles—others pivot to service-oriented jobs, such as customer support or logistics, which demand relatively lower skillsets. These inherent disparities in job types are reflected in wage structures and grading systems, allowing businesses to manage labor costs more effectively through salary adjustments rather than solely relying on increased working hours to accumulate profit.

In Company C's production model, a change during product design and customization calls for attention: Customers themselves become an integral component of the productivity. The production content and objectives and workflows are directly shaped by customer demands. Since each customer's needs are unique—and as previously discussed, human experiences are boundless—these varied requirements create an expansive demand space. This vast demand translates into an immense experiential value space.

When markets align their production to accommodate such personalized needs, the potential value generated becomes theoretically limitless. However, production remains constrained by finite resources. Imagine a market where ten companies previously focused on producing similar, standardized products. Now, these companies have shifted to creating unique offerings tailored to the specific needs of distinct target audiences. This transformation significantly enhances the value of each product by aligning it with specialized customer demand. Consequently, the diversity in demand gives rise to a new value-added space, fueled by the experiential value of these differentiated products.

As industries increasingly adopt differentiation and personalization, new sources of economic growth emerge on a macroeconomic scale for all industries.

High-income consumers, in particular, exhibit robust demand for bespoke products and are willing to pay substantial premiums for differentiation. As the national economy progresses and income levels become increasingly stratified, supply-side production methods should adapt through structural adjustments tailored to align with these distinct income segments:

(1) Low-income or lower-middle-income groups. For this demographic, businesses should focus on cost-efficient, standardized, and affordable products that address basic functional needs.
(2) Middle-income groups with flexible spending power. Companies should cater to these consumers with a diversified range of products, offering options tailored to varying preferences. Prices can scale depending on the degree to which products meet specific demands.
(3) High-income groups. For affluent customers, the emphasis should be on premium-quality and highly personalized services. These offerings create diversified service content and space for value increase.

Ultimately, consumers make purchasing decisions based on their actual spending power. For example, a low-income consumer might allocate significant resources to purchase a high-end smartphone as a symbol of individuality while economizing in other areas. Conversely, a high-income consumer with a frugal life style might choose simpler, lower-cost products for basic needs, redirecting surplus income into investments to grow their wealth. The process of consumer decision-making inherently aligns with their actual experiential needs. This alignment not only enables the market to achieve greater depth and precision in resource matching but also creates ample opportunities for diverse experiential values to be transformed into tangible economic outputs. The profound influence of experiential value lies at the core of its pivotal role in shaping the supply side of national economic activities.

For general goods, the supply-side value primarily reflects the distribution of total operating costs across each product. For manufacturers, the core challenge lies in ensuring that product sales revenue offsets total production costs, thereby maintaining sustainable and healthy operations.

In the operations of Company A, let V_S represent the product's value, C its cost, and Q its quality. This relationship can be expressed as

$$V_S = C / Q = (C_{labor} + C_{capital}) / Q$$

To ensure normal operations, the product price must not fall below V_S. However, when production exceeds demand and leads to inventory accumulation, the company incurs storage costs and risks such as product obsolescence, expiration, or degradation. Under such conditions, production costs may become unrecoverable. For operations to remain viable, sales revenue must also cover these potential losses. This means that the price of sold products must exceed their average calculated value. If the proportion of sold products is a and the proportion of inventory is b, where a + b = 1, the equation becomes

$$V_{Sa} = (C_a^{labor} + C_a^{capital} + C_b^{labor} + C_b^{capital} + C_b^{inventory}) / (Q_a + Q_b)$$

When short-term inventory levels are manageable, the pricing pressure on sold products is limited. However, as inventory builds up significantly, the sold portion a must absorb increasing production and storage costs of the inventory portion b. If pricing for sold products cannot be promptly adjusted, the company's financial health will deteriorate. To address this, the company may need to reduce production volumes to control costs.

In the case of Company B, assume it operates three differentiated production lines producing products 1, 2, and 3, with production proportions a, b, and c, where a + b + c = 1. In a simple scenario, each production line balances its revenue and costs, resulting in an overall equilibrium:

$$V_{S_1} = C_1 / Q_1 = (C_1^{labor} + C_1^{capital}) / Q_1$$
$$V_{S_2} = C_2 / Q_2 = (C_2^{labor} + C_2^{capital}) / Q_2$$
$$V_{S_3} = C_3 / Q_3 = (C_3^{labor} + C_3^{capital}) / Q_3$$

Compared to Company A, when sales of a particular product line face difficulties, Company B can dynamically reallocate resources among its three product lines, effectively mitigating risks. For instance, if Product 1 experiences a sales decline due to market-wide factors, Company B has multiple options at its disposal. It can reduce the production of Product 1, similar to Company A's approach. Alternatively, it can increase the pricing or sales volume of Products 2 and 3, leveraging the additional revenue from these lines to offset losses from Product 1. Additionally, when Products 2 and 3 are performing well, Company B can reassign workers and production resources from the Product 1 line to the other two, minimizing losses caused by idle capacity. This operational flexibility grants Company B more time and space to optimize the production of Product 1, ultimately enabling it to adapt to market changes more effectively than Company A.

Company C, however, takes a different approach. Its production volume is directly tied to order volume, avoiding the need for long-term investments in production equipment or labor. Instead, it relies on pre-arranged outsourcing agreements with external manufacturers, purchasing production services as needed at negotiated rates. As long as sales revenue offsets the cost of these services, the company maintains sustainable operations. During each production cycle, Company C can, according to the actual market situation, choose the most efficient and cost-effective production service providers to maximize savings and efficiency. From a demand-response perspective, it can quickly adapt product materials, designs, and additional features to meet changing customer preferences, launching new products that best align with market needs. Compared to Companies A and B, Company C maximizes profit potential while demonstrating superior risk management.

ii. The Role of Experience on the Demand Side

In economic activities, the demand side primarily grapples with two critical issues: purchasing power and purchasing decisions. Purchasing power is influenced mainly by consumers' income levels and the real purchasing capacity of that income, while purchasing decisions are driven by purchasing objective (consumer needs) and price levels. In terms of purchasing decisions, the impact of experience is the most direct.

Personal income distribution typically comprises four components: essential living expenses, investments, savings, and disposable income. Essential living expenses encompass the minimum necessary expenditures for basic needs such as food, clothing, housing, and transportation, along with personal income taxes and repayments for living debts. When evaluating the impact of experience on the demand side, the focus is on the distribution and utilization of disposable income across different income levels. High-, middle-, and low-income groups are classified based on their disposable income, rather than total income. Using total income as the sole criterion for assessing demand levels can lead to inaccuracies. For instance, many people with substantial incomes may face heavy financial commitments like mortgage payments, leaving them with limited disposable income and a lower quality of life. Such individuals should not be categorized as high-income since their consumption behavior does not reflect that of affluent groups. Similarly, some high-income individuals choose a frugal lifestyle and allocate only a modest portion of their income for consumption. Their consumer tier should be defined by their actual spending patterns.

Disposable income, after covering essential living costs, is typically used to improve quality of life, enhance living standards, and increase overall happiness. Since this portion of spending does not affect basic survival, it often displays certain characteristics: impulse purchases, dynamic preferences—consumer tastes can be complex and subject to change, variable demand—the quantity of demand can fluctuate significantly, and price elasticity—consumers exhibit a broad tolerance for price variations. When making purchasing decisions, consumers prioritize cost-performance (value-for-money) over price alone. Cost-performance measures the ratio of a product's perceived value to its market price. A higher ratio indicates a greater likelihood of purchase.

Here, we will separately discuss value and price, the two factors that influence cost-performance.

For the demand side, the perceived value of a product depends on its ability to satisfy consumer needs and the degree of that satisfaction. A product's value increases as it meets more needs or fulfills them to a greater extent. The perceived value to the consumer, therefore, is determined by the variety of needs addressed and the degree of satisfaction achieved. Here, an important qualification must be made: While consumer needs are often shaped by past experiences, in today's world of rapid technological innovation, many needs are stimulated by new products introduced by the supply side.

For instance, despite the presence of numerous smartphone brands, Apple's launch of the new iPhone created a fresh and exciting consumer experience. Its unique design and features reshaped user habits. When a new product inspires consumers to voluntarily adapt—learning and changing their behavior to embrace the innovation—it generates new needs, contributing to incremental demand growth. If the value provided by a specific need category n is denoted as V_i, and the degree of satisfaction for that need is represented as a_n, the relationship can be expressed as

$$V_i = f(a_n)$$

Here, a_n corresponds to the experience level (or degree of experience), as discussed earlier in the context of quantifying experiential value.

The total perceived value of the product to the consumer (V_D) is then

$$V_D = \sum_{i=1}^{n} V_i$$

The cost-performance ratio (CP) is defined as

$$CP = V / P$$

P represents the product's market price.

The evaluation of a product's value by consumers involves two critical dimensions: anticipated pre-use value and actual post-use value. The former is the primary factor influencing a consumer's decision to purchase a product they have never tried, while the latter determines whether the consumer will choose to repurchase the product in the future.

Actual post-use value assessments may occur during a trial period before the purchase or after actual use. When the actual value exceeds the anticipated value, consumers experience a sense of delight or surprise, significantly increasing the likelihood of repeat purchases. Conversely, when the actual value falls short of expectations, consumers may feel disappointed or misled, reducing the chances of future purchases. The discrepancy between anticipated value and actual value can also influence consumer behavior. Positive experiences may lead to favorable word-of-mouth recommendations, while negative experiences could deter others from purchasing the product.

Regarding commodity prices, consumers seeking experiential value often define an acceptable price range based on how effectively a product meets their needs. In cases where a fixed market price is unavailable, or where a consumer's unique preferences necessitate dynamic pricing adjustments upon average market price, price negotiations may occur. Consumers might compare multiple offers before finalizing their decision. However, tailoring products to individual needs—encompassing design, production, delivery, and after-sales service—requires substantial resource input. These include customer service agents, in-store consultants, on-site service personnel, spare parts, and more. Consequently, highly customized products are most viable in industries where the revenue per user far exceeds the costs of standard services, such as luxury travel or bespoke experiences.

Consumer decision-making also considers complementary goods and substitute goods. Complementary goods refer to items that must be used together, such as frying pans and spatulas, or shirts and trousers. Demand for complementary goods is positively correlated—purchasing one often leads to buying the other. Substitute goods refer to items that can replace each other, like tea and coffee, or ice cream and yogurt. Demand for substitutes is negatively correlated—an increase in one reduces demand for the other.

As products become increasingly differentiated, diversified, and tailored, consumer purchasing behavior tends to polarize into two extremes: On the one hand, with an abundance of varieties and choices, consumers distribute their spending across a wide array of brands and categories. On the other hand, for products with unique attributes, irreplaceability, or a technical monopoly in specific features, certain consumer groups concentrate their purchases on a single brand or product. This focused behavior, often termed the fan effect, is evident in brands like Apple and Xiaomi: Over the years, Apple has cultivated a loyal fan base through word-of-mouth; these fans not only buy iPhones but also extend their loyalty to MacBooks, iPads, and AirPods. Many act like collectors, acquiring every new release immediately. Similarly, Xiaomi has built a dedicated "Mi Fan" community in China by offering affordable, high-quality smartphones. Their admiration extends to Xiaomi's lifestyle products, including air purifiers, printers, speakers, TVs, and headphones. The fan effect endures as long as the brand maintains its differentiation. However, when this advantage diminishes, or quality issues arise, consumer loyalty erodes. The differentiation advantage is particularly notable in digital offerings. For instance, a streaming platform that secures exclusive rights to a popular TV series may dominate viewership for that content. Consumers from other platforms may temporarily switch to the exclusive provider, showcasing the power of exclusivity in shaping fan behavior.

As the variety of products continues to grow, the dynamics of complementary goods have shifted significantly: First, over time, advancements in technology and changing consumer needs have redefined complementary goods. For instance, cameras and film were once inseparable; however, with the transition to digital cameras, film is no longer required. Instead, memory cards have emerged as the new complementary goods for cameras. Second, the abundance of substitutes for complementary goods has diluted traditional interdependencies. Take frying pans and spatulas as an example: While they are typically used together, the market now offers spatulas in various materials and designs. Furthermore, innovative frying pans with non-stick or splash-proof designs may eliminate the need for spatulas altogether, allowing users to substitute them with a simple pair of long chopsticks. In such scenarios, the dependency between these two items weakens. Third, in some areas, previously simple tasks have been refined, giving rise to specialized tools and expanded demand. Consider gardening: In the past, a sunlit windowsill, flowerpot, fertilizer, and watering can suffice for growing plants. Today, consumers must consider an array of specialized tools and products tailored to specific plant needs:

(1) Flowerpots: from tall and slim to short and wide, available in clay, ceramic, or plastic.
(2) Soil: varieties with tailored compositions, such as organic blends, mineral-rich mixes, or nutrient-dense substrates.
(3) Tools: customized spades, rakes, and pruning shears in various shapes and sizes.
(4) Advanced equipment: watering cans designed for specific methods or capacities, fertilizer proportions, soil moisture meters, grow lights, and climate monitors.

This diversification requires consumers to weigh not only the price and quantity of each product but also the convenience of the buying process. For example, an online store offering a comprehensive range of tools allows customers to purchase everything they need in one seamless transaction. Convenience-focused buyers are more likely to choose such a store, bundling their purchases and paying a single shipping fee, even if the total cost is slightly higher than purchasing from multiple vendors. For these buyers, the time spent searching for products, communicating with various sellers, and managing multiple deliveries represents a significant part of their overall purchasing cost. If the added cost of a one-stop shopping experience is less than the value of the time and effort saved, these customers will naturally gravitate toward the more convenient option over the cheaper option.

Based on the influence of experiences, consumer purchasing behavior demonstrates the following characteristics:

(1) Acceptance of price flexibility. Consumers are willing to tolerate moderate price increases when they perceive the quality of the product or service justifies the cost.
(2) Diversified and differentiated demand. Experiences drive demand toward greater variety and differentiation, fostering more intricate and diverse needs. This trend opens up new market opportunities and expands the potential for value creation.
(3) Increased pricing autonomy and reduced comparability. Differentiated products have led to varying degrees of interchangeability in some and unique monopolistic traits in others. As a result, businesses enjoy greater pricing autonomy. This differentiation has also weakened the comparability and referential value between products, so consumers find it increasingly challenging to compare products directly.

(4) Shifts in complementary and substitute goods relationships.

(5) Changing consumer priorities with personal income and expenses. As disposable income grows, consumers place greater value on convenience, time savings, exclusivity, and other premium services. This shift creates opportunities for bundled offerings and all-inclusive pricing strategies that combine products with added-value services.

iii. The Role of Experience as a Bridge Between Supply and Demand

The importance of experience as a connecting force between supply and demand in socio-economic activities is becoming increasingly apparent. For experience to effectively bridge this gap, six key conditions must be simultaneously met: First, the region must surpass subsistence-level economics, enabling individuals to enjoy disposable income or capital after covering their basic living expenses. Second, society's productive capabilities and organizational structure must support the creation of personalized and customized products, with resources allocated flexibly to meet unique demands. Third, critical infrastructure, including transportation, energy, logistics, and warehousing, must be developed to ensure the swift, flexible, and efficient transfer and distribution of resources. Fourth, consumers should possess the autonomy and self-awareness to make purchasing decisions that reflect their unique preferences and values. Fifth, well-established communication technologies must enable low cost, efficient, and comprehensive access to information about products and services. Last, exposure to diverse cultures through globalization should expand perspectives, fostering cross-cultural interactions and influences. When these conditions converge, the groundwork is laid for an experience-driven economy, shaping both production and consumption dynamics.

In eras of limited economic development, both supply and demand were largely centered on meeting basic survival needs. Throughout history, economic disparities have always existed across regions and social classes. However, during periods of low overall productivity, wealth was predominantly concentrated in the hands of a small elite. It is only when society as a whole experiences a significant elevation in living standards that the pursuit of enriched experiences becomes a widespread phenomenon.

When basic human rights are secured, and individuals are endowed with dignity, financial independence, and the freedom to make autonomous choices, their aspirations for an enhanced quality of life are fully unlocked. This unleashing of individual potential drives systemic transformations in production and consumption. In such a landscape, experiences emerge as the critical bridge between supply and demand, laying the foundation for further societal progress and a fundamental evolution of production relationships. This transformative role manifests in five pivotal dimensions:

(1) Experience as the catalyst for demand creation and production innovation. Once basic survival needs are universally addressed, uncovering and catering to diverse experiential needs across varying levels becomes the driving force behind identifying and cultivating new demand.

As previously noted, the potential scope of experience is virtually limitless. Tailoring products and services to optimize experiential satisfaction not only enhances the consumer experience but also diversifies product offerings and maximizes commercial value. This dynamic creates a win-win scenario for both suppliers and consumers. In a marketplace teeming with options, businesses that prioritize profit at the expense of consumer satisfaction risk losing their hard-earned customer base. Consumers, guided by personal judgment and preferences, gravitate toward the products that best fulfill their experiential needs. Whether through rational or emotional purchasing behavior, the influence of experience is unmistakable: It generates new demand, and it spurs innovation, adaptation, and improvement in production goals, methods, and efficiencies to meet evolving market needs.

In this way, experience becomes a transformative force, driving production reform and elevating the quality of products and services.

(2) Experience fuels the enrichment and deepening of product value, creating a new space of value. As consumer needs become increasingly diverse and dynamic, products must constantly evolve to hold value that meets these shifting demands. A perfect example of this is seen in modern online multiplayer role-playing games. Early versions of these games primarily focused on character role-playing and combat, offering players a sense of immersion, excitement, and the thrill of playing a heroic protagonist. Over time, however, these games have grown in complexity and richness. New systems—such as skill trees, equipment upgrades, pet systems, housing construction, marriage mechanics, and guild dynamics—have transformed the gameplay. The virtual gaming world often surpasses real life in richness and diversity, offering opportunities to explore scenarios that are either unattainable or pose risks in reality. For example, players can engage in activities such as riding various creatures, mining, farming, animal husbandry, or crafting pharmaceuticals. They can even design and construct houses freely, following blueprints and gathering materials to bring their visions to life.

The more layers of experience (or demand) a product can offer, the greater the diversity of needs it can satisfy, and the broader its potential user base, leading to a product that is more robust and dynamic. However, this doesn't mean that simply stacking more functions will necessarily enhance the user experience. For example, with TV remotes, manufacturers often cram too many buttons, creating a complex and cluttered interface. In contrast, innovative products like Xiaomi TV and Apple TV have embraced a minimalist design philosophy for their remote controls. These remotes feature large, prominent buttons, sleek and intuitive interfaces, and a minimal number of physical keys, shifting the operation of more advanced functions to the on-screen interface. This streamlined design, being simple and user-friendly, significantly expands the product's accessibility, allowing people of diverse cultural backgrounds and age groups to operate it with ease and convenience.

Thus, the goal for suppliers is to design and arrange functions that align with users' needs and the product's unique features, maximizing the perceived experience. By doing so, they achieve greater consumer response and purchase. This leads to a new form of value creation, as consumers pay for these enriched, diverse experiences, opening up new realms of value in the market.

(3) Experience stimulates the vitality and creativity of economic participants, driving innovation in production methods. Experience, with its inherent personalization, underscores society's growing respect for individual expression and real needs. This ethos, when communicated to consumers, has a profoundly positive effect, motivating them to become more engaged and proactive. Before making purchasing decisions, consumers are increasingly given the opportunity to participate in the design process, customizing products according to their personal tastes and preferences, which sparks creativity and fuels innovation.

A prime example of this is the creation of VOCALOID's virtual idol characters in China. These characters were designed through a competition where participants submitted their designs and voted on the winning image. Subsequently, the voice recordings and music compositions for these characters were created with input from the fan community. Contributors became passionate, loyal fans of both the characters and their associated products. VOCALOID's success proves that involving consumers (the demand side) in the creation and design process not only fosters creativity but also builds a loyal community that eagerly supports the final product. These consumers form an emotional connection to the product, treating it as their own, thanks to their direct involvement.

(4) Experience strengthens the bond between supply and demand, merging both into a cyclical and iterative relationship. As the importance of experience becomes more pronounced in the consumer market, the personalized nature of experience has led to a much closer connection between supply and demand than any previous eras. Today, the final form of a product is shaped by both the supplier and the consumer. Even for products developed unilaterally by suppliers, maintaining direct engagement with consumers is crucial for integrating their purchasing behaviors and feedback into product updates and iterative improvements. To achieve this, suppliers must employ a variety of qualitative and quantitative methods to effectively gauge the real market reception of their products, as well as those of competitors. This proactive approach enables them to craft well-informed development strategies and efficiently plan subsequent production cycles.

In this process, a universally applicable and relatively standardized "user-centered" production approach has emerged, one that transcends industry boundaries. This production model is defined by three key characteristics: modularity, customer involvement, and cyclical iteration. Modularity refers to breaking down the entire production process into interrelated but independent modules. By standardizing the format of handover documentation between upstream and downstream stages, various production providers can efficiently manage and complete distinct segments of the production chain.

Customer involvement means that key stages of the production cycle—before, during, and after—incorporate customer experiences, trials, and evaluations. This participatory approach allows for timely adjustments and improvements throughout the production process, addressing core issues that may negatively affect the user experience, refining functions, and optimizing design. By integrating real customer input, suppliers can correct their limitations and biases, ensuring that the finished product delivers a high level of user satisfaction upon launch. This reduces negative post-launch feedback and minimizes rework costs.

Cyclical iteration describes a spiral progression of the production process, featuring a complete production cycle that can be dynamically adjusted based on actual time. When demand fluctuates rapidly, shorter iteration cycles and faster iteration rates are employed to respond quickly. In contrast, when demand is stable, longer cycles and more thoughtful upgrades are used. This production model is particularly prominent in internet-based product development and has proven highly effective.

(5) Experience as a glue strengthening multicultural integration across nations and ethnicities. As the internet fosters global communication, experience has become an essential catalyst for breaking down cultural barriers, easing misunderstandings, and facilitating cultural exchange. A fundamental aspect of human nature is curiosity about the new and unknown, often accompanied by apprehension and prejudice. Through experiential engagement, individuals can immerse themselves in the content, styles, and forms of other cultures, deepening their understanding and appreciation of foreign traditions and fostering greater tolerance and acceptance.

For example, in contemporary Western design, Eastern elements are frequently incorporated to appeal to the aesthetic sensibilities of Eastern cultures. Likewise, traditional Eastern crafts such as embroidery often incorporate Western techniques, like perspective and light-shadow concepts, in their compositions. Activities such as tai chi enable individuals from other cultures to connect with Chinese classical philosophy, while Western experiential exhibitions introduce Eastern audiences to new design philosophies and modes of visual communication. While verbal communication can be abstract, true understanding and cultural exchange occur only when individuals experience other cultures firsthand. As a result, experience not only plays a pivotal role in enhancing understanding but also acts as a "glue" that strengthens multicultural integration across nations and ethnic groups, helping to forge deeper, more meaningful social connections.

II. Impact of Experience on Microeconomic Analysis

What role does experience play in economic activities, and how does a change in experience levels affect microeconomic behavior? This section examines the influence of experience on microeconomic dynamics.

Microeconomics focuses on individual economic units, such as a single consumer, a single producer, a single product, and a single market. Common areas of study include individual economic behaviors and the determination of equilibrium prices. At its core is the rational individual assumption, which posits that every economic participant acts to maximize personal benefits while minimizing costs.

The classic supply and demand model in Western economics is depicted in figure 2-1.

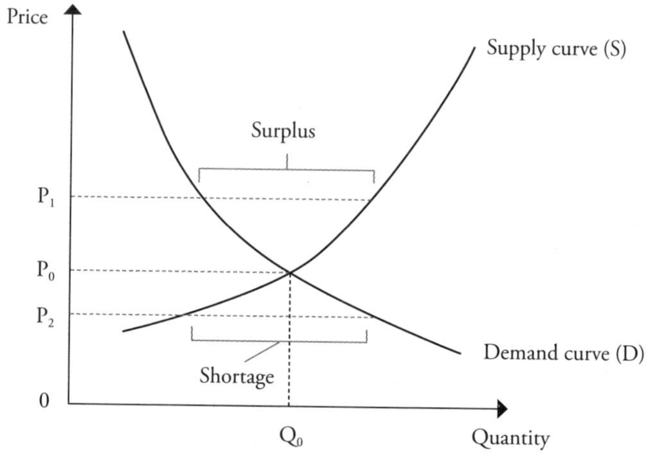

Figure 2-1 Classic supply and demand model

The (S) shows the quantity producers are able to supply at different price levels. Its upward slope reflects that higher prices incentivize increased production. The (D) indicates the maximum quantity consumers are able to buy at various price points. Its downward slope reflects that lower prices stimulate greater consumption. The two curves intersect at the point of equilibrium price and quantity (Q_0, P_0). The market mechanism refers to the process in a free market through which the price continuously adjusts until it reaches the equilibrium level.

This basic microeconomic model assumes that goods are entirely homogeneous and remain unchanged during the analysis period. However, when goods undergo frequent updates and rapid advancements, the maximum price consumers are willing to pay becomes positively correlated with the quality of experience the product provides. In such cases, the behaviors of supply and demand warrant reevaluation.

i. Behavior and Characteristics of Demand Side

1. Positive Developments in Product Experience

When product experience improves, the demand curve may exhibit the three following behaviors:

(1) Scenario A

If the enhanced experience generates only a modest consumer response, or if the price increase exceeds the willingness to pay for the improvement, the demand curve retains its downward slope but exhibits two key changes compared to when is was no improvement: The decline in purchase volume per unit price increase diminishes, reducing the curve's absolute slope; and at every price point, the demand quantity increases slightly. Graphically, the demand curve shifts rightward with a slight clockwise rotation, as illustrated in figure 2-2.

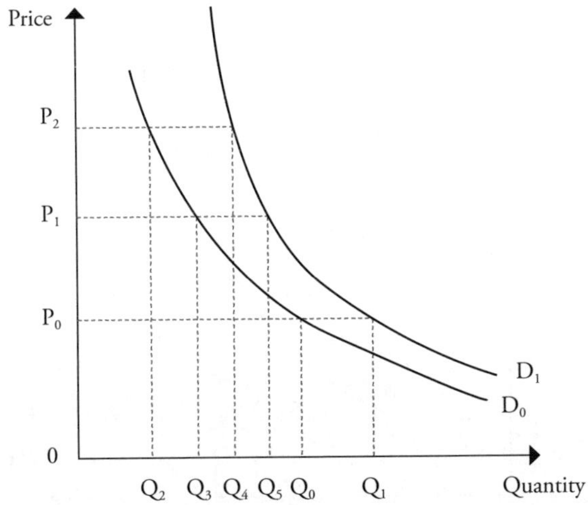

Figure 2-2 Demand curve changes (scenario A)

In the figure, D_0 represents the original demand curve. After the product is upgraded to enhance its experience, the demand curve shifts to D_1. Key observations include at any given price P_0, the demand quantity increases post-upgrade. Comparing segments, $Q_3 - Q_2 > Q_5 - Q_4$, indicating

$$(P_2 - P_1) / (Q_3 - Q_2) < (P_2 - P_1) / (Q_5 - Q_4)$$

that is

$$\Delta P_{D_0} / \Delta Q_{D_0} < \Delta P_{D_1} / \Delta Q_{D_1}$$

(2) Scenario B

In this scenario, there is a strong consumer response to experience enhancements. Consumers strongly associate an improved experience with higher value, perceiving higher prices as a reflection of increased desirability. For example, an Apple Watch may have price tiers ranging from RMB 2,565 to RMB 10,894 (RMB 3,160, RMB 4,548, RMB 5,441, RMB 5,837, and RMB 10,100) based solely on strap materials. Consumers prioritizing lifestyle and personal values may prefer higher-priced options, resulting in a demand curve where higher prices lead to increased demand instead, as shown in figure 2-3.

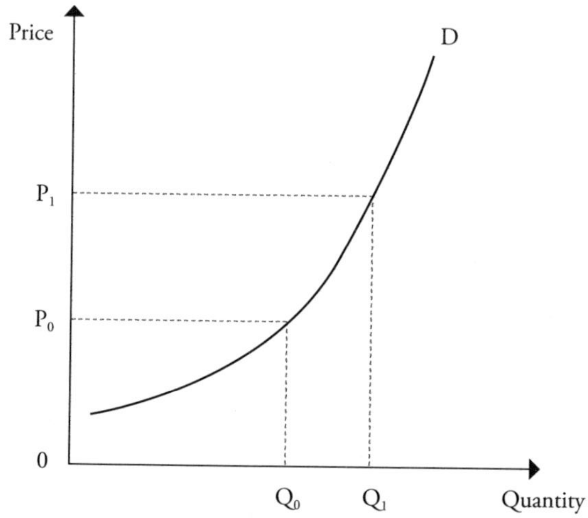

Figure 2-3 Demand curve changes (scenario B)

Luxury goods and collectibles often belong to a distinct category of products designed to cater to specific demographics, typically high-income individuals or passionate fan communities, rather than the general population. High-income consumers comprises individuals whose disposable income significantly exceeds basic living expenses. Ordinary consumption holds little appeal for them; instead, they seek unique and exclusive items to reflect their status, taste, and personal values. These consumers are often drawn to rare or specially designed products, and price increases typically do not deter their purchases. In fact, higher prices may enhance the product's appeal and perceived value. Fan communities often consist of individuals who exhibit an extraordinary and passionate devotion to products associated with specific interests. For instance, fans of movie stars or singers show unwavering loyalty by enthusiastically supporting merchandise linked to their idols. The rarer or more expensive these items are—such as limited-edition products—the higher their appeal and demand among these devoted followers. While the income levels of individual fans may not always be exceptionally high, they often dedicate a significant portion of their resources to acquiring these products. Within their financial means, they willingly bear the associated costs to express their admiration and support. Another reason for the fervent demand for such scarce items is their potential for appreciation over time. Beyond purchasing purely out of affection, fans are often motivated by the prospect of these items increasing in value, transforming them into both a symbol of personal passion and a lucrative investment opportunity.

(3) Scenario C

For certain limited-edition products, demand remains constant regardless of price changes due to strictly capped supply levels that fall far below market demand. This situation results in a unique demand curve, illustrated in figure 2-4.

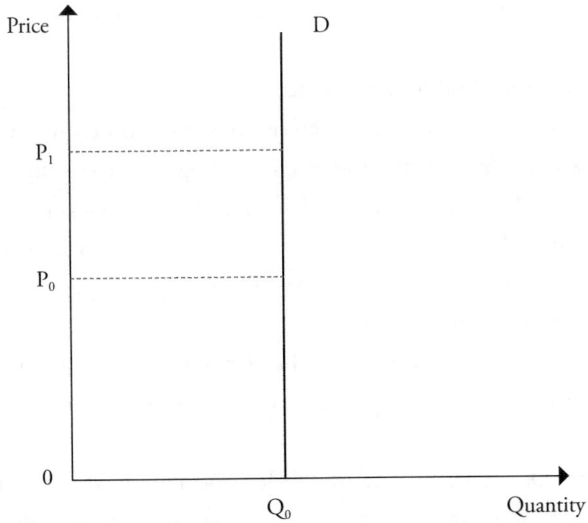

Figure 2-4 Demand curve changes (scenario C)

An extreme case of scenario C involves suppliers offering fixed quantities at a fixed price. For instance, experiential dining establishments like Ultraviolet operate with a set price of RMB 3,000 per person, accommodating only 16 guests daily. In such cases, the demand "curve" is reduced to a single fixed point defined by a specific demand level and price, as shown in figure 2-5.

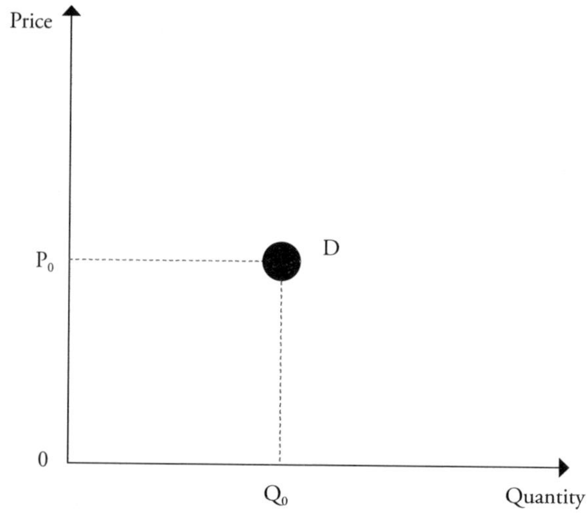

Figure 2-5 Demand curve changes (scenario C extreme case)

If product experience improves, increasing consumers' perceived value, the demand point shifts upward along the vertical line shown in figure 2-4.

2. Negative Changes in Product Experience

When the experience of a product deteriorates over time—whether due to iterative updates that result in inferior versions, stagnation leading to outdated services, or external factors such as malicious complaints causing a decline in perceived value—the demand for the product at any given price point decreases compared to its previous state. Moreover, the demand increase triggered by a unit price reduction also diminishes.

From the perspective of changes in the demand curve, this manifests as a leftward shift combined with a clockwise rotation, referred to as scenario –A, as illustrated in figure 2-6.

In this figure, D_0 represents the initial demand curve, while D_1 reflects the curve after a decline in product experience. Key observations include for any P_0, the demand quantity for updated products decreases. Additionally, since $Q_0 - Q_3 > Q_1 - Q_2$, the following relationship holds

$$(P_2 - P_0) / (Q_0 - Q_3) < (P_2 - P_0) / (Q_1 - Q_2)$$

that is

$$\Delta P_{D_1} / \Delta Q_{D_1} > \Delta P_{D_0} / \Delta Q_{D_0}$$

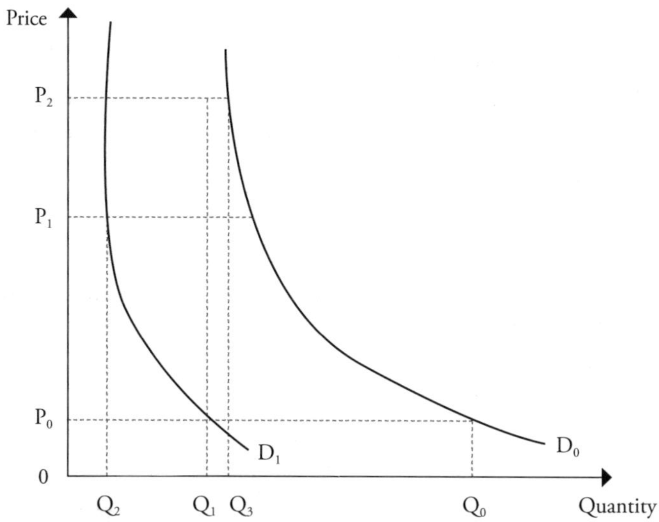

Figure 2-6 Demand curve changes (scenario –A)

In summary, as the experience of a product undergoes continuous changes over time, its demand curve will also shift accordingly, and in some cases, even change direction.

ii. Behavior and Characteristics of Supply Side

1. Positive Developments in Product Experience

When product experience improves, it generally falls into one of three scenarios: First, the supplier invests additional resources to develop new features, enhance existing functionalities, or improve the product's aesthetics. Second, the supplier does not increase resource investment (e.g., the total cost of employing labor remains unchanged) but instead makes internal adjustments to the production structure and optimizes product functionality. This could involve removing features that no longer have market demand, reallocating the saved costs to enhance core differentiated features, or using marketing and other auxiliary methods to help users better understand the product's advantages. These efforts collectively lead to an improved product experience for consumers. Third, suppliers manage to reduce production costs while simultaneously improving user experience. For example, a television remote control manufacturer might streamline functionality and remove unnecessary features, resulting in a product that is both cheaper to produce and more user-friendly.

(1) Scenario A

For this scenario, the supplier's increased investment raises production costs, which in turn increases prices at every production level Q_s. If the cost (price) per unit rises consistently with the original supply curve's slope, the supply curve shifts upward without altering its slope, as shown in figure 2-7.

Due to the law of diminishing marginal returns, the price increase resulting from each additional unit of output typically differs from that of the original supply curve. For instance, when the increase is smaller than that of the original supply curve, the supply curve shifts upward while its slope at any given point decreases, as shown in figure 2-8.

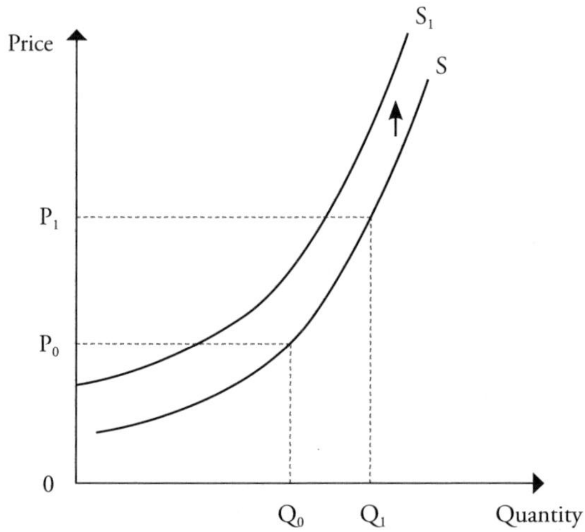

Figure 2-7 Supply curve changes (scenario A)

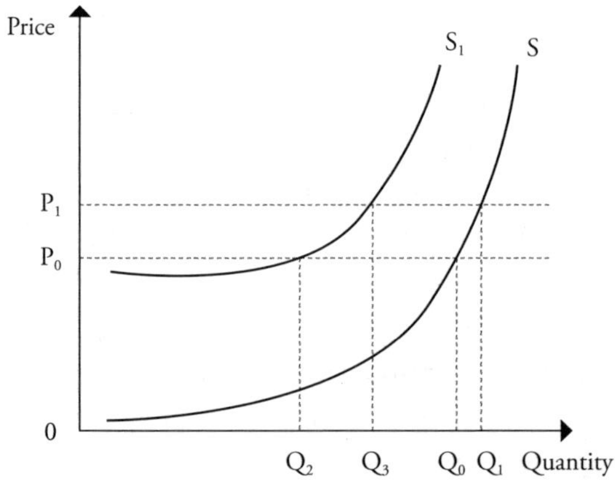

Figure 2-8 Supply curve changes (scenario A's slope changes)

Thus, since $Q_3 - Q_2 > Q_1 - Q_0$, we have

$$(P_1 - P_0) / (Q_3 - Q_2) < (P_1 - P_0) / (Q_1 - Q_0)$$

that is

$$\Delta P_{s_1} / \Delta Q_{s_1} < \Delta P_s / \Delta Q_s$$

Conversely, the opposite holds true.

(2) Scenario B

In the second scenario, product optimization and improvement do not lead to increased costs. As a result, at every level of output, the cost remains unchanged, and the supply curve does not shift.

(3) Scenario C

In the third scenario, product optimization and improvement result in reduced costs. Consequently, at every level of output, the cost decreases, leading to a corresponding reduction in price, as illustrated in figure 2-9.

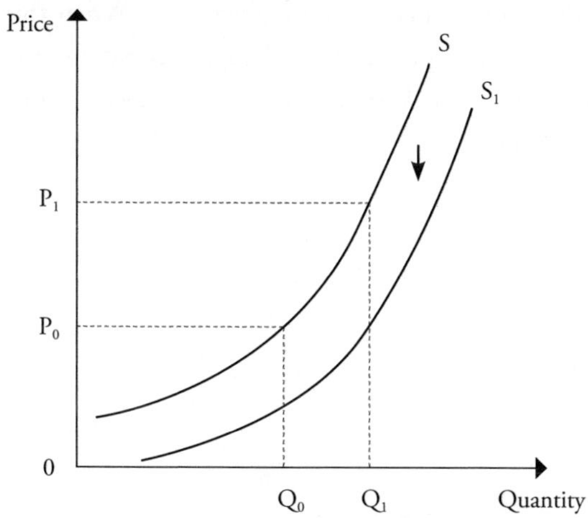

Figure 2-9 Supply curve changes (scenario C)

When the cost reduction per unit of output differs from the original supply curve, the supply curve not only shifts but may also experience a change in slope. A detailed analysis of such slope changes is omitted here.

2. Negative Developments of Product Experience

The decline in product experience can also be categorized into three distinct scenarios: First, supplier reduces resource investment, resulting in the elimination or simplification of existing features, functionalities, or product design. These changes typically lead to a diminished product experience for consumers. Second, the supplier's overall resource allocation remains unchanged, but internal production adjustments lead to the reorganization of product features. For example, well-received features may be removed to allocate resources toward other functionalities, causing dissatisfaction among users (demand side) accustomed to the eliminated features. Furthermore, public relations crises or negative publicity can significantly tarnish the product's reputation, exacerbating the decline in consumer perception and experience. Third, in some cases, rising production costs result in an unintended decline in product experience. For instance, a television remote control previously praised for its simplicity and ease of use might become cumbersome if additional, unnecessary features are added—making primary functions less accessible due to smaller or less prominent buttons.

(1) Scenario -A

In the first scenario, the reduction in product experience primarily stems from cost-cutting measures. As a result, at every production level, the associated costs decrease, causing the supply curve to shift downward. When the per unit cost reduction is smaller than that of the original supply curve, the supply curve not only shifts downward but also flattens, indicating a decrease in slope absolute value, as depicted in figure 2-10.

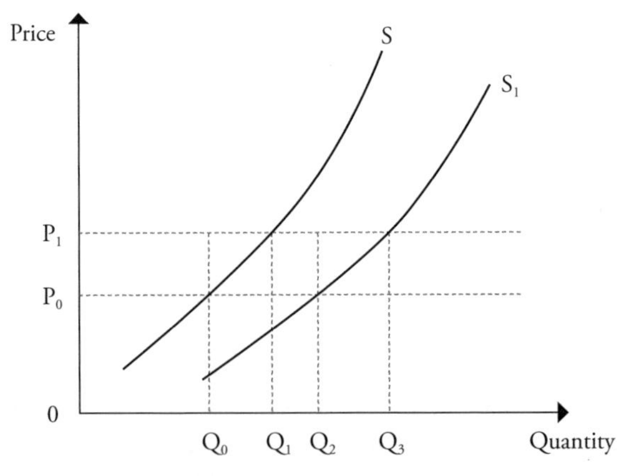

Figure 2-10 Supply curve changes (scenario –A)

(2) Scenario –B

In the second scenario, since the supplier's overall resources are not significantly reduced, production costs remain unchanged. Consequently, the supply curve stays the same.

(3) Scenario –C

In the third scenario, rising production costs are accompanied by a decline in product experience. This causes production costs to increase at all output levels, resulting in an upward shift of the supply curve.

iii. Analysis of Changes in Equilibrium Price

The preceding discussion examined various scenarios involving changes in demand side and supply-side behaviors. To provide a clearer and more concise overview, these scenarios are summarized in table 2-1.

Table 2-1 Summary of experience changes in demand and supply dynamics

			Supply					
			Positive developments in product experience			Negative developments in product experience		
			A	B	C	–A	–B	–C
Demand	Positive developments in product experience	A	(A, A)	(B, A)	(C, A)			
		B	(A, B)	(B, B)	(C, B)			
		C	(A, C)	(B, C)	(C, C)			
	Negative developments in product experience	-A				(–A, –A)	(–B, –A)	(–C, –A)

The subsequent section provides a detailed analysis of each scenario outlined in the table.

1. Scenarios of Positive Developments in Product Experience

(1) (A, A)

When both the supply side (scenario A) and the demand side (scenario A) experience positive developments in product experience, as illustrated in figure 2-11, the market equilibrium shifts from point A (Q_0, P_0) to point B (Q_1, P_1). This results in an increase in both equilibrium price and quantity.

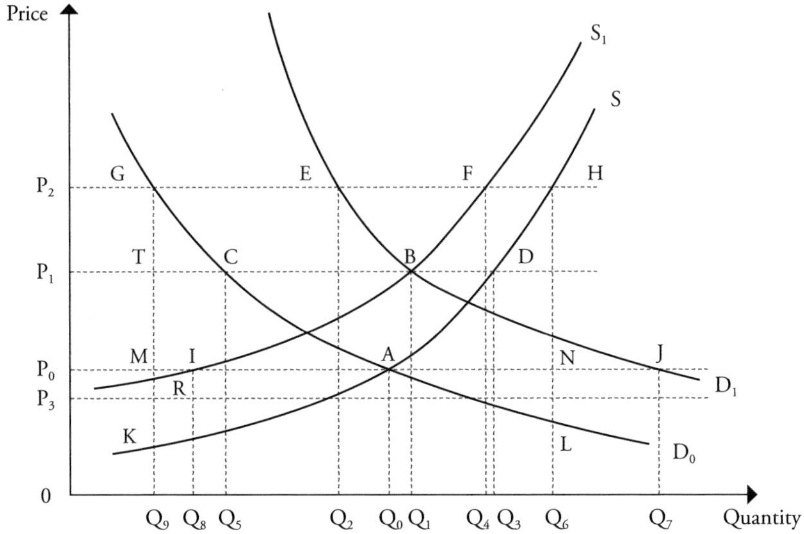

Figure 2-11 Supply-demand analysis for scenario (A, A)

The inevitable rise in equilibrium price is due to the upward shifts in both the supply and demand curves. The degree to which equilibrium quantity increases depends on the relative magnitudes of these shifts. For example, at price level P_2, before product optimization, the supply level was Q_6 (point H), which decreases to Q_4 (point F) after optimization, reflecting a production reduction of $Q_6 - Q_4$. On the demand side, the quantity demanded increases from Q_9 (point G) to Q_2 (point E), a demand rise of $Q_2 - Q_9$. From a financial perspective, the supply side reduces production costs by $P_2 \times (Q_6 - Q_4)$ and simultaneously increases revenue by $P_2 \times (Q_2 - Q_9)$. This results in a profit increase of $P_2 \times [(Q_6 - Q_4) + (Q_2 - Q_9)]$, which represents the added value from the enhancement in product experience.

From another perspective, let's take a look at producer and consumer surplus. Assume the original demand curve intersects the vertical axis at $(0, P_0^D)$ and the original supply curve at $(0, P_0^S)$. The original consumer surplus is represented by the $(0, P_0^D)$, $(0, P_0)$, and A, denoted as $S_{\triangle P_0^D P_0 A}$. The original producer surplus is represented by the $(0, P_0^S)$, $(0, P_0)$, and A, denoted as $S_{\triangle P_0^S P_0 A}$. After optimization, the new demand curve intersects the vertical axis at $(0, P_1^D)$, and the new supply curve at $(0, P_1^S)$. The new consumer surplus is represented by $(0, P_1^D)$, $(0, P_1)$, and B, denoted as $S_{\triangle P_1^D P_1 B}$. The new producer surplus is represented by $(0, P_1^S)$, $(0, P_1)$, and B, denoted as $S_{\triangle P_1^S P_1 B}$. For consumers, the increase in consumer surplus, resulting from buying at the equilibrium price, is $S_{\triangle P_1^D P_1 B} - S_{\triangle P_0^D P_0 A}$. For producers, the increase in producer surplus, resulting from selling at the equilibrium price, is $S_{\triangle P_1^s P_1 B} - S_{\triangle P_0^s P_0 A}$. As evident from the figure, the increase in consumer surplus is evidently positive. For any given output level, regardless of whether the change in producer surplus is positive or negative, as long as the combined surplus is positive, the enhancement in product experience at that output level leads to an overall increase in total market surplus. This, in turn, drives a rise in the overall value of the market.

(2) Scenario (B, A)

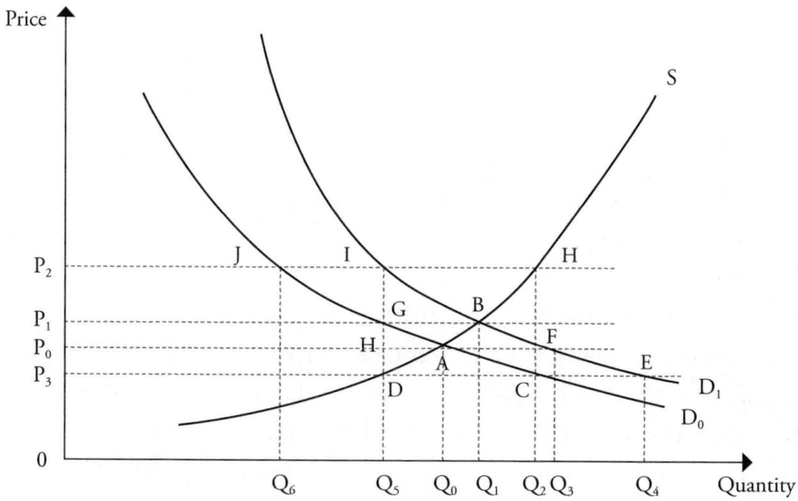

Figure 2-12 Supply-demand analysis for scenario (B, A)

When the product experience improves but the supplier's production costs remain largely unchanged, the supply curve remains stable while the demand curve shifts upward. As shown in the figure, the market equilibrium shifts from point A (Q_0, P_0) to point B (Q_1, P_1). Consequently, both the equilibrium quantity and equilibrium price increase compared to their previous levels.

When the price falls within the range of (0, P_0), for instance at the price level P_3, the original market experiences a supply shortage ranging from $Q_2 - Q_5$. Following the enhancement in product experience, the demand within each price range increases, further widening the supply shortage to the range of $Q_4 - Q_5$. The magnitude of this expansion is precisely equivalent to the extent of the rightward shift in the demand curve.

When the price falls within the range of (P_0, P_1), the original market experiences a surplus in supply. However, in the new market, this surplus transforms into a supply shortage. At any given point P within this range, the surplus in the original market combined with the shortage in the new market equals the magnitude of the rightward shift in the demand curve.

When the price exceeds P_1 and enters the range of $(P_1, +\infty)$, both the original and new markets exhibit a supply surplus. However, compared to the original market, the surplus in the new market decreases by an amount equal to the rightward shift of the demand curve. Assuming this shift is denoted as ΔD, it can be concluded that, at any price level across the entire market, the supplier's revenue increases by $P \times \Delta D$.

Similarly, let's examine the producer and consumer surplus. Assume the original demand curve intersects the vertical axis at $(0, P_0^D)$ and the supply curve at $(0, P_S)$. The original consumer surplus is represented by $(0, P_0^D)$, $(0, P_0)$, and A, denoted as $S_{\Delta P_0^D P_0 A}$. The original producer surplus is represented by $(0, P_S)$, $(0, P_0)$, and A, denoted as $S_{\Delta P_S P_0 A}$. After product optimization, the new demand curve intersects the vertical axis at $(0, P_1^D)$. The new consumer surplus is represented by $(0, P_1^D)$, $(0, P_1)$, and B, denoted as $S_{\Delta P_1^D P_1 B}$. The new producer surplus is represented by $(0, P_S)$, $(0, P_1)$, and B, denoted as $S_{\Delta P_S P_1 B}$.

For consumers, the increase in consumer surplus, resulting from buying at the equilibrium price, is $S_{\Delta P_1^D P_1 B} - S_{\Delta P_0^D P_0 A}$. For producers, the increase in producer surplus, resulting from selling at the equilibrium price, is $S_{\Delta P_S P_1 B} - S_{\Delta P_S P_0 A}$. The producer surplus increment is clearly positive, represented by the quadrilateral area enclosed by $(0, P_0)$, A, B, $(0, P_1)$. Since $S_{\Delta IGB} > S_{\Delta GHA}$ and, for any quantity such as Q_5, $IG > GH$, it follows that the consumer surplus increment is also positive. The sum of these two increments represents the value increase brought about by the improvement in product experience.

(3) (C, A)

This scenario describes a situation where the product experience improves while the manufacturer's production costs decrease. The market changes are determined by the relative magnitudes of the supply increase and the demand increase at each price level. If, at every price level, the supply increase exceeds the demand increase, the surplus supply after meeting the additional demand leads to a decline in the equilibrium price compared to the original market. This dynamic is illustrated in figure 2-13.

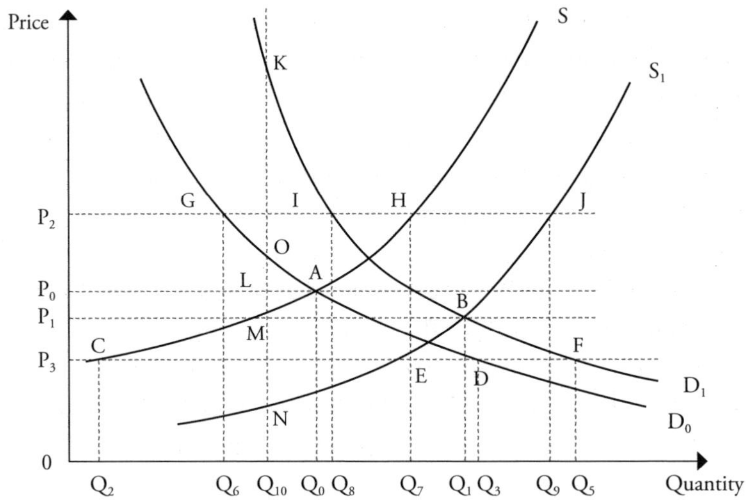

Figure 2-13 Demand and supply analysis for (C, A)

Under these conditions, the market equilibrium shifts from point A (Q_0, P_0) in the original market to point B (Q_1, P_1) in the new market. From the figure, it is evident that $Q_1 > Q_0$—equilibrium quantity increases. $P_1 < P_0$—equilibrium price decreases.

Next, let's analyze the market dynamics across price levels.

When the price fluctuates within the range of (0, P_1), for instance at the price level P_3, in the original market, there is a supply shortage represented by the segment CD, with the shortage quantity being $Q_3 - Q_2$. In the new market at the same price level, there is also a supply shortage, indicated by EF, but the shortage quantity has changed to $Q_5 - Q_7$. The segment CE, corresponding to the increase in supply $Q_7 - Q_2$, reflects the expansion of supply at the same price level, driven by reduced production costs. On the other hand, the segment DF, corresponding to the increase in demand $Q_5 - Q_3$, illustrates the boost in demand at the same price level, fueled by enhanced product experience. Therefore, at the price level P_3, the market's supply shortage has reduced by the amount CE – DF, which equals $(Q_7 - Q_2) - (Q_5 - Q_3)$. Assuming CE > DF, the reduction in the market's supply shortage is positive.

When the price falls within the range of (P_1, P_0), as shown in the figure, the market transitions from a supply shortage in the original market to a surplus in production.

When the price falls within the range of (P_0, $+\infty$), there is a supply surplus both before and after the market adjustment. For example, at the price level P_2, the supply surplus in the original market is represented by the length of line segment GH, corresponding to a surplus amount of $Q_7 - Q_6$. In the adjusted market, the supply surplus is represented by the length of line segment IJ, corresponding to a surplus amount of $Q_9 - Q_8$. If HJ > GI, the supply surplus in the market increases.

Let's further explore the changes in consumer surplus and producer surplus. We continue to assume the original demand curve intersects the vertical axis at $(0, P_0^D)$ and the original supply curve at $(0, P_0^S)$. The original consumer surplus is represented by $(0, P_0^D)$, $(0, P_0)$, and A, denoted as $S_{\triangle P_0^D P_0 A}$. The original producer surplus is represented by $(0, P_0^S)$, $(0, P_0)$, and A, denoted as $S_{\triangle P_0^S P_0 A}$. Assume the new demand curve intersects the vertical axis at $(0, P_1^D)$, and the new supply curve at $(0, P_1^S)$. The new consumer surplus is represented by $(0, P_1^D)$, $(0, P_1)$, and B, denoted as $S_{\triangle P_1^D P_1 B}$. The new producer surplus is represented by $(0, P_1^S)$, $(0, P_1)$, and B, denoted as $S_{\triangle P_1^S P_1 B}$.

For consumers, the increase in consumer surplus, resulting from buying at the equilibrium price, is $S_{\triangle P_1^D P_1 B} - S_{\triangle P_0^D P_0 A}$. For producers, the increase in producer surplus, resulting from selling at the equilibrium price, is $S_{\triangle P_1^S P_1 B} - S_{\triangle P_0^S P_0 A}$. As evident in the figure, $\triangle P_0^D P_0 A$ is a subset of $\triangle P_1^D P_1 B$, and thus, the area of $\triangle P_0^D P_0 A$ is naturally smaller. It's also easy to prove that $\triangle P_1^S P_1 B$ is larger than $\triangle P_0^S P_0 A$. Therefore, under these market changes, both consumer surplus and producer surplus have increased significantly. The total increase reflects the enhanced market value derived from an improved product experience.

When the increase in supply at each price level is smaller than the increase in demand, it indicates that all the additional supply will be sold, but there will still be unmet demand due to insufficient supply. In this case, the equilibrium price will rise compared to the original market, as depicted in figure 2-14.

In this scenario, the market equilibrium shifts from the original market point A (Q_0, P_0) to point B (Q_1, P_1). From figure 2-14, we can observe that $Q_1 > Q_0$, and $P_1 > P_0$, meaning that both the equilibrium quantity and price have increased.

When the price falls within the range of $(0, P_0)$, for instance at the price level P_3, the original market experiences a supply shortage ranging from $Q_7 - Q_2$, represented by the segment CD. In the new market at the same price, there is also a supply shortage, represented by the segment DE, but the shortage amount becomes $Q_6 - Q_7$. The segment CD corresponds to the increase in supply at the same price level (due to lower production costs), while the segment DE corresponds to the increase in demand at the same price level (due to improved product experience). Therefore, at price level P_3, the market's supply shortage has increased by the difference between DE and CD, which is $(Q_6 - Q_7) - (Q_7 - Q_2)$. Since it's assumed that DE > CD, the increase in supply shortage is positive.

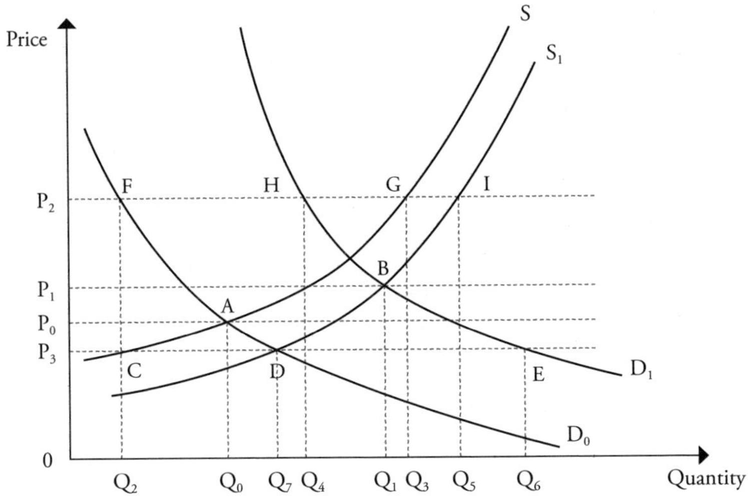

Figure 2-14 Demand and supply analysis (C, A)

When the price falls within the range (P_0, P_1), the market transitions from a surplus condition to an equilibrium state, with all surplus output being sold, resulting in corresponding revenue increases.

When the price falls within the range (P_1, $+\infty$), there is a supply surplus in both the original and new markets. For example, at price level P_2, the original market's supply surplus is represented by the length of segment FG, with a surplus quantity of $Q_3 - Q_2$. In the new market, the supply surplus is represented by the length of segment HI, with a surplus quantity of $Q_5 - Q_4$. When GH > GI, the market's supply surplus decreases.

Although the increase in output at each price level is smaller than the increase in demand, the changes in consumer surplus and producer surplus mirror the previous situation. As the proof is relatively straightforward, it will not be reiterated here.

(4) (A, B)

When the relationship between demand side price and demand shifts from a negative correlation to a positive one, the market undergoes a noticeable transformation, as illustrated in figure 2-15. Let's begin by analyzing the original market.

Assume the demand curve intersects the supply curve at point A (Q_0, P_0), where supply equals demand. When the price level is below P_0, for example, at P_1, the supply exceeds the demand, creating a surplus, represented by segment BC, with a total surplus quantity of $Q_4 - Q_1$, which cannot be sold easily.

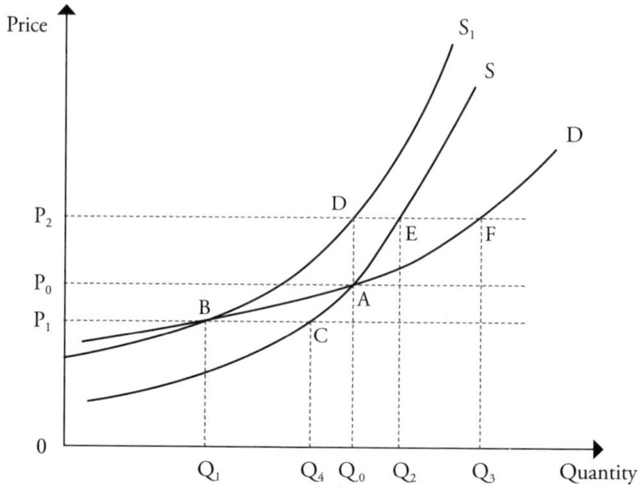

Figure 2-15 Demand and supply analysis (A, B)

In such a market environment, reducing output or lowering prices would only exacerbate the production surplus and further decrease the sale price. To reverse this passive situation, suppliers would need to increase production costs, boost output, and raise product prices. After reaching point A, the market may achieve equilibrium in terms of quantity, but neither supply nor demand is fully satisfied. As a result, production will increase, and prices will continue to rise. When the price exceeds P_0, a supply shortage arises, with demand outpacing supply. The increase in supply is insufficient to meet the demand, further driving up the market price. At this stage, the market operates in a way that whatever is produced is immediately sold.

But will the market continue expanding indefinitely? A positive slope in the demand curve typically arises from the unique characteristics of the product. Such a situation is often seen with goods that have limited availability, such as luxury items, collectibles, or limited-edition merchandise. Consequently, markets for these products generally have a production capacity limit. Let's assume this production limit is Q_{**}. In this case, to maximize profits, the supplier will continue to increase production until it reaches Q_{**}, and all of the output at Q_* will be sold. Therefore, within the range of output $[Q_0, Q_*]$, the market remains in equilibrium, with production equal to sales.

As the product experience improves and necessitates higher production costs, output at each price level decreases, exacerbating the supply shortage. This results in a higher price at each output level compared to before, with the price increase being equal to the additional production cost borne by the supplier.

Similarly, within the range [Q_1, Q_*], the market remains in equilibrium. If the supplier sets a price P_*, which is higher than the production cost at each output level, the difference between P_* and the production cost, multiplied by the output, represents the increase in producer surplus due to the enhanced product experience. For consumers, the willingness to accept higher prices stems from their perceived value, which exceeds the market value. The difference between the expected value and the actual price, multiplied by the quantity purchased, represents the increase in consumer surplus. Therefore, the total market value resulting from the improvement in product experience is the sum of the increase in producer surplus and the increase in consumer surplus.

At this point, another crucial factor that warrants attention is the relationship between the slopes of the demand and supply curves. We will explore these two scenarios in greater detail in the following section.

(5) (B, B)

When the slope of the demand curve becomes positive and improvements in product experience do not result in changes to the supply curve, this situation can be divided into two distinct cases, illustrated figure 2-16(a) and figure 2-16(b). Figure 2-16(a) represents the case where the slope of the supply curve is greater than that of the demand curve. Figure 2-16(b) represents the case where the slope of the supply curve is less than that of the demand curve.

Assume the supplier's maximum output is Q_*.

For the figure 2-16(a), when output is less than Q_1, at every level of demand, the price consumers are willing to pay exceeds the supplier's production cost. For

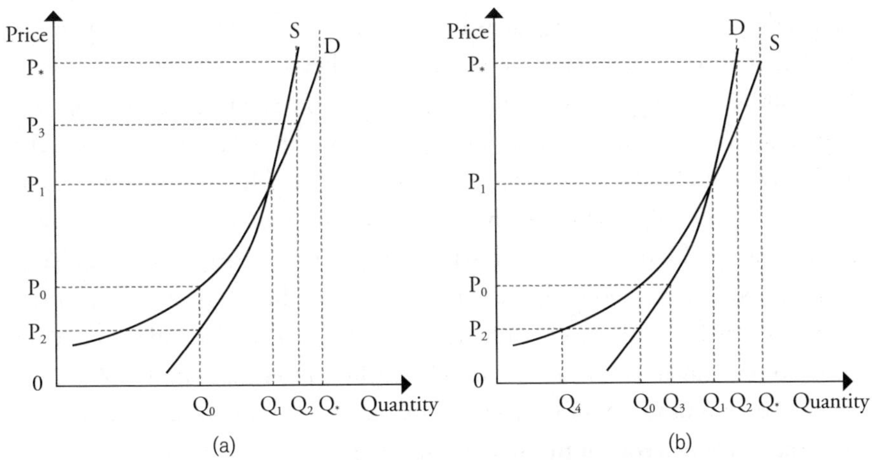

Figure 2-16 Demand and supply analysis (B, B)

example, at Q_0, if suppliers sell at price P_2, consumers gain a surplus of $P_0 - P_2$. If suppliers aim to maximize revenue, they sell at P_0, gaining a producer surplus of $P_0 - P_2$. The market price, determined by suppliers, will stabilize at (Q_0, P_0). Suppliers will expand production to increase sales and revenue until reaching Q_1, where the supply and demand curves intersect at (Q_1, P_1), achieving equilibrium. When the output is greater than Q_1 but less than Q_*, suppliers can continue producing, but the marginal increase in production cost exceeds the marginal price consumers are willing to pay. From a price perspective, at every price level, demand exceeds supply. What actions will both sides take?

For instance, at price P_*, consumers demand Q_*, which is greater than Q_2, but at this production cost level, suppliers can only provide Q_2. As a result, suppliers will only sell at Q_2, and consumers will purchase all these products. The market behavior in this case occurs along the supply curve. There will be a supply shortage of $Q_* - Q_2$, and suppliers will continue production until reaching Q_*. Assume the price corresponding to Q_* on the supply curve is P^S_*, and the market will ultimately reach equilibrium at (Q_*, P^S_*).

To avoid confusion, let us revisit the situation when the demand is Q_2. At Q_2, the production cost for suppliers far exceeds the price consumers are willing to pay, so suppliers will not produce Q_2 units of products for the market. Instead, they will produce according to the maximum price consumers are willing to pay at Q_2, which is P_3, as their production cost. This leads to output lower than Q_2, causing a supply shortage. As there is still unmet market demand, suppliers will continue producing, raising market prices to stimulate consumer demand until reaching equilibrium at (Q_*, P^S_*).

For figure 2-16(b), when demand is less than Q_1, for example, at Q_0, the supplier's production cost P_0 exceeds the price consumers are willing to pay P_2. Suppliers won't fully produce Q_0. Instead, they will produce Q_4, based on P_2, resulting in a supply shortage of $Q_0 - Q_4$. To maximize profits, suppliers will continue production and raise market prices as production costs rise. This gradually reduces the supply shortage until the supply and demand curves intersect at (Q_1, P_1), achieving balance. When output exceeds Q_1, at every production level, consumers' willingness to pay exceeds suppliers' production costs. Suppliers set prices based on consumer willingness to pay, earning producer surplus equal to the difference between sales prices and production costs. To maximize profits, suppliers will continue producing until reaching the maximum output Q_*. Assume the consumer price at Q_* on the demand curve is P^D_*; the market behavior at this point is (Q_*, P^D_*).

In conclusion, regardless of whether the slope of the supply or demand curve is steeper, the market reaches equilibrium at Q_*. There are differences in the path to equilibrium: When the supply curve slope is steeper, equilibrium is reached along the supply curve at (Q_*, P_*^S). When the demand curve slope is steeper, equilibrium is reached along the demand curve at (Q_*, P_*^D). For further insights, readers are encouraged to explore section 4 for a deeper discussion on equilibrium outcomes with differing slopes.

(6) (C, B)

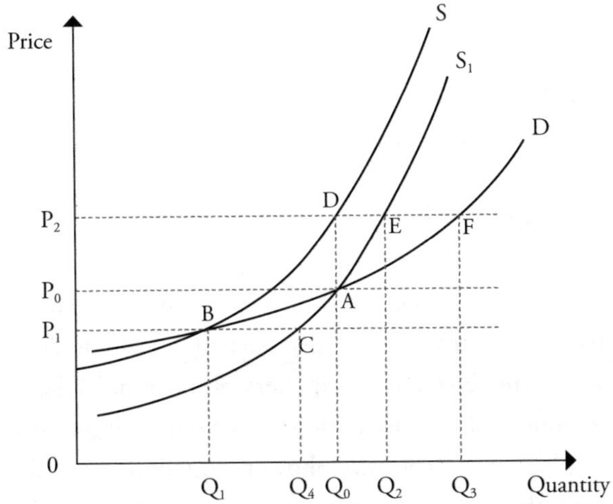

Figure 2-17 Demand and supply analysis (C, B)

This section examines the scenario where the supply curve shifts downward. Assume the supplier's maximum production capacity is Q_3. Here, we analyze the case where the slope of the supply curve is steeper than that of the demand curve first. The reverse case can be proven similarly.

According to the previous analysis, when the slope of the supply curve is greater than that of the demand curve, the market equilibrium occurs along the supply curve at the maximum production level. Assume that the original equilibrium is (Q_3, P_*^S), and the new equilibrium after the shift is $(Q_3, P_*^{S_1})$. Since the supply curve shifts downward, $P_*^S > P_*^{S_1}$, indicating a decrease in the equilibrium price by $P_*^S - P_*^{S_1}$. Production cost reductions alleviate supply shortages at all production costs above P_1. The reduction in shortages equals the horizontal rightward shift of the supply curve.

(7) (A, C)

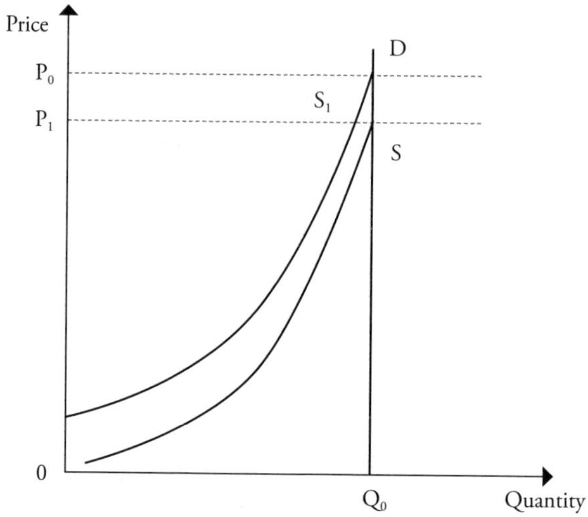

Figure 2-18 Demand and supply analysis (A, C)

This case represents an extreme scenario of (4), (5), and (6). Here, the demand curve is perfectly vertical to the quantity axis Q, meaning demand remains constant regardless of price changes. Suppliers produce only the fixed demand quantity. The minimum selling price corresponds to the reduced production cost. Suppliers can set a higher market price above production costs according to the actual demand, with the surplus becoming producer profit.

(8) (B, C)

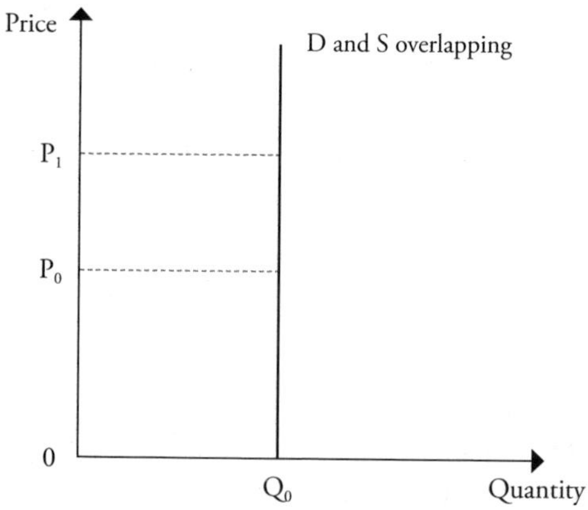

Figure 2-19 Demand and supply analysis (B, C)

This case further simplifies case (7). Both the demand and supply curves are perfectly vertical to the quantity axis Q, implying that demand and supply quantities are constant regardless of price changes. Market prices are determined primarily by suppliers.

(9) (C, C)

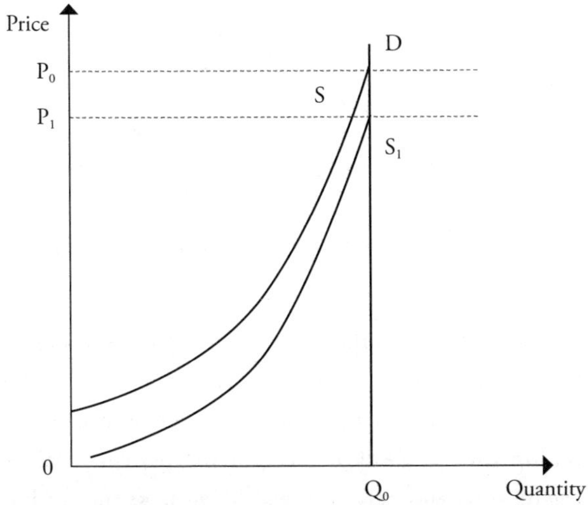

Figure 2-20 Demand and supply analysis (C, C)

This case is similar to case (7) but involves a reverse shift in the supply curve.

2. Scenarios of Negative Developments in Product Experience

(1) (–A, –A)

When product experience deteriorates, the demand curve shifts leftward. At every price level, the quantity demanded decreases. At every quantity level, the price consumers are willing to pay also decreases. In the (–A, –A) scenario, the decline in product experience results from reduced production costs, causing the supply curve to shift downward as well.

First, let's take a look at when the supply curve shift is greater than the demand curve shift, as shown in figure 2-21. Market equilibrium moves from the original point A (Q_0, P_0) to point B (Q_1, P_1). Although the equilibrium price decreases, the equilibrium quantity increases.

When prices fall within the range (0, P_1), both the original and the new markets exhibit excess demand at each price level, meaning the quantity demanded exceeds the quantity supplied, resulting in supply shortages. How-

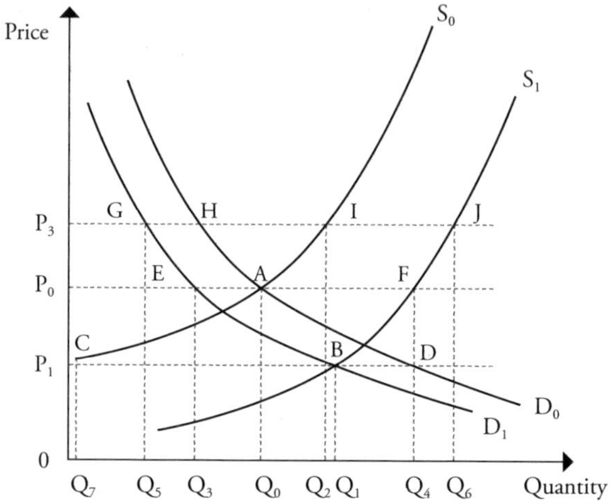

Figure 2-21 Demand and supply analysis (−A, −A)

ever, compared to the original market, the extent of the shortage is reduced in the new market. For prices between (P_1, P_0), the original market still shows a supply shortage, while the new market now experiences excess supply, leading to inventory buildup due to declining product experience. When prices rise above P_0, both the original and new markets show excess supply, but the surplus is more severe in the new market. A large volume of unsold goods results in declining net profits.

From the perspective of consumer and producer surplus, let us assume that the original demand curve intersects the vertical axis at (0, P_0^D), and the original supply curve intersects it at (0, P_0^S). The consumer surplus in the original market is represented by the area of the triangle formed by points (0, P_0^D), (0, P_0), and point A, denoted as $S_{\triangle P_0^D P_0 A}$. The producer surplus is represented by the triangle formed by (0, P_0^S), (0, P_0), and point A, denoted as $S_{\triangle P_0^S P_0 A}$.

Now suppose the new demand curve intersects the vertical axis at (0, P_1^D), and the new supply curve intersects it at (0, P_1^S). The new market's consumer surplus is the triangle formed by (0, P_1^D), (0, P_1), and point B, denoted as $S_{\triangle P_1^D P_1 B}$. The producer surplus is represented by the triangle formed by (0, P_1^S), (0, P_1), and point B, denoted as $S_{\triangle P_1^S P_1 B}$. For consumers, the change in consumer surplus when purchasing at the new equilibrium price is expressed as $S_{\triangle P_1^D P_1 B} - S_{\triangle P_0^D P_0 A}$. For producers, the change in producer surplus when selling at the new equilibrium price is expressed as $S_{\triangle P_1^S P_1 B} - S_{\triangle P_0^S P_0 A}$. As shown in figure 2-21, the change in consumer surplus is clearly positive. Whether the change in producer surplus is positive depends on the specific values. If producer surplus also increases, this suggests that the negative impact of the decline in product experience is outweighed by the positive effects of reduced production costs.

When the supply curve shift is smaller than the demand curve shift, see figure 2-22.

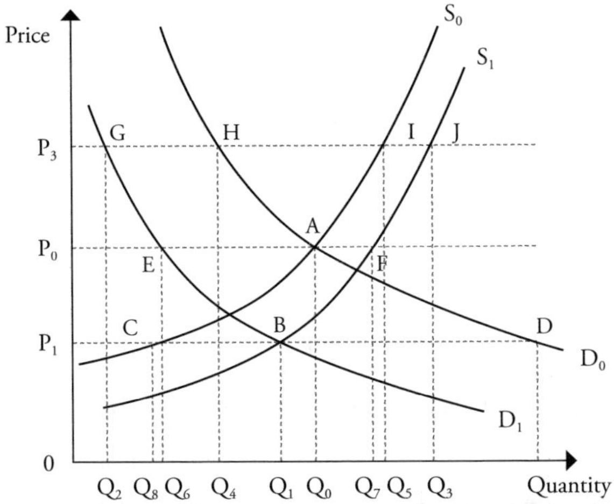

Figure 2-22 Demand and supply analysis (B, B)

Since the extent of demand reduction is greater than the extent of supply reduction, we find that the same market equilibrium point changes from A (Q_0, P_0) to B (Q_1, P_1), but both equilibrium price and quantity decrease. For prices in (P_0, $+\infty$), for instance, at price P_3, oversupply exists in both the original and new markets. However, in the new market, the surplus increases compared to the original. For prices in (P_1, P_0), the original market experiences undersupply, whereas the new market shifts to oversupply. For prices in (0, P_1), both markets experience undersupply. However, the shortage is less severe in the new market. Conclusively, the decline in product experience reduces supplier sales and revenue, representing the value lost due to the negative shift in experience.

From the perspective of consumer surplus and producer surplus, the previous assumption stands. Both consumer surplus and producer surplus decrease, and the sum of these decreases quantifies the market value lost due to the drop in product experience.

(2) (-B, -A)

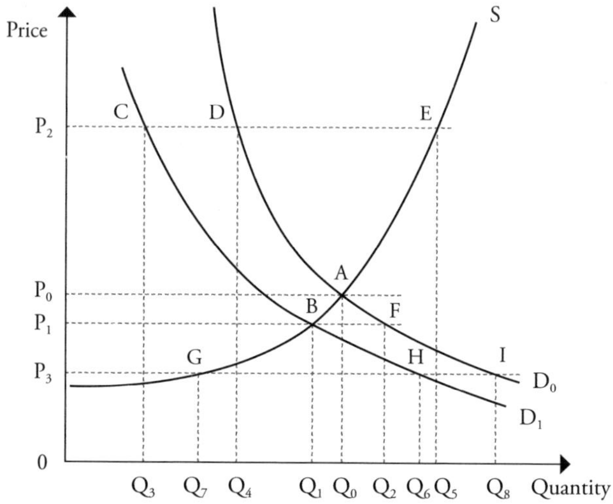

Figure 2-23 Demand and supply analysis (−B, −A)

This case depicts a scenario where product experience deteriorates while production costs remain unchanged, causing the demand curve to shift leftward and the supply chain to remain unchanged. At this time, the market equilibrium shifts from A (Q_0, P_0) to B (Q_1, P_1). Both equilibrium price and quantity decrease.

For prices in (P_0, $+\infty$), oversupply occurs in both the original and new markets due to unsold inventory. However, the new market experiences more severe oversupply, whose increase is manifested as the leftward shift of the demand curve. For prices in (P_1, P_0), the market transitions from undersupply to oversupply. For prices in (0, P_1), both markets experience undersupply, but the shortage is less severe in the new market, whose increase is manifested as the leftward shift of the demand curve.

Obviously, there is reduction in both consumer surplus and producer surplus, whose total reflects the market value lost due to the deterioration in product experience.

(3) (-C, -A)

This scenario involves a decline in product experience, shifting the demand curve leftward, while production costs increase, causing the supply curve to shift upward.

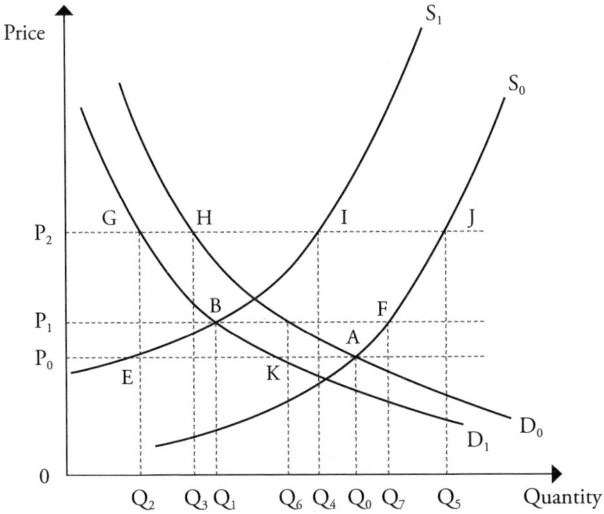

Figure 2-24 Demand and supply analysis (−C, −A)

First, let us examine the case where the upward shift of the supply curve exceeds the downward shift of the demand curve, as shown in figure 2-24. The market equilibrium shifts from A (Q_0, P_0) to B (Q_1, P_1). The equilibrium price increases, while the equilibrium quantity decreases. For prices in (0, P_0), at each price level, the corresponding quantity demanded exceeds the quantity supplied in both markets, which therefore experiences undersupply, but the shortage is more pronounced in the new market. For prices in (P_0, P_1), the original market experiences oversupply, while the new market transitions to undersupply. The impact of the decline in product experience is smaller than the impact of changes in production costs. For prices in (P_1, $+\infty$), oversupply exists in both markets, but less severe in the new market.

From the perspective of consumer surplus and producer surplus, assume original demand curve—intersects the vertical axis at (0, P_0^D), original supply curve—intersects the vertical axis at (0, P_0^S), new demand curve—intersects the vertical axis at (0, P_1^D), and new supply curve—intersects the vertical axis at (0, P_1^S). The original consumer surplus then is the area of triangle $S_{\triangle P_0^D P_0 A}$, and the new is the area of triangle $S_{\triangle P_1^D P_1 B}$. The original producer surplus is the area of triangle $S_{\triangle P_0^S P_0 A}$, and the new is the area of triangle $S_{\triangle P_1^S P_1 B}$. For consumers, the increase in consumer surplus obtained when they pay the equilibrium price can be represented as $S_{\triangle P_1^D P_1 B} - S_{\triangle P_0^D P_0 A}$. Similarly, for producers, the increase in producer surplus earned when selling at the equilibrium price can be expressed as $S_{\triangle P_1^S P_1 B} - S_{\triangle P_0^S P_0 A}$. As shown in figure 2-24, both the consumer and producer surplus changes are negative. The sum of these negative changes quantifies the total market value loss caused by the decline in the product.

When the supply curve shift is smaller than the demand curve shift, as shown in figure 2-25.

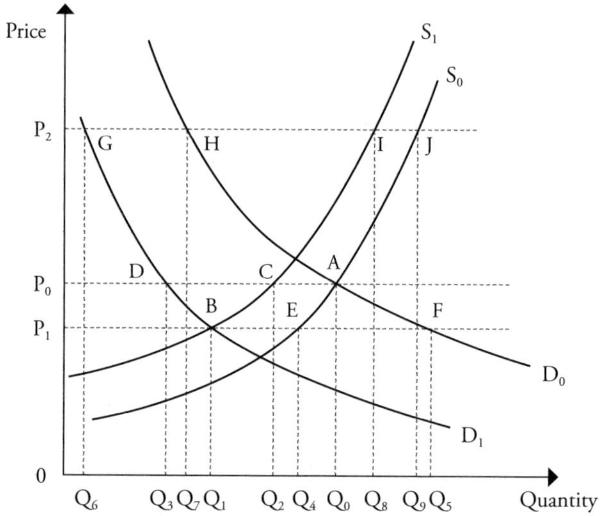

Figure 2-25 Demand and supply analysis (−C, −A)

When the downward shift of the demand curve exceeds the upward shift of the supply curve, the following changes occur: The market equilibrium shifts from A (Q_0, P_0) to B (Q_1, P_1). Both the equilibrium price and quantity decrease. For prices in (P_0, $+\infty$), for instance, at price P_2, oversupply exists in both the original and new markets. In the new market, the oversupply is more severe. For prices in (P_1, P_0), the original market experiences undersupply, while the new market transitions to oversupply. For prices in (0, P_1), both markets experience undersupply. The new market exhibits a less severe shortage, indicating a decline in product experience significantly reduces supplier sales and revenue, representing the value loss attributable to the decline in product experience.

When observing from the perspective of consumer surplus and producer surplus, we have adopted the previous assumptions. It can be found that both the incremental consumer surplus and the producer surplus are negative, and the total market value loss can also be used to characterize the amount of reduction in market value due to the decline in experience.

iv. The Relationship Between Experience and Utility

In microeconomics, utility is a concept akin to experience, referring to the satisfaction consumers derive from goods. Indifference curves and their corresponding utility functions, derived from the varying levels of satisfaction provided by different combinations of goods, serve as core components of microeconomic analysis. When analyzing real-world economic activities, three significant issues with utility theory become apparent:

First, the fundamental principle of utility theory asserts that, regardless of the specific combination of goods a consumer selects, if they are willing to pay the same total price for different combinations, those combinations can be considered equivalent in terms of satisfaction. However, this principle is based on the assumption that a consumer's overall perception or level of satisfaction derived from a combination of goods is fully reflected in their willingness to pay, and that this perception remains relatively stable over short periods. In practice, however, even for the same combination of goods, individuals' perceptions and willingness to pay are subject to continuous change. At any given moment, the price a person is willing to pay is shaped by expectations formed from past experiences. As these expectations evolve in response to the actual experience of consuming the goods, attitudes toward the same combination can shift significantly. This issue becomes even more pronounced with the increasing variety of goods and the rapid pace of product iteration and optimization. Under such conditions, capturing and stabilizing indifference curves and combinations becomes increasingly difficult, making the practical application of utility theory highly challenging.

Second, the fundamental methods of measuring utility—cardinal utility theory and ordinal utility theory—fail to fully address the core issue of quantifying utility. At the heart of economic analysis lies the quantification of economic factors; without such quantification, it becomes challenging to effectively capture and describe the state and evolution of these factors. This lack of quantification hampers subsequent analysis, leaving it without a solid mathematical foundation.

Third, utility, in its most literal sense, often refers to "usefulness," representing the level of satisfaction derived from "practicality." However, through the earlier discussion of experience, we find that satisfaction with a product goes beyond mere practicality and extends to "emotional" fulfillment as well. For example, in traditional economic utility theory, products like clothing and food are often used to illustrate how different combinations of goods meet consumer needs. If a consumer is equally satisfied with a combination of 5 units of clothing and 2 units of food, as they are with 2 units of clothing and 5 units of food, we would consider the consumer's indifference curve for clothing and food to be represented by a line or curve connecting these two points. In reality, however, the sheer abundance of goods and the notable differences in quality present a range of choices for both clothing and food. When selecting products, consumers not only consider whether the item meets basic needs, such as filling their stomach or providing warmth, but also whether it offers enjoyment or reflects their personal taste. This insight reveals that experience is a broader and more encompassing concept than utility alone. In the context of economic decision-making, when consumers base their choices on more than just the practical utility of a product, but also on various other influential factors, experience becomes a far more meaningful economic element than utility. Consumer decisions rooted in experience encompass not only practical utility and emotion but also all the potential human feelings that may arise from a product. As society's focus shifts from basic survival needs to higher-level aspirations, the significance of these influences becomes even more pronounced.

Building on the analysis above, we confidently put forward the following proposition: Experience serves as a more effective indicator than utility for measuring consumers' satisfaction with a product. This advantage manifests in four key areas:

(1) Experience is more easily quantifiable and offers a more comprehensive account of consumer perception. As discussed in earlier sections, there are various methods, tools, and techniques for quantifying experience—ranging from the micro level (an individual's response to a specific product) to the macro level (public attitudes). As long as a valid conversion relationship can be established between experience and the value of goods, experience can serve as a meaningful economic variable within economic analysis.

(2) Experience treats individual differences in response to similar goods as essential factors. Unlike utility, which primarily reflects the price consumers are willing to pay, experience takes into account variations in how consumers perceive different items within the same product bundle. For example, consider a purchase totaling RMB 1,000: RMB 500 is spent on clothing, RMB 200 on food, and RMB 300 on cleaning supplies. The clothing includes two T-shirts in different patterns and a pair of jeans; the food includes two boxes of bread and some fruit; the cleaning products consist of toothpaste, laundry detergent, and disinfectant. In this scenario, the consumer feels the clothing is of great value, the food is reasonably priced, but the cleaning products are clearly more expensive than before—yet still necessary. Although the total

expenditure is RMB 1,000, the experience across categories varies. The price paid does not necessarily reflect maximum satisfaction, but rather a compromise after weighing pros and cons. Even when two different product bundles cost the same—say, RMB 1,000—the consumer's experience can differ, even for the same individual.

(3) Experience captures the dynamic nature of consumer perception more effectively. Because consumer feelings about products are constantly evolving, experience can not only reflect how a consumer feels at the moment of purchase but also track changes in perception over time. In this sense, experience is a dynamic and quantifiable metric.

(4) Experience encourages attention to the deeper motivations behind decision-making, leading to a more accurate understanding of the market. Consumers often have underlying reasons for their purchasing decisions that cannot be fully explained by the prices they pay. This is especially true in markets with repeat purchases and competing alternatives. Understanding these deeper motivations is critical to retaining existing customers and attracting new ones. If a product fails to continuously meet a certain need, consumers are likely to leave, making it difficult to predict future behavior based on past data. Similarly, if a product does not respond to emerging consumer needs, past buyers may turn to competitors. As a result, producers cannot afford to maintain a fixed product model or production structure—they must continuously monitor the market and adjust their strategies in real-time to capture new opportunities. Both production and consumption thus become dynamic processes, and market equilibrium along with other economic variables evolves accordingly.

Building on the findings above, we propose a detailed methodology for replacing the concept of utility with that of experience as a core metric in economic analysis. Utility is traditionally described through combinations of goods and their associated prices. However, the concept of experience offers a richer and more comprehensive framework.

Experience includes not only the composition of product combinations and the distinct characteristics of each product category but also the perceived experience level of each individual product. In essence, experience can be represented as a detailed data matrix for a product combination, encompassing both quantitative and qualitative aspects. This approach captures not only the quantity of each product but also its specific attributes and the unique satisfaction it delivers.

The distinctions between the information encapsulated by utility and experience are highlighted in tables 2-2 and 2-3.

Table 2-2 Product combination for measuring utility (template)

Utility			
	Quantity	Price	Total
Product 1	3	500	1,500
Product 2	5	20	100
...			
Product n	2	1,000	2,000

Table 2-3 Example of product combination for measuring experience

Experience								
Dimension 1	Dimension 2	Dimension 3	Dimension 4	Dimension 5	Dimension 6	Dimension 7		Dimension 1
Product category	Product	Material parameters	Function	Features and advantages	Appearance	Price	...	Experience level
Category 1	Product 1	(example)	(example)	(example)	(example)	(example)	...	(example)
	Product 2	(example)	(example)	(example)	(example)	(example)	...	(example)
	Product n	(example)	(example)	(example)	(example)	(example)	...	(example)
Category 2		(example)	(example)	(example)	(example)	(example)	...	(example)
...	...	...	...	...	...	...	...	...
Category n		(example)	(example)	(example)	(example)	(example)	...	(example)

As seen, experience encompasses all information captured by utility while adding richer details specific to each product. In the digital age, every parameter of a product is meticulously documented and stored in the form of data, enabling seamless calculation, processing, and management through advanced computational tools.

v. Findings

The analysis above explored the 12 possible market transformations caused by changes in product experience within single-product markets. From a broader perspective, we observe the following findings: Variations in product experience levels significantly impact the total market value of goods. Although the extent of these changes depends on the slopes and shifts of supply and demand curves, the relationship between experience and market value has been established. As product iterations accelerate, experience continues to influence markets, even causing sustained shifts in total market value. For economic participants operating in experience-sensitive markets, acknowledging these changes is essential. Businesses and individuals must adapt to the dynamic nature of supply-demand relationships influenced by experience: For businesses, focus on ensuring sustainable operations and innovation to meet evolving consumer needs; and for consumers, optimize decision-making to satisfy personal preferences in the most effective way. Based on this analysis, we propose the bold idea that experience, rather than utility, should serve as the core economic metric for measuring consumer perceptions.

III. Impact of Experience in Macroeconomic Analysis

Macroeconomics delves into the broader patterns of economic behavior within society and the cumulative effects they generate. To explore these dynamics, macroeconomics examines the overall functioning of the economy, focusing on key aspects such as total output, income levels, price stability, and employment rates. The most critical indicators for assessing macroeconomic performance include Gross Domestic Product (GDP), national income growth, unemployment rates, inflation or deflation trends, and price fluctuations. Additionally, factors such as changes in fiscal deficits, trade imbalances, and interest rates also play a significant role. This section will offer a preliminary analysis of how experiential factors influence macroeconomic outcomes.

i. When Does Experience Become Significant?

As human society advances, each historical stage nurtures a level of productivity, means of production, and production relations uniquely suited to its developmental needs. These elements collectively shape the economic activities of their time. In turn, economic theories emerge as systematic analyses and generalizations of these activities, forming conceptual frameworks to guide economic behavior. Similar to the progression of physics—from Newtonian mechanics to Einstein's relativity, quantum mechanics, and string theory—economics evolves through theories reflective of its era's defining characteristics.

In the primitive, slave, and feudal societies, despite regional and temporal variations, economic activities predominantly aimed to meet basic needs such as food and shelter. Agriculture formed the backbone of national economies, supplemented by handicrafts, light industry, and, to a limited extent, heavy industry. Although wealth disparities existed, luxurious lifestyles were largely confined to the ruling classes and nobility, with the majority of the population subsisting at minimal levels.

As discussed earlier, experience is closely intertwined with levels and types of needs. When living standards are low, limited income is allocated primarily to essential needs like food, clothing, and shelter, leaving little financial capacity for pursuing higher-order aspirations. However, with the advent of the Industrial Revolution, the dismantling of feudal systems, and rapid advancements in science and technology, society witnessed exponential growth in productivity, fundamentally transforming the structure of wealth: The working class gradually accumulated wealth through wage labor; the middle class emerged and expanded, forming a significant societal segment; and the affluent elite gained access to an explosion of investment opportunities and financial instruments.

These shifts led to a substantial increase in overall societal wealth, elevating disposable incomes across all social strata. This growth, combined with the increasing specialization of industries and an expanding variety of goods and services, dramatically broadened consumer choice. As options multiplied, so did the capacity to fulfill more diverse and elevated needs. Society transitioned from a focus on basic survival to a pursuit of quality living, personal expression, and self-actualization. Only when society evolves to such a stage does experience emerge as a crucial factor influencing economic life.

Regarding economic analysis, exploring experience's impact in macroeconomics necessitates a specific level of societal development as a backdrop. However, even within the same era, economic conditions can vary significantly across regions and time periods. While this has been previously mentioned, it is worth reiterating: The influence of experience on economic activities relies on the following foundational conditions:

(1) The region's economic development must have surpassed the stage of merely meeting basic subsistence needs, allowing individuals to possess a certain level of disposable income.

(2) Social productivity and production relations should have progressed to a stage that facilitates personalized and customized products, with the capability for flexible resource allocation within a defined range.
(3) Critical infrastructure, such as transportation, energy, logistics, and warehousing, must be sufficiently developed to ensure the rapid, flexible, and efficient transfer and distribution of resources.
(4) Individuals should possess an awakened sense of self-awareness, enabling independent decision-making based on personal preferences and desires.
(5) A robust communication and networking infrastructure is essential, enabling individuals to access product and service information comprehensively, efficiently, and at a low cost.
(6) The global exchange of ideas and cultural integration should have broadened perspectives, enriched consumer cognition, and transformed needs, resulting in more diverse and sophisticated demands.

ii. The Impact of Experience on National Income Components

The core measure of national economic activity is GDP. From the expenditure approach, GDP is calculated using

$$GDP = C + I + G + (X - M)$$

C refers to total individual (or household) consumption expenditure, I represents gross private domestic investment, G stands for government purchases, and X – M denotes net exports (exports minus imports).

From the income approach, GDP is calculated as

$$GDP = C + S + T + K$$

C stands for consumption, S for savings, T for taxes, and K represents income received by other countries from the domestic economy.

As people move beyond meeting basic survival needs, individual consumption begins to include happiness and self-actualization, leading to changes in both consumption structure and volume. In economics, the Engel coefficient, which measures the proportion of food expenditure in total household spending, has been used as a key indicator of economic disparity. However, when discussing the impact of experience on consumption, the expenditures required to meet basic living needs should include not only food but also essential costs such as rent (or home purchase), utilities (water, electricity, gas, and property management fees), transportation, communication, and medical expenses.

Basic living expenditure = Minimum food expenditure + Minimum housing expenditure + Minimum transportation expenditure + Minimum communication expenditure + Minimum medical expenditure

Disposable income = Total individual income + Savings – Basic living expenditure

This disposable income represents the actual resources individuals can allocate toward improving their quality of life and meeting higher-order needs. The aforementioned minimum expenditure thresholds should align with the region's social development level. Only when the majority of residents have disposable incomes greater than zero can they engage in experience-driven consumption, making this factor a key area of examination.

From a fundamental standpoint, individuals with disposable income above zero form the primary focus of experience-based consumption analysis. When this population grows to a significant scale of influence, experience becomes a crucial macroeconomic factor requiring attention in economic studies. Experience primarily influences consumption-related decisions, indirectly shaping broader economic activities. From an income perspective, it has a direct impact on C, S, and K, while T remains unaffected. From a macroeconomic perspective, experience is closely tied to demand, particularly consumption demand. Changes in the structure and form of consumption demand necessitate adaptive changes on the supply side, thereby indirectly influencing supply dynamics.

In subsequent sections, we will delve deeper into these areas of impact, exploring both direct and indirect influences of experience on economic activities.

iii. The Impact of Experience on Demand Side

1. Influence on the Demand Space

Experience plays a pivotal role in expanding total demand and fostering demand diversification. As national income levels rise significantly, individuals gain greater disposable income and benefit from a more diversified income distribution structure. Human needs at various levels collectively shape the overall demand space. Building on prior microeconomic discussions of production methods, this section explores consumer demand at a macroeconomic level by categorizing it into different tiers.

During the planned economy era, industrial production adhered strictly to state-mandated macroeconomic plans. Consumer goods, such as basic necessities, were standardized in design and specifications. For instance, households used identical patterned bedsheets, curtains, enamel cups, bowls, and washbasins, and even children played with uniform plush toys.

As the economy transitioned to a market-driven model, foundational goods and services inherited from the planned economy remained prominent due to their acceptable quality and low cost. This type of demand is referred to as the first level: the consumption of basic goods and services focused on affordability. This category encompasses food, clothing, transportation, and other essentials, representing the minimum requirements for basic living. Social relief and minimum living standards are typically calculated based on the prices of these goods and services.

With rising incomes, residents allocate surplus income to improve living standards beyond basic needs. At this stage, consumers seek differentiation and variety in goods and services.

In dining, the focus shifts from merely eating enough to eating well, emphasizing health and flavor. In clothing, the emphasis is on style and uniqueness. Similar elevated preferences emerge across other lifestyle domains. This stage is defined as the second level: consumption of mid-value, differentiated goods and services. Achieving this level signifies a moderately prosperous society where basic needs are thoroughly met, and surplus income is available for enhancing quality of life.

With further socioeconomic development, some individuals achieve higher incomes, leading to affluence. At this stage, spending on basic necessities occupies a smaller proportion of overall expenditure, while lifestyle-enhancing and luxury goods and services become more dominant. Consumers at this level seek novelty, personalization, and self-expression through their purchases. Exploring diverse cultures and values through travel. Discovering unique and intriguing products. Prioritizing comfort and quality in daily life, with a focus on material excellence, craftsmanship, and customer service. This stage represents the third level: consumption of high-value, personalized goods and services.

Finally, when individuals attain complete financial freedom, allowing them to make unrestricted choices about their consumption, they ascend to the fourth tier of the consumption hierarchy. This stage is characterized by a desire for bespoke, self-expressive goods and services tailored precisely to their needs. These consumers gravitate toward exclusivity, customization, and limited editions, demanding offerings uniquely crafted to suit their preferences. At this level, their willingness to pay spans a wide range, as they possess the means to invest in unparalleled services and superior quality that set them apart.

As consumer demand transitions from the first to the fourth level, on top of addressing survival needs, it creates a richer and more diverse demand space, significantly enhancing the economy's value potential. For instance, consider a standard mass-produced dish like sweet and sour pork compared to a customized version tailored to an individual's preferences. Although production costs may be similar, the personalized dish carries greater value. The premium it commands reflects the added value derived from an expanded demand space. On a macroeconomic scale, this evolving demand space raises critical questions: Can limited resources, such as land, achieve greater total value through refined demand management and resource allocation? Can stimulating new demand spaces improve overall living standards and happiness without increasing pressure on land production?

A potential concern with expanded value is the risk of rising prices, which could strain low- and middle-income groups. However, as previously analyzed, consumption levels align closely with income levels. Meeting basic subsistence needs remains a priority when balancing societal demand structures. The growth in demand space and corresponding value creation primarily targets consumers with greater purchasing power. Therefore, the extent of demand expansion must align with overall economic development levels while ensuring regional balance. While ideally every individual has infinite potential needs, not all have the means to realize or fund them.

2. Impact on Current and Future Income Distribution

From the perspective of income predictability, individuals can be categorized into three distinct groups:

(1) Individuals with accurate predictions of both current and future income. This group typically includes people employed in stable positions, such as government, state-owned enterprises, or public institutions. They enjoy fixed incomes, face minimal unexpected disruptions (e.g., company closure), and do not plan to change jobs in the near term.

(2) Individuals with accurate short-term income predictions (up to three years) but uncertainty beyond that. Examples include private-sector employees

who anticipate career changes or variations in their income trajectory in the medium term.
(3) Individuals unable to accurately predict their future income. This category often comprises self-employed individuals or those who frequently switch jobs.

From the perspective of daily expense proportions, individuals can also be divided into two categories:

(1) Individuals with stable daily expense proportions. This group generally includes individuals with a conservative or steady temperament, or older individuals who exhibit a more measured approach to finances.
(2) Individuals with variable daily expense proportions. These individuals prefer flexibility in financial decisions, enjoy trying new experiences, and often adopt a "you only live once" mindset. They are typically younger or more dynamic in their financial behavior.

Although real-world scenarios are more complex, analyzing these primary types allows for a better understanding of broader variations. By combining the above classifications, six possible scenarios emerge, each analyzed below:

(1) Accurate income prediction with stable expense proportions. In this scenario, individuals have a clear prediction and calculation of their total income, enabling meticulous planning and allocation of resources for now and the future. After setting aside funds for retirement, risk reserves, and essential living expenses, the remainder is considered disposable income, available for consumption or investment. Assuming rational behavior, individuals aim to maximize their lifetime experiential satisfaction using this disposable income. This creates a value space corresponding to total disposable income and an experiential demand space reflecting experiential needs.

The extent to which goods in the economic market satisfy the experiential demand within this value space directly impacts the fulfillment of this group's preferences and potential needs. The more effectively these needs are met, the greater the proportion of their income that is converted into consumption expenditure. It is important to note that this value has a fixed net worth. When consumption expenditure represents a higher proportion during one period, it will inevitably decline in subsequent periods, thereby establishing an upper limit to the total demand of this group.

(2) Accurate income prediction with variable expense proportions. In addition to the characteristics previously outlined, this scenario introduces a flexible value space for disposable income. Allocations for retirement funds, risk protection, and basic daily expenses can fluctuate, increasing or decreasing based on actual consumption demands. From the perspective of this group's overall income capacity, their maximum income boundary can exceed the level described in scenario (1), potentially reaching their total income. This means that consumers might opt to sacrifice future consumption to maximize their experiential satisfaction during a specific period. Their primary objective is to optimize overall experiential satisfaction and fulfill demand within the confines of their total income. Consequently, the total market demand generated by this group aligns closely with their total income.

However, much like in scenario (1), their total income is finite. As such, their overall demand has an upper limit, necessitating careful and strategic allocation over the course of their lifetime.

(3) Short-term income predictability (up to three years) with stable expense proportions. For individuals in this group, while short-term income is foreseeable, long-term income remains uncertain. This often leads to a conservative approach to spending, with higher savings rates to prepare for potential future risks, cutting down current expenses.

When their saving and expense proportions are fixed, the maximum demand they bring to the market is limited to their current disposable income. Generally, strategies to enhance their market demand include improving social security systems to reduce future risk concerns, thereby encouraging reduced savings and higher spending; raising medium- and long-term income expectations to instill confidence in their financial future, promoting increased consumption in the present.

(4) Short-term income predictability (up to three years) with variable expense proportions. Unlike scenario (3), individuals in this group exhibit flexible expense proportions. Savings for future risks may vary based on their financial circumstances. Their maximum demand potential is their entire current income, though debt-financed consumption is also a possibility.

This group may be tempted by innovative or high-value products that promise exceptional experiences, tempting them to prioritize immediate consumption over future stability. For example, an innovative, high-tech product exceeding expectation may prompt them to make substantial purchases, even at the cost of future consumption, which causes a reduction in experiential satisfaction in subsequent periods. Overall, their total demand aligns with their income levels and their pursuit of optimal experiential satisfaction at different points in time.

(5) Unpredictable future income with stable expense proportions. The income uncertainty of individuals in this group is the highest, leading to conservative financial behavior. They maintain high savings rates to guard against potential future risks and focus on affordable, essential goods and services, minimizing luxury consumption. These individuals prioritize financial security over experiential satisfaction, seeking a balance between the two yet the former weighing more. Only when their savings reach a level that ensures long-term stability do they engage in more experience-driven consumption.

(6) Unpredictable future income with variable expense proportions. Similar to those in scenario (5), individuals in this category need to maintain savings to address future risks. However, their outlook is more optimistic, allowing for greater flexibility in adjusting daily expense proportions. These individuals strike a balance between ensuring future financial security and fulfilling present experiential needs.

The analysis above highlights the characteristics and dynamics of demand-value spaces across different consumer groups. It is essential to clarify that when discussing demand-value spaces influenced by experiential needs, we refer to the portion of consumer income that remains after covering basic living expenses and future financial safeguards.

For instance, in China's first-tier cities like Beijing, Shanghai, and Guangzhou, high living costs consume most, if not all, of the income for middle class and low-income groups. Many households even resort to debt to meet their current living expenses. Despite having relatively higher-income levels, these individuals often lack the means to engage in experiential consumption. On the other hand, individuals whose income and savings exceed the requirements for basic living and retirement possess a surplus that enables them to participate in experience-driven consumption. Their demand for high-quality goods and services becomes a vital contributor to economic growth. This consumption drives the redistribution of wealth, as affluent groups' surplus income flows to other segments of society through the provision of premium services. For the affluent, this redistribution offers access to more comfortable and aesthetically pleasing goods and services, fulfilling their diverse needs. For the market, this demand stimulates innovation and production, creating new supply chains and employment opportunities. These opportunities, in turn, improve income levels across a broader population through wage redistribution.

Thus, the emergence of new value spaces driven by experiential demand represents a significant source of economic momentum. By fostering demand in a resource-constrained environment, these spaces serve as a critical engine for optimizing resource allocation and stimulating economic activity.

iv. The Impact of Experiential Demand on Supply Side

Experiential demand has profound effects on the supply side, primarily in two areas: Transforming supply methods: The expansion of demand-value spaces drives a shift in production and sales models, evolving from standardized production to differentiated production and ultimately to demand-driven manufacturing. Repurposing surplus inventory: It inspires innovative approaches to reprocess and create secondary value from overproduced goods.

1. Evolution in Supply Methods

(1) Evolution of Production Methods

The evolution of production methods in human society can be categorized into five major stages based on the roles of humans and machines:

Stage 1: pure manual labor. Before the Industrial Revolution, all goods were produced through manual labor. While tools were developed to aid production, the primary driver of productivity was human effort. And low productivity levels limited societal focus to basic survival needs such as food and clothing. Except for a small number of skilled artisans creating luxury goods (such as architectural carvings, jewelry, etc.) for the elite, most labor was simple and repetitive. The labor process predominantly depended on the physical exertion of workers, with production levels influenced not only by human effort but also significantly by environmental and climatic conditions. Given the limited ability to withstand natural disasters and the generally low levels of productivity, society's overall output remained extremely constrained.

The scarcity of resources often sparked conflicts among different groups, with larger-scale disputes escalating into full-blown wars. These wars not only heightened instability in production and distribution but also played a pivotal role in shaping distinct social hierarchies within human society. Those who managed to mobilize large groups of people, establish armed forces, and secure absolute dominance rose to become the ruling class. Individuals directly or indirectly associated with this ruling elite—often through blood ties in early societies—were stratified into various levels of nobility, with their status determined by the closeness of their connections. Supporting the ruling and noble classes were the upper echelons of the military, forming the warrior class, which aided in the armed conquest and governance of allocated territories.

The vast majority of the populace, however, were relegated to being slaves or subordinates, deprived of ownership rights to land or assets. Additionally, there emerged a merchant class that operated fluidly across societal strata, engaging in trade to sustain their livelihoods.

Despite the limited variety and quantity of societal labor products, resources were disproportionately directed toward the ruling class, intensifying the already significant gap between the rich and the poor. Although a modest middle class existed, the overwhelming majority of the population struggled to fulfill their basic living needs.

Excessive oppression by the ruling class often incited rebellions led by the warrior class and the lower classes, resulting in social upheaval until a new regime emerged and restored stability. These recurring phenomena were fundamentally rooted in the low levels of productive forces and the severe scarcity of resources. During this period, the concept of "value space" was largely defined by the pursuit of basic survival needs, many of which remained unattainable for the majority.

Another distinctive feature of this stage is the influence of manual labor on production, leading to a wide variation in product quality and relatively low overall output. This was primarily due to the limited capabilities and skills of the labor force. Agricultural products were subject to the conditions of the land, climate, and farming techniques, resulting in a significant disparity in the quality of yields. Similarly, the quality of handicrafts and light industrial products varied based on the skill level of workers and production techniques. The merchant class skillfully capitalized on these discrepancies, purchasing goods at low prices and then creating added value through market transactions to earn profits.

For the ruling and noble classes, the focus was on the production of essential goods such as food, clothing, and precious metals from their lands. Once these fundamental needs were reliably met, they had the leisure and inclination to pursue novelty and entertainment. To fulfill these higher-level desires, they turned to the merchant class, acquiring goods and services that catered to their refined tastes. This created a demand for a wide range of service industries, including entertainment (such as music, dance, acrobatics, and clowns), wellness and healthcare (such as bathing, massages, and medicine), transportation (including boat and vehicle manufacturing), and industries that enhanced daily life, such as architecture and interior design.

However, despite occasional miraculous achievements (such as monumental buildings), the development of these industries remained relatively underdeveloped, largely due to isolated regional cultures and the overall limitations of social production.

Stage 2: simple machines and low-to-mid-level manual labor. With the onset of the Industrial Revolution, machines began replacing some of the manual labors in social production. From the steam age to the electrical era, and later the biotechnology and aerospace age, the extent and sophistication of machine labor gradually increased. The division of labor between humans and machines underwent transformative leaps.

This stage, primarily covering the steam and early electrical eras, is defined as the simple machines and low-to-mid-level manual labor. During this period, machines replaced specific forms of labor—those conducive to standardized production or tasks unsuitable for humans due to low productivity or harsh conditions (e.g., high temperature or pressure). Production processes were fragmented into discrete steps, interconnected by chains of operations.

The purpose of this fragmentation was to delegate all tasks that could be mass-produced to simple-function machines, while leaving tasks beyond the capacity of machines—such as assembling parts—to be performed by manual labor. A typical production chain consisted of machines and workers playing complementary roles in different segments. As a result, human labor became focused on specific, repetitive tasks. For instance, workers performing tasks like screwing bolts became increasingly skilled through repetitive practice, achieving higher efficiency than in earlier eras.

Additionally, the repetitive nature of these tasks ensured that labor hours directly correlated with increased output, unaffected by the complexities of earlier production methods. To boost production, machines could operate around the clock, supplemented by the maximum possible labor hours from workers. Given the low-skill requirements of such labor, even children, women, the elderly, and individuals with disabilities could participate in production.

This stage marked the zenith of labor exploitation, with relentless utilization of human labor. Such intensive resource accumulation fueled an explosive increase in production output. However, this approach had significant drawbacks: The relentless pursuit of quantity led to a lack of diversity in product forms. Excessive exploitation of land and human resources resulted in unsustainable practices. When overexploitation reached critical levels, and low-end workers could no longer secure basic living necessities, societal tensions reached breaking points.

The adverse effects of this production model were evident in the environmental degradation it caused, leading to severe health crises. Despite these challenges, the value of production had inherent limits: Total production was capped by population size and the stagnation of machine technology. While industry improved living standards, it also drove advancements in weaponry. This empowered rulers to expand their ambitions, enabling them to invade and plunder lands previously out of reach. On a global scale, such ambitions triggered large-scale resource conflicts, culminating in world wars. World wars devastated labor forces, destroyed existing production infrastructure, and imposed heavy reparations on defeated nations. These factors collectively limited production output during this stage and highlighted the inherent constraints of this model.

At this stage, with capital increasingly concentrated in the hands of the ruling elite, the entire productive capacity of the lower class is subjected to even greater exploitation, leaving their basic livelihoods unprotected. The disparity between the rich and the poor becomes more extreme. In the realm of social consumption, the proletariat can only afford to meet their basic survival needs, and during certain periods, even these essentials cannot be guaranteed. Meanwhile, luxury and indulgence are entirely monopolized by the ruling and capitalist classes. The market's value space is predominantly focused on catering to the demands of high-end groups, with this extravagance built upon and sustained at the expense of the hunger and deprivation of others.

As social tensions intensify, proletarian revolutions erupt to varying degrees across industrialized nations. The fundamental aim of these uprisings is to reset the socio-economic distribution structure through armed resistance, ensuring that the majority can achieve basic sustenance in terms of food and clothing. Once this objective is realized, and some of the seized resources can meet general living needs, the nascent regime can stabilize as long as it maintains this balance. Consequently, the mode of production evolves accordingly.

Stage 3: advanced machines and mid-to-high-end mental labor (emergence of demand-value space). As time continued to advance into the late electrical era and the era of biotechnology and aerospace, scientific and technological progress far exceeded earlier expectations and achieved breakthrough developments. With the computational power of electronic computers increasing in accordance with Moore's Law, the resulting gains in productivity have been both substantial and far-reaching.

In agriculture, technological advancements have brought about a transformation toward precision-based production methods. Through biotechnology, it is now possible to optimize species at the genetic level and to exercise finely tuned control over the conditions of their growth. This includes the regulation of light (such as intensity, specific spectral wavelengths, and the ratio of light to darkness), water (including moisture levels in the medium and humidity of the environment), nutrients (precisely balanced fertilizers containing nitrogen, phosphorus, potassium, and trace elements tailored to specific species), pest and disease control (various protective agents), and temperature (strictly managed through greenhouse systems). These advancements have led to simultaneous increases in both productivity and yield.

In industry, the capabilities of machines have improved dramatically. With electronic computers serving as central control systems, humans can now manage machine operations with great precision and coordination. Most repetitive manual tasks can be handled by machines, and many previously hazardous jobs that posed risks to human safety can now be performed through mechanized labor. As a result, human roles in production shift from physical labor to intellectual tasks.

Human labor has become increasingly stratified based on levels of education. For those with lower educational attainment, as machines progressively replace jobs involving simple, repetitive tasks, they are often left to seek employment in service-oriented roles in urban or rural areas—such as cleaning staff, restaurant servers, construction workers, domestic helpers, couriers, and movers.

Beyond these roles, an expanding array of jobs requires higher levels of education and training. As machines take over much of the production process, the primary role of human workers shifts toward tasks involving planning, strategizing, creativity, and design. In pursuit of profit maximization, humans are tasked with identifying developmental patterns and emerging needs, as well as organizing production and distribution chains accordingly.

Such work typically demands a strong command of technical tools, interdisciplinary knowledge, higher-level cognitive skills, a broad worldview, and keen observational abilities. According to individuals' specific qualifications and capabilities, society offers a diverse range of job positions suited to match those varying levels of competence.

From this stage onward, society witnesses a transformative leap in overall productivity, enabling total output to better meet the essential needs of the population. As the majority of people achieve basic living standards, higher-order human desires begin to surface, creating new value space. Even average workers, after covering their fundamental needs for food and clothing, find themselves with discretionary income, which they use to enhance their quality of life, indulge in leisure activities, and seek personal fulfillment.

Economic independence allows individuals to be respected as autonomous beings, fostering the development of unique personal identities. This newfound freedom enables people to make choices based on their preferences, determine the types of goods they wish to acquire, and pursue distinctiveness as a way to assert their value. Higher-income individuals, meanwhile, begin to aspire to more elevated goals, including influencing larger communities or societal progress. At this stage, the importance of personal experiences starts to resonate with a broader population, no longer confined to the elite. As these advanced needs scale, they generate significant economic value and expand new market opportunities. Consequently, production evolves to cater to these emerging demands, shifting away from foundational methods toward a more consumer-centric approach.

As for production structures, producers adapt their strategies to maximize efficiency and profitability. Tasks where machines excel in both productivity and cost-effectiveness are increasingly automated, reducing dependence on low-skill, repetitive manual labor. As education levels rise and the cost of human labor increases, producers aim to minimize the use of low-end human labor, keeping its costs under control.

Simultaneously, producers expand their hiring of highly educated individuals, despite their higher costs. These professionals contribute critical observation and creativity, ensuring that products and services remain relevant to evolving consumer needs, thereby maintaining and growing revenue streams. In addition, producers strengthen their marketing and branding teams to forge strong connections between products and consumers. These teams help bridge gaps when product updates lag behind market trends, employing strategic marketing techniques to mitigate potential disruptions. This approach provides a buffer for both production and sales, enabling producers to adjust and sustain market presence.

This stage serves as a critical juncture where traditional production methods, dominant in the previous era, continue to play a significant role while new production methods driven by emerging demands rapidly gain ground. The new production methods driven by emerging demands exhibit a snowball effect: The introduction of new products and services reshapes consumer perceptions, which in turn stimulates additional demand and further expands the demand space. These innovative production approaches are thriving, steadily broadening their influence and exerting an increasingly significant impact on economic activities.

However, this highlights a challenge of reconciling and aligning past practices with future advancements. The previous stage witnessed a significant overproduction of goods, leading to vast inventories with insufficient demand to absorb them. This surplus created severe challenges for producers, pushing many into survival crises. At the same time, emerging producers—largely disconnected from the excess output of traditional industries—frequently faced situations of undersupply.

This duality resulted in a paradoxical market landscape. On the one hand, numerous manufacturers struggled to offload their overproduced goods, confronting financial ruin and widespread employee layoffs. On the other hand, markets for new products and services, predominantly driven by small and medium-sized enterprises, were overwhelmed by the unpredictable preferences and demands of consumers. Some innovative products, despite being priced at a premium, remained in short supply, while others that initially enjoyed popularity were quickly discarded and forgotten. Consequently, many emerging enterprises found themselves unable to establish stable profitability despite their relentless efforts.

The simultaneous struggles of traditional industries and the instability of new enterprises created widespread employment insecurity and chaotic pricing dynamics. This fragile equilibrium was further destabilized by external factors such as inflation, volatility in capital markets, and shifts in tariff policies, injecting additional uncertainty into the broader market system.

The fundamental solution to bridging the gap between traditional producers and emerging producers lies in achieving effective integration. For traditional producers, two critical strategies must be adopted: Convert existing surplus inventory into products that align with current market demands, and accelerate the overhaul of production methods to adapt to new market dynamics and consumer needs. For emerging producers, the focus should be on enhancing resilience to market risks. This can be achieved by forming integrated clusters of enterprises, allowing for greater flexibility in responding to shifting demands and reducing friction in the process.

Additionally, a new class of intermediary producers is expected to emerge. These producers will play a crucial role by identifying and addressing gaps between the traditional and emerging production sectors. As a new type of supplier group, their primary function will be to repurpose surplus inventory through resource reallocation, reprocessing, and reproduction, aligning these resources with new market needs.

Another manifestation of this intermediary group is the rise of outsourced support manufacturers. These entities will handle production tasks that are inefficient or unsuitable for end-consumer-facing companies. By supplying products or components at a predetermined cost, these manufacturers enable contracting firms to remain profitable as long as final sales revenues cover procurement costs.

These support manufacturers act as bridges, connecting surplus material resources from the traditional sector with specialized requirements of downstream businesses. They leverage expertise in niche areas to achieve production efficiency and differentiation, generating sales revenue through their unique capabilities. This intermediary network promotes optimal resource allocation, smoothens economic operations, and creates employment opportunities, becoming a vital component of the economy.

Stage 4: intelligent machines and human demand creation (growing prominence of demand-value space). The evolution of AI technology has fundamentally reshaped production methods on the supply side. During this phase, machine intelligence achieves a transformative milestone—tasks that once relied exclusively on human creativity and intelligence can now be executed by machines. When machines begin to evolve autonomously—through self-learning, self-optimization, and self-creation—entirely new methods, technologies, and production processes emerge, independently developed by machines.

This shift profoundly redefines the human-machine relationship. Historically, humans maintained absolute control over machines, dictating their behavior and fully anticipating their outputs. However, as machines become increasingly intelligent and creative, the results they produce may deviate from initial human intentions. Assuming humans retain fundamental control mechanisms (e.g., power management), these divergences can expand human cognition, further broadening the scope of demand.

From this point forward, the interaction between supply and demand becomes increasingly dynamic. Human needs drive production, while the diversity of products, in turn, stimulates awareness and creates new demand. This continuous expansion of demand space fosters the growth of corresponding value spaces, unlocking new avenues for economic development.

However, the exponential growth of this "snowballing" effect introduces significant challenges: As the demand snowball grows, what happens if physical resources, such as land, fail to keep pace with production needs? How will differences in the speed and scale of demand growth across regions impact global economic stability?

Regarding the first question, when the availability of land-based resources fails to match the pace of increasing demand, it is inevitable that demand will naturally stratify and segment. By categorizing the population based on income levels, the extent to which each segment's needs are met will face inherent limitations. However, these limitations are not imposed by external authority but rather arise from individuals self-regulating their consumption within the boundaries of their financial means.

For instance, when individuals aspire to fulfill high-tier experiential needs that exceed their financial capacity, their consumption patterns will naturally adjust downward to align with their affordability. As this adjustment becomes widespread within a particular income group, new forms of low-tier production will emerge to cater to this demographic. Such production focuses on minimizing the additional costs associated with high-quality services, reducing product quality, and consequently lowering prices until they align with the purchasing power of lower-income groups, thus satisfying their basic living requirements.

When stratification and segmentation are no longer sufficient to meet basic living needs—especially when even the lowest tiers of demand are elevated due to external environmental influences—the second challenge arises. Significant disparities in demand between regions, coupled with uncontrolled population growth, could trigger large-scale conflicts over the redistribution of resources within human society. When the degree of social stratification and job differentiation can no longer meet people's growing living needs—even among the lowest tiers of society, whose expectations are increasingly stimulated by broader environmental influences—a second major issue may arise. This occurs when significant disparities emerge in the demand space across different regions, or when population growth becomes uncontrollable. Under such conditions, humanity may face another large-scale conflict over the redistribution of resources.

Such conflict can manifest in various forms—not only as conventional warfare involving physical weapons but also as information warfare, driven by technological competition through information systems, and economic warfare, carried out via economic erosion and capital control. These conflicts ultimately serve several purposes: to reduce populations that exceed environmental and systemic carrying capacities, to drive a more balanced allocation of resources across regions, and to reshape the global demand space and its corresponding value structures.

An alternative resolution lies in advancements in space exploration, leading to the discovery of habitable environments beyond Earth and enabling human migration. Such developments could fundamentally alleviate the pressure on Earth's resources. However, this would elevate the challenge of resource allocation to an interstellar scale—a topic that lies outside the scope of this book.

At this stage, our focus is that production becomes predominantly driven by machines, with humans assuming supporting roles. Intelligent machines are capable of autonomously delivering creative product designs and service solutions, efficiently matching production methods and resource allocations to fulfill human needs. This shift significantly reduces the necessity for human labor—both physical and cognitive—on the supply side.

Human involvement becomes focused on overseeing machine operations and managing the relationship between resource consumption and output. As machines take on the majority of production tasks, most individuals may no longer need to work to sustain their lifestyles. This transition marks humanity's progression into the next phase: fully demand-driven production.

Stage 5: fully demand-driven production (dominated by the demand-value space). In this stage, all societal production is initiated by demand, with each person's requirements being uniquely tailored. Under this ideal scenario, the demand-value space achieves its maximum expansion.

When individuals no longer need to work for income to meet their needs, and income itself becomes unnecessary, the concept of currency may ultimately vanish. If humanity successfully navigates the challenges of wars, maintains absolute control over machines without being displaced by them, and avoids catastrophic resource extraction practices, this stage may become a reality.

At this juncture, human aspirations will transcend physical survival and reproduction, shifting entirely toward intellectual and spiritual pursuits. Material desires will lose significance, leaving only the pursuit of profound and meaningful experiences. Value will no longer be quantified by money, wealth, or numerical metrics but instead by intangible spiritual fulfillment.

Thus, human society will complete a transformative journey from materialism to spirituality. Production will no longer address material needs but will cater solely to the aspirations of the mind and spirit. What such a society would look like is beyond today's imagination.

(2) Evolution in Sales Methods

Sales methods are another thing that the rise of consumer experience has transformed. Products and services must connect with consumers through sales, and this process, whatever product it is, traditionally consists of four main stages: information sharing (awareness stage), trial and validation (trust stage), purchase and usage (confirmation stage), and post-sale support and word-of-mouth (judgment stage).

Each stage is inherently linked to experience. Over time, these stages have become richer and more diverse in both content and form, and so has experience.

The structure of these sales stages is deeply tied to the way individuals process and engage with new products. The primary goal of sales is to educate consumers about the benefits of a product, inspire interest and trust, and ultimately encourage purchase. For businesses, the ideal outcome is repeat purchases, ensuring a consistent revenue stream.

Therefore, the core of the entire sales process is to generate consumer purchase intent, with all sales techniques, methods, and strategies centered around this goal. As consumers transition from basic consumption to experience-driven consumption, sales methods must also evolve to meet market demands.

Unlike basic consumption, experience-driven consumption focuses on the diversity of needs a product can satisfy and its unique characteristics compared to numerous similar products. When introducing products to consumers, the information conveyed by the seller must include not only the product's basic attributes but also its irreplaceable features.

For example, consider the act of selling bread. In the past, a salesperson only needed to communicate basic information such as price, quantity, and sweetness level to meet consumer needs—because the primary goal for most consumers was simply to "fill their stomachs at the lowest possible cost." In the era of experiential consumption, however, this is no longer sufficient. In addition to the basic details, salespeople now need to highlight several added-value features: the uniqueness of ingredients (ensuring food safety and consistent flavor), attractive and varied presentation (suitable for social events and gatherings), appealing and health-conscious taste (delivering flavor while managing sugar, salt, and other health-related factors), specially designed products for particular groups (such as sugar-free bread for people with diabetes), and overall value-for-money. Of course, due to resource constraints, no business can excel in every area. However, companies must establish at least one or two standout differentiators to distinguish themselves from competitors. This leads to natural market segmentation, with each business formulating market strategies based on its unique strengths. Sales strategies are closely tied to the characteristics of the company's products. In the field of sales, businesses refine their messaging, visual presentation, and marketing language to highlight the distinctive features of their offerings.

In addition to the message delivered by salespeople, advancements in technology have revolutionized traditional sales channels, which historically fell into two main categories: In-store sales—consumers visited physical outlets or retail stores to make purchases, and field sales—sales representatives traveled to promote and sell products.

In the past, limitations in transportation and communication meant producers could not directly connect with consumers across regions. Intermediaries filled this gap. However, even after undergoing subcontracting, redistribution, and intermediary involvement, the core sales methods remained predominantly twofold: physical stores and sales representatives. Except that these sales channels may be under the jurisdiction of intermediaries rather than producers themselves.

Stores aim to maximize product presentation, arranging a variety of goods according to their space capacity and showcasing samples from different product lines for consumers to explore. While these stores provide an environment for consumers to experience and test products, their primary objective is to drive purchases—encouraging customers to complete transactions on-site.

Sales representatives offer a more flexible alternative. When stores face geographical constraints and seek to expand their reach, they rely on these representatives to access remote or underserved regions, uncover new customer bases, and scale their sales volume. However, deploying sales representatives involves costs, and their availability is inherently limited by numbers and capacity. Consequently, cross-regional sales expansion traditionally depended on a strong operational foundation in the local market.

The rapid advancements in transportation and internet communication have dramatically transformed these traditional sales structures. Among the internet's most profound impacts is its facilitation of explosive information growth and accelerated dissemination. This innovation has empowered consumers to access product information across geographical boundaries at virtually no cost and even make cross-regional purchases seamlessly.

As a result, physical stores have gradually shifted their focus, evolving from sales hubs to experiential spaces. Factory stores, for instance, not only continue selling products but also offer immersive experiences that allow consumers to observe and participate in the production process. By witnessing production firsthand, consumers develop trust in the brand more quickly and effectively.

These experiential engagements, characterized by their rich and enjoyable nature, encourage consumers to share details about the products and production processes with others through word-of-mouth. For businesses, this acts as a cost-free, organic promotional channel. Additionally, recommendations based on personal experience are inherently more credible and persuasive when shared with friends and family, far surpassing the influence of unfamiliar sales representatives.

Meanwhile, purchasing behavior has shifted significantly to online platforms. With the rise of robust logistics services, consumers can now enjoy convenient, customized delivery options, including scheduled home delivery. The internet has not only made sales processes more accessible and efficient but has also substantially accelerated the speed of product transactions.

The internet has revolutionized access to product information, but it has also introduced a new challenge: Consumers are no longer limited to learning about a single company's products. They can now easily compare offerings from across the market. This expanded access means consumers consider and evaluate a broader range of factors before making purchasing decisions.

Moreover, because this information is publicly available, competitors can effortlessly obtain details about a company's products, including specifications, user reviews, and marketing strategies. This transparency has fueled rampant imitation and replication in the marketplace. Innovative marketing campaigns, creative designs, and even unique product features can be quickly copied, while differentiated advantages are easily eroded.

As a result, strategies that rely solely on external packaging—encompassing branding, promotional messaging, product aesthetics, and manufactured public opinion—are becoming increasingly ineffective. To establish a lasting foothold, businesses must cultivate irreplaceable core advantages. These may include exceptional R&D capabilities, patented technologies, unique corporate cultures, or exclusive access to specialized resources. Such advantages are inherently difficult to replicate and, in some cases, protected by patent laws that provide recourse against infringement.

In the era of experiential consumption, the market often dazzles with a whirlwind of fleeting trends and momentary successes. Some businesses may achieve temporary gains by creating or chasing viral sensations or employing unconventional tactics. This creates the illusion that wealth, business success, and overnight fame are easily attainable. Media amplification of extraordinary success stories only perpetuates this misconception, obscuring the true complexities of the market.

However, this surface-level brilliance is often fleeting. Today's celebrated trend can be forgotten within a week. Companies that exhaust their resources chasing these transient phenomena risk losing sight of their consumers' genuine needs. For early-stage businesses, this misdirection often results in wasted resources and unsustainable operations.

Experiential consumption, by contrast, is rooted in real, tangible demand. Each layer of consumer need is richly diverse, providing businesses ample opportunities to carve out niches that align with their strengths. By focusing on these areas and delivering deeply and effectively, companies can secure their place in the market.

Experiences, by their very nature, are grounded in authenticity and substance. Long-term success belongs to those who invest in advancing technology, crafting high-quality products and services, and meeting real consumer needs. Such companies not only endure but thrive, becoming indispensable players in the market. The kind of supply we value is precisely this: meaningful, reliable, and enduring.

v. The Introduction of the Experience Index

Since experience influences both microeconomic aspects—such as demand, supply, and market equilibrium—and macroeconomic dimensions, including demand side and supply-side economics, it is reasonable to believe that its impact is universal, permeating all levels of economic activity. When this impact becomes significant enough to demand attention, a formal economic concept is needed to describe it and serve as the foundation for further analysis. To address this necessity, we propose the concept of an experience index.

Although the term may appear to be a simple combination of words and might have been mentioned in various contexts, here, it is introduced as a novel economic concept, more than just a term and implying a comprehensive research framework.

1. The Connotation and Scope of the Experience Index

The experience index is a quantitative metric designed to measure levels of experience. Developing and measuring such an index requires answering several fundamental questions: Who or what is being measured? In what context (including time and space)? Which aspects of the experience are being assessed? What methods and conditions are required for measurement?

Each of these questions has countless possible answers, making the experience index, in its broadest sense, highly inclusive. It encompasses all interactions between humans and the world. Human life itself consists of continuous exchanges with the external environment—whether with people or objects. As long as the senses are engaged, experiences are formed. Experiences make up our life. Hence, studying experience is tantamount to studying human activity itself. For every level, method, and purpose of human activity, there exists a corresponding level, method, and purpose of experience.

Our focus, however, is specifically on human experiences. Interactions among non-human entities, such as animal-to-animal or animal-to-object interactions, are excluded. Instead, we examine interactions between humans and between humans and their environment. Ultimately, all experiences stem from individual perceptions. Each person can be regarded as an "experience field," and the collective human experience as the interaction of these fields with each other and the external world.

Within each experience field, the foundational elements—human senses, emotions, and shared traits—are constant. However, their states are ever-changing, influenced by environmental factors and past interactions. This dynamic can be likened to a ball bouncing randomly within a confined space. Depending on the surroundings, the ball may collide with various objects, leaving marks of varying intensity. Some marks are superficial; others create small, recoverable dents, while some cause irreversible damage, such as cracks. The ball carries these marks as it moves forward, altering its future collision path. For instance, impacts on irreversible dents might shift its angle of movement, while the expansion of certain cracks could lead to air loss, reducing its overall elasticity. Meanwhile, smaller dents might gradually recover to their original state through opposing forces ...

Similarly, human interactions with the world shape and reshape their experiences. Unlike a ball, which interacts solely through surface impacts, humans experience the world through their five senses—sight, hearing, smell, taste, and touch. While the marks left on a ball are purely external, human experiences leave imprints both in sensory memory and consciousness. Memories stored in sensory organs become reflexes, while impressions in consciousness involve more complex cognitive processes.

These cognitive processes, discussed in chapter I as the four forms of perception, include the following:

(1) Recognitional perception. The fundamental identification of "what" the object is.
(2) Discriminative perception. The evaluation of whether the object elicits a positive or negative feeling—judging it as good or bad.
(3) Analytical perception. A deeper, reflective stage where earlier judgments are reconsidered in light of past experiences. This involves confirming, refining, or overturning previous conclusions, often with varying degrees of complexity.
(4) Operational perception. The final stage is where a decision is made based on the analysis, influencing subsequent verbal and physical actions.

Individual differences in processing these layers of perception result in diverse attitudes and interpretations. The differences we observe among individuals fundamentally arise from their unique processing habits. These variations shape distinct ways of thinking, resulting in diverse attitudes and interpretations of the same situations or concepts. These variations, when accumulated over time, shape different personality, worldviews, life perspectives, and values. Yet, despite this diversity, patterns do exist. These cognitive habits since infancy and evolve continuously, with judgments of good versus bad serving as their foundation despite various forms.

Through the accumulation of judgments on the direction and intensity of what is deemed good or bad, combined with the interplay of perceptions among various elements, individuals develop their core impressions of things. The initial impressions formed by sensory inputs influence people's immediate reactions to stimuli, while accumulated impressions shape their subsequent responses. The extent to which a message is accepted or endorsed depends more on these impressions than on the sensory inputs themselves. Even when information is rejected, it may linger in sensory memory and consciousness, potentially being reassessed (rejected information becomes accepted or accepted information becomes rejected) as circumstances or perspectives change.

This dynamic underscores the immense complexity involved in studying human experiences. While psychology is often built on observable behaviors and physiological responses (e.g., facial expressions, blood flow, body movements), it assumes that all thoughts eventually manifest through actions. While effective, this approach raises a critical question: Do behaviors and physiological responses 100% represent inner experiences?

What about the unexpressed thoughts and emotions—an integral part of human experience? How can we accurately capture an individual's true attitude toward something? What methods can we use to gain a complete understanding of human experiences?

It is crucial to address potential biases that may arise during the measurement of individual experiences. Enhancing measurement accuracy relies on minimizing both the probability and impact of these biases. Three common forms of bias include the following:

(1) People lie.
(2) People may overstate or understate the intensity of their experiences, even if their responses are directionally truthful.

(3) People often struggle to precisely grasp their own "feelings," especially when trying to differentiate between experiences of similar intensity.

First, let's talk about lies. Lies are characterized by a discrepancy, or even opposition, between the verbalized content and the individual's true thoughts. This discrepancy arises from cognitive processing and has identifiable roots. In early childhood, individuals typically express their genuine desires without deception. However, as cognitive abilities develop and when expressing the truth results in unexpected negative consequences, individuals may begin to subconsciously adopt lying as a coping mechanism.

Lying often stems from a distortion of true intentions, aiming to align with others' preferences to gain positive feedback such as recognition, affirmation, or praise. This behavior is frequently accompanied by fear, worry, or anxiety about potential negative reactions to honesty.

Children who often face rejection or opposition in early communication with family are particularly prone to forming lying habits. In some cases, children who feel undervalued may fabricate stories to gain attention, sometimes by disparaging others who receive more favor. Similarly, children with a heightened sense of arrogance or conceit may resort to lying. These smart children, for instance, may create elaborate narratives to convince others, ultimately manipulating them to accept their ideas and act as told.

Lying also becomes a method for controlling others, a tool often employed by individuals with strong control desires. Lies also pervade strategic and tactical conflicts due to their goal-driven nature. The so-called master tacticians or brilliant military strategists often excel in deception, crafting temporal and spatial illusions to mislead adversaries and seize control. Regardless of its form, the underlying driver of lying is often the desire to gain favor. During-experience level measurements, participants may lie in three primary scenarios:

(1) Insecurity. Participants feel uneasy or defensive due to the environment.
(2) Fear of losing incentives. Participants worry that failing to express appreciation or praise might result in the loss of rewards, such as gifts or stipends.
(3) Peer influence. Participants are swayed by the opinions (both positive and negative) or behaviors of others, leading to responses that do not reflect their true feelings.

Since experience level measurements typically involve voluntary participation and mild scenarios, extreme incidents are rare. Thus, apart from these three factors, there are usually no strong motivations for participants to lie. Additionally, these issues can be mitigated with thoughtful interventions by organizers.

Organizers generally find it manageable to address these three concerns. Experience measurement is typically conducted in environments designed to make participants feel at ease—this might be in their own homes, in a specially decorated experience room with a home-like atmosphere, or in familiar settings such as a café, restaurant, or park. Through thoughtful environmental design and the warm, friendly demeanor of the hosts, participants' apprehensions are usually alleviated with ease. For those worried about not receiving a gift, clear communication can help—explaining that the purpose of the measurement is to collect accurate data rather than to fulfill performance targets or other agendas. As for concerns about being influenced by others, organizers can opt for one-on-one measurement sessions whenever possible, minimizing the risk of peer influence on participants' responses.

Let us now delve into two significant challenges: the tendency of individuals to amplify or downplay their judgments and the inherent difficulty humans face in precisely evaluating subtle distinctions in sensory experiences. When an individual forms a strongly polarized opinion about something—either extreme fondness or aversion—they often exaggerate this sentiment in their behavior and expressions. Conversely, when the sentiment is moderate or weak, they are inclined to understate or conservatively assess their evaluation.

This phenomenon becomes evident when individuals rate different aspects of their experiences using scoring scales. People typically gravitate toward five levels of evaluation and struggle to discern finer gradations between these levels with precision. These five levels are commonly expressed as: very good, good, average, poor, and very poor. Practical experience indicates that these categories allow individuals to convey their true experiential levels with reasonable accuracy. Consequently, employing a five-point scale is an effective approach for measuring experiences.

The experience index provides a multidimensional evaluation of a particular subject, combining both qualitative and quantitative data to achieve a comprehensive assessment. Quantitative analysis, supported by large sample sizes, ensures accurate representation of overall experience levels. Meanwhile, qualitative insights uncover the deeper influencing factors and perceptions behind these evaluations, helping to refine and validate the findings from quantitative research.

For qualitative analysis, sampling a group of 10 to 12 individuals is sufficient to meet most investigative needs. Quantitative surveys, on the other hand, typically involve sampling 10% to 20% of the user base. Large-scale quantitative data analysis leverages technical tracking mechanisms to encompass the entire production and sales process. Technologies such as blockchain can trace a product's full life cycle, enabling comprehensive data acquisition. Detailed methodologies for these measurements can be found in section 6 of chapter I.

2. Experience Index in Microeconomics

In microeconomic analysis, the focus lies on individual enterprises, specific products, and their related production and consumption behaviors, along with market price trends. Within this scope, the experience index quantifies public perceptions of either a particular product or an enterprise as a whole. Based on the target of measurement (product or enterprise), the experience index in microeconomics can be categorized into three key dimensions: product experience index, enterprise experience index, and brand experience index.

(1) Product Experience Index

This measures the experience level associated with a specific product, whether it be a tangible good, a virtual item, or a service. The product experience index serves as the foundational unit of analysis in microeconomics. Consumer perceptions of a product's experience level evolve over time. Thus, when measuring this index, the focus is on capturing the collective experience level of consumers in the market within a specific timeframe. Depending on the duration of this timeframe, the index can be further classified as short-term product experience index—reflects the experience level over a relatively brief period, typically within six months, provided no significant disruptive events occur to drastically alter perceptions; and long-term product experience index—reflects experience levels over extended periods exceeding six months, particularly when fundamental changes in the product result in notable shifts in public perception.

Short-term indices capture instantaneous levels of consumer experience, whereas long-term indices track trends and transformations over time. Collectively, the product experience index serves as a reliable metric of consumer sentiment toward a product. It comprehensively encapsulates feelings and evaluations, functioning as a direct indicator of a product's popularity in the market. This index can also be correlated with sales data to derive actionable insights.

Additionally, enterprise management teams can leverage the experience indices of their product portfolio to conduct comparative analyses and monitor market performance in a more intuitive manner. The structural framework of the product experience index is outlined in table 2-4.

Table 2-4 Structure of the product experience index

Product experience index	Qualitative insights	Types of needs the product fulfills
		Product usability
		Product strengths and weaknesses
	Quantitative sampling surveys	Customer preferences
		Purchase intentions
		Willingness to recommend
	Quantitative big data analysis	Monitoring of financial performance
		Monitoring of sales data
		Monitoring of production and operational data
		Monitoring of external public opinion

(2) Enterprise Experience Index

This measures the overall experience level consumers associate with a particular enterprise. A key contributor to this index is the performance of the enterprise's products, as the public primarily becomes acquainted with an enterprise through its offerings. Other influential factors include the company's involvement in public welfare, promotion of corporate culture and values, media coverage, financial transparency, and market performance.

This index is useful not only for microeconomic analysis and cross-enterprise comparisons but also for broader applications in industrial and macroeconomic studies, as the fundamental unit. It is particularly crucial for assessing the market performance of small and micro-enterprises. When these businesses lack product maturity or reliable financial metrics for future development prediction, the enterprise experience index serves as a vital tool for investors to gauge future potential. Therefore, the index can contribute to enterprise credit ratings, forming a key dimension for evaluating creditworthiness. The structural framework of the enterprise experience index is outlined in table 2-5.

(3) Brand Experience Index

This measures the overall experience level consumers associate with a specific brand. While brands are often linked to specific enterprises, the relationship can vary significantly due to the diversity and complexity of corporate structures. This index focuses exclusively on the brand, which may encompass sub-brands

Table 2-5 Structure of the enterprise experience index

Enterprise experience index	Overall experience	Brand awareness
		Reputation and public opinion
		Customer loyalty
	Product experience	Qualitative insights
		Quantitative sampling surveys
		Quantitative big data analysis
	Cultural experience	Corporate values
		Culture and organization
		Social responsibility and contributions

managed by multiple enterprises. It represents a collection of products, with its value extending beyond the sum of individual product experiences.

In economic contexts, a brand's influence—driven by its identity, philosophy, and values—frequently surpasses that of the enterprise behind it. Prominent brand symbols in commercial areas, often accompanied by year marks, evoke trust and loyalty in consumers. Brand recognition often serves as the first filter in purchase decisions. Even when narrowed down by product category, brand reputation strongly influences the final choice. Consumers tend to gravitate toward established, reputable brands with a rich history, equating these attributes with quality and reliability. Compared to individual products, brands typically elicit a stronger, more cohesive experiential impact. The structural framework of the brand experience index is outlined in table 2-6.

3. Experience Index in Macroeconomics

At the macroeconomic level, the experience index manifests through various perspectives. To analyze the overall demand across industries, the industry experience index is employed. For studying the experiences of consumers with a basket of essential goods, the product bundle experience index provides meaningful insights. These indices enable us to assess the rationality of industrial structures and guide strategic adjustments. Ultimately, the national economic experience index serves as a measure of the overall experiential quality of a national economy. Cross-country comparisons of this index can inform strategies for international economic relations.

Table 2-6 Structure of the brand experience index

Brand experience index	Overall experience	Brand awareness
		Reputation and public opinion
		Customer loyalty
		Customer preference
		Trustworthiness
	Cultural experience	Corporate values
		Culture and social image
	Experience of products under the brand	Qualitative insights
		Quantitative sampling surveys
		Quantitative big data analysis

(1) Industry Experience Index

This reflects the collective consumer experience level within a specific industry. It gauges the extent to which the industry's supply meets total consumer demand and provides an aggregated evaluation of the consumption experience.

Since industries collectively shape the national economy, the industry experience index plays a crucial role in guiding strategic adjustments for industrial layouts. This index surpasses traditional industrial economic indicators by offering nuanced insights into how effectively consumer needs are being fulfilled.

When paired with demographic data, the industry experience index, which includes attitudes, analysis of causes, and evaluation, enables detailed analyses of industry performance across regions, income levels, age groups, genders, and other parameters. Such correlations provide valuable input for national industrial strategies and planning. The structural framework of the industry experience index is outlined in table 2-7.

(2) Product Bundle Experience Index

This serves as the experiential counterpart to the consumer price index (CPI). Similar to CPI, it aggregates the experience indices of over 200 essential consumer goods into a weighted composite score. While CPI tracks price levels, the product bundle experience index captures the experiential aspects of these goods.

The effects of inflation and changes in purchasing power, often overlooked in the CPI, are vividly captured in the product bundle experience index. This

Table 2-7 Structure of the industry experience index

Industry experience index	Overall experience	Quality of industry outputs
		Demand fulfillment
		Reputation and public opinion
	Social impact	Social responsibility
		Environmental protection
	Industry structure	Balance
		Health
	Related enterprise experience (weighted aggregation)	Overall experience
		Product experience
		Cultural experience

index reflects the overall consumer experience shaped by these factors, offering a nuanced understanding of how a basket of essential goods impacts daily life. It not only highlights the actual state of supply and demand but also uncovers quality issues in supply and other practical aspects of consumer experience.

When specific groups express significant dissatisfaction with the quality of certain products, the product bundle experience index can identify these issues by analyzing the relevant product scores. This targeted approach enables precise problem identification and resolution.

The versatility of the product bundle experience index lies in its ability to adapt to different product bundle categories. For example, while traditional stock market indices focus primarily on price, experience-based counterparts could provide a broader perspective. By incorporating additional dimensions, these indices offer investors deeper insights, helping them make more informed decisions. The structural framework of the product bundle experience index is outlined in table 2-8.

(3) National Economic Experience Index

This measures the overall experiential level of a nation's economy. Unlike the GDP, which quantifies total income levels, this index evaluates the level of experience that the economy provides to its residents. It highlights issues often overlooked by GDP growth, such as environmental pollution, imbalanced industrial structures, and declines in residents' quality of life.

Table 2-8 Structure of the product bundle experience index

<table>
<tr><td rowspan="10">Product bundle experience index</td><td rowspan="3">Product 1 experience</td><td>Qualitative insights</td></tr>
<tr><td>Quantitative sampling surveys</td></tr>
<tr><td>Quantitative big data analysis</td></tr>
<tr><td rowspan="3">Product 2 experience</td><td>Qualitative insights</td></tr>
<tr><td>Quantitative sampling surveys</td></tr>
<tr><td>Quantitative big data analysis</td></tr>
<tr><td colspan="2">...</td></tr>
<tr><td rowspan="3">Product n experience</td><td>Qualitative insights</td></tr>
<tr><td>Quantitative sampling surveys</td></tr>
<tr><td>Quantitative big data analysis</td></tr>
</table>

When assessing living standards across varying levels—poverty, modest prosperity, affluence, or intermediate stages—both income and experiential level must be considered. Real-life examples abound where individuals with middle to high incomes lead arduous and unsatisfying lives, demonstrating that financial wealth does not necessarily translate into happiness. This disparity underscores the persistence of hidden societal challenges that hinder the improvement of life quality, even as incomes rise. Higher income does not necessarily lead to greater life quality.

The national economic experience index is envisioned as a tool to provide a truthful, objective, and effective portrayal of the actual quality of life experienced by all residents. As economic growth reaches certain levels, the focus naturally shifts from mere output expansion to enhancing overall life quality and happiness—a pursuit far more vital than economic growth itself.

At the macroeconomic level, the interplay between material and spiritual well-being remains a dialectical unity. If GDP represents the material aspect of the economy, the national economic experience index embodies its spiritual dimension. Both are indispensable to depict a complete picture of a nation's economic life. The structural framework of the product bundle national economic experience index is outlined in table 2-9.

4. The Evolution and Advancement of Experience Indexes

As with all other factors of human progress, experience indexes at every level must evolve alongside society's growth and transformation. With the passage

Table 2-9 Structure of the national economic experience index

<table>
<tr><td rowspan="17">National economic experience index</td><td rowspan="7">Demand side experience</td><td>Overall happiness</td></tr>
<tr><td>Demand fulfillment</td></tr>
<tr><td>Demand satisfaction</td></tr>
<tr><td>Quality of life</td></tr>
<tr><td>Work-life balance</td></tr>
<tr><td>Physical health metrics</td></tr>
<tr><td>Life expectancy</td></tr>
<tr><td rowspan="3">Supply-side experience</td><td>Enterprise health</td></tr>
<tr><td>Production technology advancements</td></tr>
<tr><td>Supply balance</td></tr>
<tr><td rowspan="2">Social security experience</td><td>Basic social security (e.g., pensions, unemployment, healthcare, maternity, education)</td></tr>
<tr><td>Support for vulnerable populations</td></tr>
<tr><td rowspan="3">Natural environment experience</td><td>Air quality experience</td></tr>
<tr><td>Water quality experience</td></tr>
<tr><td>Ecological environment experience</td></tr>
<tr><td>Safety experience</td><td>Food and material safety</td></tr>
</table>

of time, human needs expand in both scope and depth. Each era demands its own unique experience indexes, tailored to the characteristics and aspirations of that time. Yet, in whichever era, despite the differences in form and content, the fundamental purpose of experience indexes remains unwavering: to represent the overall experience level of people's life.

These indexes are intricately interconnected and mutually influential, forming an organic system with an inherent pattern of development. While reflecting regional, ethnic, and cultural diversity, they also share a universal core. Across all cultures, the shared mission is to enhance human welfare and elevate collective happiness, making experience indexes a bridge that transcends geographic, ethnic, and cultural boundaries.

Experience indexes express a profound commitment to the spiritual dimensions of human existence. They are inextricably linked to material metrics—distinct in function yet harmonious in purpose. Imagine a future where national economies shift their focus from mere income levels to the happiness and well-being of every citizen. Picture a world where industries, enterprises, and individuals prioritize not just material exchanges but the enhancement of others' experiences and joy. Envision a society where the wealth of material production is allocated in ways that ensure every individual can live a fulfilling and contented life. Perhaps such a vision represents the ultimate ideal.

IV. Era of Experience, Experience Economy, and Experience Economics

i. Definition of the Era of Experience

An era is characterized by distinct and defining features that emerge during a specific historical period. For example, geologists divide Earth's history into periods like the Archean, Proterozoic, Paleozoic, and Mesozoic, based on noticeable differences in geological components. Similarly, in human society, eras are often classified along two primary dimensions: First is economic evolution—categorized by the progression of production tools, such as the Stone Age, Bronze Age, Iron Age, Steam Age, Electrical Age, and Information Age. Second is political systems—defined by societal structures, including the Primitive, Slave, Feudal, Capitalist, and Socialist societies. In specialized fields, eras are sometimes delineated based on their unique disciplinary focus. For instance, in the history of economic thought, periods are identified as the Enlightenment Era, Classical Economics Era, Neoclassical Era, Keynesian Era, and so on. These categorizations are defined by prevailing theories rather than strict historical timelines.

The concept of the Era of Experience deviates from these traditional frameworks, focusing on the evolution of human needs. There was no such concept before because historically, experience was not regarded as a key factor in economic dynamics. However, as income levels rose and consumption shifted from basic necessities to experiential demands, experience-related economic activities emerged as prominent and mature phenomena, necessitating the introduction of this term.

When experiential consumption evolves and reaches a significant level of growth, the introduction of the concept of the Era of Experience becomes essential to encapsulate and define the unique characteristics of this period. Accordingly, we propose the following definition for the Era of Experience:

The Era of Experience refers to a period when human experience becomes a core element driving economic activities. During this time, societal actions—whether individual, communal, or national—are oriented around enhancing collective and individual experiential well-being.

The Era of Experience emerges in regions where economic development reaches a specific threshold. At any given historic moment, disparities in economic progress mean that while some countries or regions have entered this era, others may still be in earlier developmental stages. Even within a single nation, regional differences in development levels may exist. The Era of Experience does not necessarily align with other categorizations, such as the Information Age or political eras.

For example, during the Information Age, many regions worldwide remain in poverty, struggling to meet basic survival needs and are far from entering the era of experience. Conversely, in certain historical periods, such as the feudal era, experiential economic behaviors might have existed among the wealthy elite but were insufficient to define an Era of Experience. To truly qualify as such, the majority within a region must participate in experience-driven consumption and production activities.

ii. Conditions and Characteristics of the Era of Experience

Like other human eras, regions entering the Era of Experience exhibit specific foundational conditions and defining characteristics.

In the realm of politics, a region must be peaceful, free from the disruptions of war, natural disasters, or political conflict. Peace provides the foundation for steady growth and the development of experiential economies. While experiential economic activities may exist among affluent groups during periods of instability, such activities are often volatile and subject to external disruptions. Turbulence typically leads to the redistribution of economic resources through plundering or upheaval, destabilizing income structures. Therefore, political peace and steady progress are indispensable prerequisites for the Era of Experience to flourish.

In the realm of science and technology, regions that have transitioned into the Era of Experience exhibit remarkable technological advancements both internally and externally. These areas boast expansive communication networks, the widespread use of electronic computing, and highly efficient logistics systems. Production technologies have evolved to enable flexible, personalized customization and assembly processes, supported by advanced methods for collecting, processing, and refining diverse raw materials. Sensor technologies facilitate multidimensional monitoring, enhanced by robust big data storage, scheduling, and control systems, enabling real data collection across various scenarios.

Economically, these regions are characterized by well-established financial institutions, sound regulatory frameworks, and a diverse array of financial products, providing individuals and businesses with versatile and dynamic capital allocation methods. The market offers a rich variety of goods tailored to meet specific and segmented needs, while income levels surpass basic subsistence, granting individuals discretionary income and the freedom to allocate it based on personal preferences and aspirations.

In terms of lifestyle and values, in this region, self-awareness has blossomed, with individuals increasingly prioritizing personal growth and the exploration of complex, multidimensional needs. The principle of equality is deeply entrenched, empowering people to choose how they participate in production and earn income based on their unique abilities, talents, and values. Flexible work schedules and self-directed employment are becoming a trend, reflecting a shift from past eras where income was paramount to a balanced focus on earnings and leisure. People now seek to harmonize work and relaxation, emphasizing personal fulfillment. Each individual is recognized as an independent, autonomous entity capable of making decisions with minimal external influence. This sense of autonomy often relies on economic stability; the ability to earn sufficient income through one's efforts forms the bedrock of individual independence.

Culturally, these developments have fostered a high degree of inclusivity, transcending ethnic, national, and regional boundaries. This inclusivity enables the widespread exchange and integration of diverse cultural elements and ideas, broadening horizons and deepening knowledge. The resulting cultural interplay sparks inspiration and fuels new demands, driving innovation and transformative shifts in production. Such dynamics also contribute to the global optimization, growth, and evolution of culture.

As these facets continue to develop, the defining traits of the Era of Experience become increasingly evident. This era is marked by three core characteristics:

(1) The diversification and refinement of human needs.
(2) An explosive increase in the variety and richness of social production.
(3) Significant advancements in production and distribution efficiency.

The cumulative progress across these dimensions lays the groundwork for these defining features.

iii. Defining the Experience Economy

The concept of the experience economy is widely credited to B. Joseph Pine and James H. Gilmore, authors of the 1999 book *The Experience Economy*. The authors posited that "experience" would become the fourth economic offering—after "products," "goods," and "services"—emerging as a new and vital source of economic value. Since then, scholars worldwide have delved into the experience economy and its related fields. However, a universally accepted definition has been elusive.

We propose the following definition of the experience economy: The experience economy refers to the totality of economic activities centered on human experiences as the primary source of value, with the creation and enhancement of experiential value at its core.

The experience economy differs fundamentally from traditional goods- and service-based economies. While traditional economic activities are rooted in the production and exchange of goods and services, the experience economy places human experience at the forefront. In this framework, goods and services are tools to fulfill experiential needs rather than ends in themselves. Traditional economic value is measured through pricing mechanisms in transactions, whereas the value in the experience economy is determined by the extent to which goods or services satisfy experiential demands. When the fulfillment of such demands is quantified effectively, this quantification provides a new metric for assessing value—referred to as experiential value.

The experience economy differs from the traditional goods economy due to the distinction in their primary focus and core value proposition, leading to both connections and divergences.

In a traditional context, an object becomes a commodity only when it possesses exchange value—this value arising because someone else has a demand for it. Exchange value, therefore, reflects human needs or, more precisely, is an expression of demand or demand itself. However, in practice, the exchange value of a commodity often falls short of addressing the full spectrum of human needs.

Take, for example, a loaf of bread: While it might satisfy the need to "eat," it may not completely fulfill the desire to "feel full." Its taste, texture, freshness, or preparation might fail to provide an enjoyable experience. Additionally, concerns about ingredients or storage could compromise its safety, failing to ensure "eating safely." Often, people tolerate varying levels of discomfort or dissatisfaction based on the price they are willing to pay and the urgency of their need. But under ordinary circumstances—when one is neither starving nor constrained by exorbitant costs—people naturally gravitate toward food that offers a better eating experience. Preferences differ widely: One person may prioritize size, another texture, and yet another may abandon bread altogether for an alternative.

These diverse, personalized demands collectively constitute the experiential value of individuals. This illustrates a critical insight: A commodity's exchange value is merely a subset of the broader set of human needs. The gap between this subset and the full set of demands changes dynamically as human needs evolve. For instance, the same loaf of bread might satisfy hunger in childhood but fall short in adulthood. Beyond quantity, qualitative preferences like taste can shift with age, circumstances, or even mood. Adding to this complexity is the fact that individuals may not always fully understand their needs until encountering a product and realizing whether it meets their expectations—whether it is "delicious" or "not delicious."

Herein lies a fundamental distinction of the experience economy: its rapid variability and immense diversity. These characteristics reflect a demand space that is constantly shifting, spontaneous, and inherently unpredictable. From this perspective, production detached from consumer needs is inherently meaningless. No static model can adequately capture the infinite uncertainties of human desires. Consequently, the experience economy demands an unwavering focus on the consumer—respecting, understanding, and involving them directly in the production process.

This inevitable shift in production creates a human-centered approach that not only respects consumer individuality but actively empowers them to express their preferences and engage in the creative process. In turn, consumers feel a newfound sense of respect and significance, motivating them to contribute actively and articulate their desires. Economic activity, therefore, transforms into a consumer-driven and consumer-oriented endeavor.

Such a profound shift in the essence of economic activity inevitably permeates every facet of human life and society. The experience economy serves as a catalyst for an entirely new economic system, one centered on experiential value. This emerging system represents a natural progression from the goods economy—much like how the Industrial Revolution redefined productivity, this transformation has the potential to drive sweeping advancements across human society.

To study and understand this groundbreaking economic paradigm, it is imperative to establish a systematic framework. Thus, we propose the bold introduction of the concept of experience economics.

iv. Definition and Fundamental Framework of Experience Economics

Experience Economics is the discipline that studies the comprehensive economic system built around experiential economic activities. Its research framework is broadly divided into two main components: the theoretical foundation of experience economics and the study of experiential economic activities.

1. Theoretical Foundation

This component involves foundational research on the core subject of experience economics: experience. It encompasses characteristics analysis, categorization, quantification model and its application, and the development of associated theories, such as happiness theory and value theory. It also defines the framework and concept of experience economics itself:

(1) Concept and scope of experience economics

- Concept and definition: clarifying key concepts and definitions within the field
- Research scope: defining the boundaries of the study
- Research paradigm: explaining the methods, tools, goals, and approaches used in research
- Research framework: summarizing the discipline's structure, progress, and future directions

(2) Experience

- Experience theory: conducting a holistic investigation of human experiences, closely linked to psychology, human factors, and related disciplines
- Quantitative assessment of experience (methods, tools, and models): analyzing mathematical methods and principles for quantifying experiences, developing classification models, and designing measurement approaches and tools

(3) Happiness theory

- Elements of happiness: exploring the origins of human happiness and its relationship to experiences
- Fundamental principles: identifying the underlying principles of human happiness
- Morality and ethics: examining the social moral and ethical implications arising from understanding the fundamental elements and principles of experience and happiness

- Happiness strategies: offering strategic guidance for maximizing happiness at both individual and societal levels

(4) Value theory
- Value generation: analyzing the origins of experiential value, its influencing factors and different scenarios
- Value measurement: mathematical methods and principles for measuring experiential value and their characteristics
- Value structure: exploring the components and dynamics of experiential value
- Value enhancement: examining factors that contribute to value growth, stability, or decline, as well as trends, change volume, change rate, and other factors
- Value transformation: analyzing the conversion of experiential value into exchange value, including methods, rates, relationship and influencing factors

2. Study of Experiential Economic Activities and Decision-Making
This component focuses on analyzing the specific impacts and manifestations of experiences within economic interactions. This involves conducting both independent and integrated analyses of various categories of economic participants. The scope includes examining demand, supply, and equilibrium, performing in-depth analyses of diverse scenarios, exploring the interconnections among participants, and devising strategies or optimal approaches for participants to engage effectively in economic activities.

(1) Individual (human) level. This analyzes the economic behaviors of individuals, including consumers, producers/laborers. Small family (less than five members) units are also included.
- Demand: classifications and characteristics of demand
- Supply: classifications and characteristics of supply
- Equilibrium: analysis and categorization of equilibrium states

(2) Individual (commodity) level. This studies the economic behavior of individual entities that participate in economic activities by offering tangible or virtual goods with monetary value (such as physical items, services, or virtual products). It includes studying the behavior of entities as providers of goods and services, as well as their behavior as demanders (such as procuring basic

materials from other economic units), along with an analysis of their equilibrium conditions.

- Demand: classifications and characteristics of demand
- Supply: classifications and characteristics of supply
- Equilibrium: analysis and categorization of equilibrium states

(3) Collective (enterprise) level. This refers to entities that operate collectively to produce goods or services and generate profits to meet the income, individual value realization, and other needs of their members. These entities can be traditional businesses with physical office spaces or groups of individuals engaged in production collectively through network-based communication without a centralized office location.

- Demand: classifications and characteristics of demand
- Supply: classifications and characteristics of supply
- Equilibrium: analysis and categorization of equilibrium states

(4) Collective (industry) level. This refers to a group of businesses with shared characteristics in the production of goods or services, along with closely connected upstream and downstream enterprises. Industries can be classified from diverse perspectives or across multiple dimensions.

- Demand: classifications and characteristics of demand
- Supply: classifications and characteristics of supply
- Equilibrium: analysis and categorization of equilibrium states

(5) National level. This refers to a specific administrative region with independent sovereignty. Analyses at the national level typically fall under macroeconomic analysis, as they consider the national economy as a whole to understand economic patterns and achieve structural balance. Evaluating a nation's overall demand, overall supply, income levels, and employment serves as the foundation for formulating national economic development strategies, closely linked to other national policies, including those related to politics, society, culture, and the environment.

- Total demand: classifications and characteristics of demand
- Total supply: classifications and characteristics of supply
- Equilibrium: analysis and categorization of equilibrium states

(6) Global level. This refers to the study and analysis of human economic activities from a global perspective, emphasizing the overall dynamics and rela-

tionships between different regions. Global economic analysis is grounded in national economic assessments and primarily focuses on understanding the behavioral patterns and trends of regions, individual nations, and alliances of nations.

- Global demand: classifications and characteristics of demand
- Global supply: classifications and characteristics of supply
- Equilibrium: analysis and categorization of equilibrium states

(7) Economic relationship analysis. This refers to analyzing and researching the economic relationships between participants across various dimensions, offering insights, recommendations, and guidance on the strategies these participants employ in their economic activities.

- Individual (human) and individual (commodity): relationships, strategies for both, and equilibrium
- Individual (human) and enterprise: relationships, strategies for both, and equilibrium
- Enterprise and industry: relationships, strategies for both, and equilibrium
- Industry and nation: relationships, strategies for both, and equilibrium
- Nation and global: relationships, strategies for both, and equilibrium

CHAPTER III

Transformation of Traditional Enterprises in the Experience Economy

In today's rapidly evolving digital age, one significant issue that has drawn widespread attention in the ongoing reform of national economies is the transformation of traditional enterprises. With the market constantly shifting, new products and technologies emerging, and short-lived wealth creation stories unfolding, companies are left grappling with the challenge of maintaining their long-term viability. In this new era, the critical questions arise: Should enterprises undergo transformation? If so, where should they direct their transformation, and how should they do it? In this chapter, we explore these questions through the lens of the experience economy.

Before diving into the topic of transformation, it is essential to first clarify what constitutes a traditional enterprise. Without a clear definition of the research subject, it becomes impossible to address the issue of transformation effectively. Broadly speaking, traditional enterprises can be defined in several ways: The first category refers to businesses associated with cultural traditions, where their products and services reflect characteristics of ancient Chinese culture, such as century-old brands, folk crafts, and intangible cultural heritage. The second category contrasts traditional enterprises with internet companies, referring to those whose management and operational models differ from those of internet-based companies, and whose products and services evolve at a slower pace compared to the rapid changes of the digital world. The third category describes larger companies with slower decision-making processes, complex organizational structures, and dependence on resource monopolies for growth, in contrast to the emerging, smaller, faster, and more agile businesses. The fourth category encompasses enterprises in agriculture, industry (including manufacturing), and services that rely on conventional methods of production, operations, and sales. These stand in contrast to emerging industries that adopt innovative business models, such as those seen in modern service sectors.

The term traditional is inherently juxtaposed with new, and as we discuss traditional enterprises, we inevitably draw a comparison with new enterprises. The concept of traditional enterprise transformation carries with it the assumption that the operational methods of traditional enterprises are outdated, inefficient, or lagging, while the methods of new enterprises are deemed advanced, modern, or innovative. However, when viewed objectively, the operational methods of businesses themselves are not inherently good or bad. Instead, the success or failure of a business often lies in how well its operations align with the changing needs and realities of the times. When the evolution of society and economic systems introduces new operational models, traditional businesses that cannot adapt may encounter challenges such as stagnant sales, declining customer loyalty, and loss of long-term clients. However, businesses that analyze and optimize their operations in line with the demands of the current era can revitalize their existing frameworks. Therefore, the transformation of traditional enterprises should not be seen as a rejection of their core existence, but rather as an optimization of their methods—whether in production, operations, or sales—to better suit the new market landscape.

In this chapter, we focus on a particular subset of traditional enterprises, distinguished by certain defining features. These companies are often large in scale, with complex organizational structures and lengthy decision-making processes. Their product updates and iterations tend to be slower, and their leadership is often older, with many decision-makers aged 40 or above. These enterprises have historically thrived by relying on resource monopolies. Examples of such businesses include large state-owned enterprises, multinational corporations, and sizable private firms. In this context, the term traditional enterprise is used in a narrower sense to refer to these specific types of organizations.

I. Challenges Facing Traditional Enterprises in the New Era

As internet-based enterprises rise rapidly, traditional businesses face significant challenges, chief among them being how to adapt to the ever-evolving demands of the market. With an ever-expanding array of products, consumer preferences have become increasingly nuanced and segmented. Products created under conventional models often fail to meet modern user expectations, both in appearance and functionality. Witnessing emerging companies quickly dominate the market with their new products and earn consumer acclaim, traditional enterprises are growing increasingly anxious.

Traditional businesses find their market share eroding as competitors seize opportunities. Rushing to release new products often leads to disappointing results, while developing novel features requires substantial time and resources. Adding to their woes, emerging companies excel in identifying market needs and offer attractive salaries that lure top talent—not just young professionals but also experienced experts and key personnel from traditional enterprises—further enhancing their competitive advantage.

On an operational level, traditional enterprises, constrained by their size and complexity, rely on multilayered reporting and approval chains to manage risks. Reports from front-line staff typically reflect the latest market dynamics, yet mid-level managers in these lengthy and cumbersome decision-making chains often fail to fully comprehend the context or urgency of such updates. With an aging leadership cohort, these managers frequently lack an understanding of younger demographics and emerging trends. Their conservative outlook and aversion to risk further slow decision-making, creating significant resistance at each level of approval.

As decisions crawl through these bureaucratic layers, competitors with agile and efficient mechanisms launch new features and designs, further tightening their grip on the market. Front-line staff in traditional enterprises struggle to overcome increasing barriers to business development. Rigid performance evaluation systems severely limit their ability to respond flexibly to market changes, resulting in difficulties meeting KPIs. The root cause lies not in staff efforts but in outdated products, services, and overly stringent management frameworks that restrict their ability to innovate or adapt.

For instance, many companies in the animation and gaming industries employ managers who lack personal experience with anime or gaming. When younger employees propose creative ideas, these uninformed managers, relying on assumptions, make decisions that are disconnected from actual market needs. This detachment inevitably leads to products that fail to resonate with users, creating a fundamental marketing challenge.

Products that fail to engage consumers at a core level inevitably struggle in the marketplace. Even if short-term tactics manage to attract some attention, consumers quickly abandon such offerings in favor of genuinely compelling alternatives. Conversely, products that deeply resonate with users are inherently more resilient. They can withstand temporary setbacks, such as negative publicity, and ultimately recover their scale and momentum over time, maintaining a solid foundation for sustainable growth.

Therefore, the essence of transformation for traditional enterprises lies in fundamentally shifting their mindset to prioritize the study of users and human needs. All other challenges faced during transformation are secondary and will naturally resolve as efforts to address this core issue deepen.

Traditional enterprises often falter because of insufficient research into user needs. Products developed based on outdated models frequently fail to resonate with consumers, leading to poor sales performance. In response, enterprises typically resort to a few common strategies, each with inherent limitations:

(1) Marketing tactics. Enterprises often rely on short-term promotions or incentive-based strategies to boost user attention and sales. However, these approaches have two significant drawbacks: Promotions and rewards require substantial cost investments. Beyond financial outlays, lengthy approval processes within traditional enterprises often delay marketing campaigns, causing missed opportunities during critical market windows. Users acquired through subsidies tend to leave once the incentives are reduced or removed. If the product itself lacks appeal or fails to build loyalty, these users quickly move on, resulting in lower repeat purchases and diminishing long-term marketing returns.

(2) Product optimization. In attempts to emulate successful competitors, enterprises may rush to develop similar features. However, this process requires time, and the long decision-making chains typical of traditional enterprises exacerbate delays. Additionally, a poor understanding of user needs often leads to poorly informed decisions. The result? Products that may look similar to competitors on the surface end up greatly different. These discrepancies may not be immediately noticeable but become evident during actual user interactions. As a result, products that appear visually similar to competing offerings may still fail to resonate with users. Furthermore, truly differentiated core functionalities cannot be achieved merely through surface-level design mimicry. For example, precision facial recognition technology in photo editing applications is a result of years of R&D by companies with significant intellectual property. To achieve similar levels, competing enterprises must either invest heavily in their own research

or collaborate with these innovators, which often means sharing revenue. In cases where such technologies are monopolized, competitors face steep costs and dependency challenges.

(3) Cost reduction. To alleviate pressure from declining sales, enterprises often turn to cost-cutting measures. However, reducing already strained front-line personnel or marketing resources weakens promotional efforts, exacerbating challenges. Similarly, cutting resources in product operations—such as design, development, or data analysis—hinders innovation and product updates, further weakening long-term competitiveness.

(4) Erosion of confidence. The cumulative drawbacks of these strategies erode management's confidence in their products. Poor performance metrics heighten pressure on business units, perpetuating a vicious cycle. As more business lines encounter similar issues, failures are often attributed to individual employees—such as sales staff being unmotivated or lacking creativity—rather than addressing systemic flaws. This misattribution sustains rigid structures and alienates capable front-line employees.

(5) Seniority-based culture. The entrenched "seniority-first" culture further aggravates these problems. Younger employees are frequently dismissed as inexperienced, too young, or unorthodox, causing their opinions—the ones often most attuned to modern consumers—to be ignored. This bias silences innovative voices, stifles enthusiasm among the younger workforce, and accelerates their attrition. As a result, enterprises that cling to rigid traditions continue to struggle in an evolving market.

The persistence of outdated practices in traditional enterprises stems from a history of success built on monopolistic strategies, aggressive bundling, and high-pressure marketing tactics. These methods once yielded remarkable results, leading managers to assume, perhaps naively, that sticking to the old playbook would guarantee continued high growth and rapid development. Consequently, all their efforts were focused not on studying the characteristics of new markets, new demands, and new user groups, but on restoring their former resource monopolies and reviving outdated practices like cold calls and aggressive bundling that users had already rejected. They stubbornly believed that intensifying these efforts would guarantee renewed success.

This attitude inevitably clashed with the realities of a rapidly changing marketplace. Today, consumers have an abundance of choices, making it easy to find products that are not only more visually appealing but also more user-friendly.

Emerging alternatives often come with personalized features and superior service, empowering consumers with unparalleled autonomy in their purchasing decisions. They can choose the one that suits them best by comparing products and using them through their own personal experience. Businesses dictating consumer behavior through forceful tactics are no longer acceptable.

As this shift unfolds, consumers are becoming more self-aware and protective, rejecting intrusive and passive marketing strategies. Traditional enterprise managers, observing the success of new products, attribute it not just to product quality but to diverse marketing techniques. In response, they pour resources into studying these methods, only to achieve limited success. The reason is clear: Each product's path to market dominance is unique, difficult to distill a pattern. This lack of actionable insights often leads to blind investment in marketing, further entrenching resistance to innovation and experimentation when these efforts fail.

When we recognize that insufficient research into user needs is the fundamental cause of poor market performance for any product, the entire strategy and approach for enterprise transformation can undergo a fundamental shift. Addressing a single critical aspect can trigger revolutionary changes in other areas. This aspect is building a professional team dedicated to user research.

Such a team must conduct thorough, frequent, and ongoing investigations into the real needs of diverse target groups. Research methods were briefly introduced in chapter I, section 6. Here, it is particularly important to emphasize that research should be multi-layered, moving from surface-level observations to deeper insights. Take dietary preferences as an example, understanding daily caloric needs is only the beginning. Research should also explore nutritional composition, taste preferences, visual appeal, and the convenience and safety of packaging. Beyond these product attributes, it's essential to investigate how dietary habits are formed, life experiences that shape preferences, emotional attachments to specific items and the reasons behind, interactions with family and friends, and shared values.

When we focus on human needs as the core of their research, questions naturally arise, leading to deeper and more meaningful insights, which ultimately pave the way for a profound understanding of the fundamental characteristics of a key target group's needs. Armed with this knowledge, enterprises can create products tailored to actual needs (which may not always align with expressed expectations, as people often misjudge their true requirements). This approach provides enterprises with a genuine and objective demand basis for production.

Such products inherently align with market needs, ensuring strong sales without the inefficiencies of overproduction. Standardized production can be reserved for universal components and intermediate materials, while final products are customized based on specific demands. This strategy minimizes inventory backlogs and reduces costs.

When a dedicated user research team consistently supplies business lines with an abundance of first-hand user data, every level of enterprise decision-making gains a solid foundation. This becomes particularly crucial when allocating resources across different business units. By integrating user research findings with performance metrics, companies can make objective, data-driven decisions to balance resource distribution. Moreover, professional insights from a specialized team carry far greater authority and credibility than scattered, informal feedback from individual employees. By employing multidimensional and multi-group investigation methods, the team delivers well-rounded analysis and recommendations that are far more persuasive.

Through the team's efforts, business units can gain a deep understanding of how users perceive their products well before planning updates or iterations. This enables them to identify both obvious and subtle issues early on, ensuring that product development plans are targeted and purposeful. As a result, these plans focus directly on solving users' specific problems, leading to tangible improvements and more effective optimizations.

Beyond this practical impact, the team's ongoing work continually channels the voice of the user throughout the organization. Over time, this subtly fosters a user-centered mindset across the company. As business units, middle management, and even back-end support teams embrace principles like "production exists to serve the user" and "the core of enterprise value lies in the value it delivers to users," these ideas begin to influence every aspect of operations.

For example, consider the issue of overly lengthy decision-making processes. When the entire organization—from executives to entry-level staff—understands that such delays impede service speed and efficiency, ultimately damaging customer satisfaction and the company's reputation, a collective consensus emerges to address the problem. This shared understanding, held by the majority of employees, becomes a powerful driving force for systemic reform. Unified by this vision, the company can push forward meaningful changes in its structures and processes.

With everyone working together, creativity flourishes. The organization begins to develop dynamic, market-responsive operating mechanisms, which evolve and improve through practical testing. Along the way, performance metrics naturally shift from being quantity-driven to quality-focused, as products lacking quality cannot sustain long-term user loyalty. These changes are not theoretical; they are compelled by market forces, creating a feedback loop that aligns enterprise mechanisms with real-world needs, endowing the organization with vitality and resilience.

One profound yet often overlooked effect of this transformation is the impact on interpersonal relationships within the company. As employees adopt user-focused and human-centered values, traditional barriers—such as departmental silos, hierarchical divisions, and internal conflicts—begin to dissolve. Team members become more inclined to care for one another and to listen attentively, fostering deeper understanding and collaboration. This focus on human connection generates immense cohesion, creating a positive feedback loop that drives the organization forward.

This unified effort also enables the company to create greater societal value by aligning its offerings with the diverse needs of humanity. Simultaneously, it enriches the life experiences of every employee. Such a transformation embodies the ideal vision for the modernization of traditional enterprises.

Ultimately, there are no universally good or bad business models or products—only those that are either well-suited or poorly matched to their intended needs. Therefore, the goal is not to blindly improve products or overhaul systems but to focus on aligning offerings with the diverse and evolving demands of users. This approach unlocks opportunities to repurpose overproduced inventory while fostering the efficient and precise creation of new innovations tailored to real-world needs.

As industries like energy recycling and reuse experience exponential growth, we can look forward to a meaningful slowdown in the rise of global energy consumption. This transformative path is the true thorough traditional enterprise transformation.

II. Building a Professional User Experience Team in Traditional Enterprises

Establishing a professional user research team from scratch in traditional enterprises involves two primary approaches: First, top-down approach. A centralized department is first established at the corporate headquarters. This department then gradually extends its talents and resources to branch offices, supporting their creation of teams. Second, bottom-up approach. Business units or product teams begin by independently hiring professionals. Over time, as their collective expertise grows, a centralized department is formed at the corporate level to integrate and manage these efforts.

Depending on the organizational structure, three models can emerge: centralized matrix model, consulting firm model, and enterprise blue army model. These models, combined with the two developmental approaches mentioned above, can be flexibly adopted at different stages of the enterprise's evolution to suit specific needs.

i. Composition of a Professional User Experience Team

A user experience team (UX team) is a specialized group dedicated to the "user-centered" philosophy. Their primary mission is to deeply understand and address users' real needs while uncovering value space derived from the user experience. Within the organization, they fulfill several critical roles:

(1) User advocates. As representatives of the user, they rely on long-term tracking to voice user concerns and ensure these insights are communicated effectively to other members of the enterprises.

(2) Product innovators. By continuously monitoring user needs, the team generates creative ideas and recommendations for product improvements, delivering these insights to product development teams through detailed user demand reports and other channels.

(3) Product optimization advisers. The team analyzes which features and functions of the product/service resonate with users and identifies gaps where the product/service fails to meet real user needs, providing precise, research-backed suggestions to drive product refinement.

(4) Bridging products and users. Throughout a product's life cycle, whether it's a newly developed product or an updated version of an existing one, gathering authentic user feedback is essential. Companies employ various methods to engage with users, such as inviting select customers to visit stores, mailing product samples for remote testing, or collecting insights through phone interviews and surveys. In these scenarios, the UX team plays a pivotal role by planning and executing these activities in alignment with the needs of both the enterprise and its users. To ensure the smooth implementation of these efforts, the team must maintain reliable channels for ongoing engagement with external users. These channels may include offline retail locations, online platforms, and social media tools, enabling the UX team to recruit a diverse and sufficient user base for participation when required.

(5) Evangelists. Promoting a "user-centered" philosophy across the organization, the team designs and delivers training programs tailored to different employee levels. They are also responsible for building a professional user experience talent pool, managing professional skill certification, and related tasks. This includes recruiting new employees, providing training, and facilitating the upskilling and development of existing staff.
(6) Business monitors. Adopting the perspective of real users and functioning as an independent third party, they routinely evaluate user experiences, monitor business operations, and ensure follow-through on resolving identified issues. By implementing administrative measures—such as integrating user experience metrics into key business performance assessments—they effectively expose and address practices that infringe on user rights or result in significant negative experiences.
(7) Trend trackers. User needs reflect the overall product dynamics of the industry, highlighting its developmental direction and emerging trends. The UX team is responsible for identifying these trends promptly and sharing insights with other members of the organization, ensuring the enterprise's production and operational modes remain up-to-date.

Product experiences can generally, by experience level, be categorized into visual aesthetics and usability. Accordingly, the fundamental qualifications of the team members are divided into specialized categories, which can be adjusted to align with the nature of the products or services provided. These categories include the following:

(1) Psychological researchers. Often graduates in sociology or psychology, these professionals specialize in exploring the deeper motivations and reasons behind human behavior. Using scientifically validated methods and advanced tools, they analyze both conscious and subconscious factors to uncover users' true needs and desires.
(2) Physical behavior analysts. Experts in disciplines like human-computer interaction, material science, physiology, and medicine belong to this category. They focus on the physical aspects of user behavior, such as changes in physiological indicators, muscle and skeletal movements, and reflex responses. Their work aims to evaluate and enhance the comfort and functionality of products or services during use.
(3) Sensory experience specialists. Researchers in this group focus on researching sensory-specific experiential characteristics. For products with distinct, inde-

pendent physical forms, it is crucial to align professionals with the sensory dimensions those products engage. For example, a simple desktop speaker involves both visual aesthetics and auditory performance. The research team for such a product should include experts in visual design and auditory perception. These specialists possess a sharper eye for detail and a broader sensitivity to nuances than the average individual. For instance, professionals with expertise in visual perception can ensure the product's universal accessibility, considering users with varying visual conditions such as color blindness, partial vision impairment, or blindness. Similarly, those with a deep understanding of artistic aesthetics can identify subtle, unique color relationships within a product's visual elements. Given that a product's user base is typically diverse, with various demographic segments represented across the population, such considerations significantly enhance its potential applications. Each additional factor accounted for during the design and research process broadens the product's usability, elevates its value, and unlocks new market opportunities.

(4) Data analysts and modelers. They are specialists in data analysis and mathematical modeling. Given that user demand research involves substantial data collection, analysis, and mining—often leveraging big data and cloud computing tools to capture user behavior insights—these experts are an indispensable component of the team. Their responsibilities include processing user-derived data, developing indicator frameworks, analytical and presentation models, and crafting comprehensive data reports. In an era marked by rapid advancements and the pervasive application of AI, data analysts hold a critical role within the UX team.

(5) Additional specialists (as needed). Based on project requirements, other professionals may be included. For instance, when managing vast data sets or creating tools for business platform management, technical experts in platform development and maintenance might be necessary. These roles can be filled by external consultants or internal teams, depending on the company's specific needs.

ii. Centralized Matrix User Experience Organizational Structure

The centralized matrix user experience organizational structure involves establishing a specialized user experience department at the group headquarters. This department focuses on recruiting and developing middle and top-tier user experience professionals. Subsidiaries and branches are equipped with corresponding user experience departments that directly interface with the headquarters. Key managerial roles and core staff in these subsidiary departments are directly appointed and managed by the headquarters. This structure is characterized by the following features:

(1) By centralizing the recruitment of specialized talent, the headquarters can swiftly assemble a sizable team capable of handling certain professional tasks and delivering targeted solutions for critical business challenges within a shorter period of time.
(2) The user experience department operates independently from business and other departments, maintaining a status equal to or higher than other departments. In some cases, it may report directly to the general manager. This independence ensures the department can objectively and accurately represent real user needs. It can uphold fairness and impartiality only if it functions as a truly independent third party, free from any vested interests or affiliations with business departments. Reports and insights generated by the department are submitted directly to the general manager, serving as key inputs for strategic decision-making.
(3) All personnel in branch-level user experience departments are fully managed by the headquarters. When the evaluation, performance incentives, and salary of department personnel are unaffected by branch offices, and their core tasks are entirely assigned by the headquarters, these individuals can effectively provide impartial oversight of branch operations based on directives from the headquarters.
(4) By establishing UX teams across all branches, the organization ensures effective implementation of headquarters' directives. In cases where a branch faces resource constraints, the headquarters can reallocate personnel across regions for seamless support. Given the nature of user research—which often requires diverse samples from multiple locations—this widespread network enables simultaneous and coordinated execution of tasks. This management style with widespread coverage is crucial for operational effectiveness.
(5) For enterprises aiming to strengthen user experience management, integrate it into performance evaluation frameworks, and implement professional grading for user experience specialists, maintaining the UX team as an independent third-party entity is crucial to achieving effective and unbiased management.

This organizational structure is particularly suitable for large state-owned or private enterprises with extensive branch networks across multiple provinces or cities. These enterprises are typically vast in scale, with a significant workforce and extensive operations. Establishing dedicated departments within each branch ensures direct responsiveness. Furthermore, such organizations often wield strong centralized control at the group level, making them well-suited for implementing structured, command-and-direct reform mechanisms.

In this context, as long as the leadership prioritizes user experience strategically and elevates its status within the organization, policies can be effectively executed at the branch level. If the corporate headquarters simultaneously introduces a matrix of user experience branches while refining complementary management systems—such as performance evaluation frameworks, talent management strategies, and decision-making processes—it can markedly accelerate the adoption of a user-centric philosophy across the enterprise.

Given their considerable societal influence, these organizations have the potential to disseminate forward-thinking concepts to the public, creating substantial ripple effects. Often serving as industry leaders, they are uniquely positioned to spearhead paradigm shifts within their respective sectors. As a result, this structure stands as one of the most powerful and effective organizational models available.

However, implementing a centralized matrix structure requires robust support from top leadership. Enterprises, where understanding of user experience principles may be limited, might question the time- and resource-intensive nature of this approach.

Moreover, the success of this structure hinges on the capabilities of the UX team leaders. As an emerging department, failure to demonstrate immediate results during trial phases could lead to skepticism, eroding confidence and derailing reforms. These potential challenges must be addressed accordingly during practice.

iii. Consulting-Firm-Style User Experience Organizational Structure

The consulting-firm-style UX organizational structure involves establishing a dedicated subsidiary within the corporate group. This subsidiary operates under the unified management of the headquarters while remaining independent of other branches. Functioning as a professional rating agency, it provides standardized, modular, and systematic UX services with publicly listed pricing. The key service categories are as follows:

(1) User experience evaluation. This service focuses on assessing the current UX performance of existing business operations. It provides targeted, tiered

recommendations for improvement, encompassing developing indicator systems, designing data collection tools and methodologies, organizing and executing evaluations, and delivering detailed reports.

(2) Targeted UX enhancements. Addressing specific issues identified during evaluations, this service offers professional guidance in areas such as interface design, visual aesthetics, interaction methods, and in-depth user research to uncover root causes.

(3) Brand experience planning. This service supports comprehensive brand strategy development, including visual identity, brand philosophy and culture, and communication planning.

(4) Business innovation. Designed to help businesses identify differentiation advantages over competitors and build a business with core competitiveness, this service provides creative solutions grounded in user demand research.

Additionally, the subsidiary can deliver services such as UX index rankings, industry-level UX analysis reports, insights into user demand trends, and specialized research for particular industries or verticals.

By publicly listing its service pricing, the subsidiary ensures fairness and transparency. When the professional UX management system becomes an integral part of the group's overall business framework, every major business line requires UX oversight. This growing and continuous demand for UX services across business lines ensures that the subsidiary generates consistent revenue to sustain its operations.

Beyond meeting internal corporate needs, the subsidiary can also expand into external markets, unlocking new business opportunities. Competing in the marketplace further drives improvements in the subsidiary's service quality and professional expertise over time.

The consulting-firm-style UX organizational structure is less reliant on mandatory group-wide reforms and maintains a more detached relationship with business lines. Consequently, its ability to promote UX principles across the organization is limited and heavily influenced by the understanding, acceptance, and commitment of individual branches to a "user-centric" philosophy.

When establishing a professional UX team from the ground up, many employees within the organization may initially have a limited understanding of UX principles, necessitating a gradual and step-by-step process of adoption. A consulting-firm-style approach offers flexible and adaptable service options, allowing for both evaluations from a purely user-centric perspective and in-depth, targeted guidance to enhance specific business aspects. This flexibility provides branch personnel with a broad range of tailored solutions.

For teams with a limited understanding of user experience principles, a gradual introduction of relevant methods and processes can help them ease into the concept. For those with some familiarity and a willingness to explore further, a wider range of more in-depth services can be provided. Meanwhile, teams facing urgent needs can be supported with tailored, more directive reform plans to ensure a smooth transition. However, while this consulting-style organizational structure offers significant flexibility, it inherently lacks the robust control mechanisms found in more centralized models.

iv. Enterprise "Blue Army" Organizational Structure

The "Blue Army" is a concept used in contrast to the "Red Army." If the Red Army represents front-line business personnel focused on selling products, the Blue Army embodies an internal team acting as users to evaluate and challenge the Red Army's efforts. This organizational structure involves forming a team that penetrates various business lines and evaluates products from a user-centric perspective. Through regular testing and feedback, this team helps identify and resolve user experience issues before products or services are released to the market.

The key to the effectiveness of the enterprise Blue Army lies in its members' ability to maintain a user-centric mindset, free from the influence of business-driven thinking. This ensures they can accurately and objectively reflect the genuine attitudes of discerning and critical users in a real market environment.

Unlike other organizational structures, the enterprise Blue Army organizational framework embeds UX personnel directly into various business lines. The responsibilities of Blue Army members may be undertaken by existing business staff following training or by new team members recruited for the role. The Blue Army model is the most flexible among organizational structures, but its lack of a robust and independent management hierarchy diminishes the independence of its members in representing the user perspective.

If performance evaluations for these members are conducted by the business lines they are embedded in, the business lines' own performance metrics can exert significant constraints. When conflicts arise between business growth targets and user experience goals, direct managerial pressure often forces UX considerations to yield to growth-focused performance indicators. Consequently, UX issues risk being downplayed, sidelined, or ignored, relegating them to a secondary, non-essential status.

To address this, when business line management is relatively decentralized and a more flexible enterprise Blue Army structure is necessary, it is crucial to ensure that the Blue Army is overseen by a functional department or specialized UX department outside the direct control of the business units. Key aspects of the Blue Army members' roles—such as performance evaluation, bonus incentives, and rank assessments—must remain under the exclusive purview of an independent authority rather than the business units they are embedded in.

At the same time, since these personnel work daily alongside business staff, their performance should be partially assessed through feedback and evaluations from the respective business units. This feedback should be collected by the independent management department and used as a foundational input for assessing Blue Army members' contributions.

This dual-evaluation management system serves as a vital tool for maintaining balanced oversight and regulation of Blue Army members' performance. It allows business departments to provide objective and accurate assessments of the Blue Army's contributions and value. These evaluations complement the independent management department's appraisal of members' skills and job performance. Such an approach facilitates the planning of targeted training and development programs while ensuring that issues arising during implementation are promptly identified and effectively addressed.

The Blue Army structure is ideal for organizations with minimal control layers, flexible business operations, and quick adaptability to market changes. This structure is characterized by its flexibility rather than strict enforcement, making it ideal for adapting to the evolving needs of business lines. It allows for the dynamic dissection, reorganization, and redistribution of resources as business lines develop. However, due to the relatively weaker enforcement, it is crucial for companies to establish policies, mechanisms, processes, and standards that safeguard the Blue Army's independence. For example, the reports generated by the Blue Army could be empowered to be submitted directly to the CEO through an independent management department, ensuring that the true voice of the users is effectively conveyed.

As the Blue Army grows and matures, enterprises can implement a more centralized approach to manage these personnel according to specific needs. Especially when various specialized talents within the team develop individually, enterprises should establish tailored management, training, and promotion systems that allow these professionals to continuously hone and elevate their expertise.

v. Top-Down Development Model

The concept of "top" and "down" in the top-down model refers to the hierarchy within an enterprise. "Down" represents grassroots levels—frontline employees directly interacting with consumers—while "top" refers to the highest management level. Between these two extremes lies a broad spectrum of middle management, which can be further divided into lower-tier middle management, closer to the grassroots, and upper-tier middle management, closer to senior leadership.

The top-down development model involves the highest level of management first introducing the concept of UX management and defining relevant arrangements. Middle management collaborates to create corresponding plans, which are then cascaded down the hierarchy for execution.

The hallmark of this approach is its command-driven nature. Senior leadership recognizes the strategic significance of a "user-centered" philosophy, orchestrating unified directives from the top. Branches and lower-level units are tasked with adopting and implementing these strategic objectives. This model's administrative enforcement ensures unparalleled effectiveness, enabling swift and efficient progress in organizational transformation.

However, its mandatory nature can also lead to surface compliance without genuine alignment as directives percolate down the hierarchy. Lower-level employees might implement systemic reforms as required by their superiors, but the results may not fully align with the reform's objectives. This discrepancy is particularly pronounced when grassroots personnel lack the necessary professional skills or have yet to embrace the new mindset. Challenges may arise in execution, such as inconsistencies in implementation methods, content, or outcomes. Moreover, tensions between reformed and unreformed processes can create operational conflicts when reform measures are not fully implemented.

Such issues can generate friction throughout the reform journey. When the benefits of reform are not immediately evident and existing systems are disrupted, companies might experience a temporary decline in performance. This turbulence can also result in the loss of key personnel. In the face of such pressures, a company's ability to stay resolute and continue implementing transformative measures amid an increasingly competitive market hinges on the sustained collective efforts of its entire workforce. The process of transformation, therefore, serves as a profound test of the company's cultural strength.

Reform inevitably disrupts established interests, creating friction and altering the status quo for some employees. To maintain stability, a strong and cohesive corporate culture is essential as a stabilizing force.

In the long run, adapting to shifting market demands through transformative change is an unavoidable necessity. Although challenges and setbacks are inevitable, transformation remains the foundation for sustainable growth and the pathway to renewed prosperity. By guiding employees to fully understand the underlying issues, the objectives of reform, and the potential obstacles that may arise, companies can cultivate widespread support, thus ensuring that the reform process unfolds with greater fluidity and effectiveness.

vi. Bottom-Up Development Model

Unlike the top-down approach, the bottom-up development model is a more commonly observed pathway in organizational transformation. This model originates at the grassroots level, where a few frontline departments or individuals recognize the importance of understanding user needs amid rapidly changing market conditions. In response, they proactively acquire relevant knowledge, recruit specialized talent, and begin implementing user-centered practices within their respective business units.

As these efforts yield positive results, their successes are shared across teams. Much like a spark igniting a wildfire, these concepts, methods, and practices gradually gain traction and are adopted by more teams. Over time, grassroots departments organically cultivate their own "Blue Army" teams, creating a ripple effect that extends throughout the organization. Since these teams emerge naturally within business lines, they are inherently aligned with operational objectives, enabling them to effectively harness their expertise to drive business growth.

However, UX teams formed through a bottom-up approach often face significant challenges. They frequently lack substantial authority. Spread across various business units, these teams remain relatively small and fragmented, making it difficult to consolidate their efforts into a unified force. Additionally, their professional skills are rarely developed within a structured framework, leading to inconsistent levels of expertise. While these teams may demonstrate gradual progress, they often struggle to gain enterprise-wide recognition or support, which hinders their development.

This vulnerability makes them highly susceptible to external disruptions, potentially leading to disbandment. Even teams that manage to endure often find themselves in a prolonged state of stagnation, with limited opportunities for growth or advancement.

When assessing a company's transformation pathway, solutions should be thoughtfully tailored to align with the company's unique circumstances and current stage of development, carefully integrating the most appropriate elements from the outlined models. For organizations where frontline teams have already embraced user-centric principles and demonstrate strong user awareness, strategic leadership from the executive level can accelerate these grassroots efforts and foster rapid growth. On the other hand, for organizations with limited user awareness, large-scale operations, or entrenched legacy systems, initiating transformation from the top through targeted administrative directives may be necessary to establish a cohesive framework.

Ultimately, there is no one-size-fits-all approach. Each organization must critically evaluate its current situation and creatively adapt or combine elements from these models. By doing so, they can chart a transformation path that aligns with their unique needs and objectives.

III. User Experience Production Process and Team Composition

What does a "user-centered" production process look like in a real enterprise? What roles should a professional UX team comprise, and how do these roles contribute throughout the production process? How can we evaluate the value and contribution of each team member? These are critical, practical questions that businesses face at a micro level.

In this section, we delve into these topics using the smartphone app production process as a case study. Smartphone apps have seen rapid development in recent years, and this product form has been widely adopted across industries. We will introduce the current UX production processes and team structures, which many businesses have implemented, offering valuable insights to those interested in building a professional UX team.

To provide some context, we begin by briefly discussing smartphone apps. Following that, we will break down the production process of such products, focusing on the roles and functions of participants at each stage.

i. Introduction to Smartphone Application Products

According to the 41st Statistical Report on Internet Development in China, published by the China Internet Network Information Center in January 2018, as of December 2017, the number of mobile internet users in China reached 753 million, an increase of 57.34 million compared to the end of 2016. The proportion of internet users accessing the web through mobile phones rose to 97.5%, up from 95.1% in 2016, continuing a strong upward trend. The report highlights key developments in the mobile internet sector:

(1) Diversification of service scenarios. Mobile application platforms now integrate social networking, information services, finance, transportation, and various public services, forming unified service ecosystems with broader reach and greater influence.
(2) Accelerated increase of mobile terminals. Smart devices centered around smartphones are at the heart of the Internet of Everything, driving innovations like connected cars and smart homes, and creating more personalized, intelligent application scenarios.
(3) Continuous expansion of mobile data. As population growth slows and user numbers stabilize, the vast amount of mobile data, deeply coupled with big data technologies, provides new opportunities for innovation and value extraction for the mobile internet industry.

According to iiMedia Research's 2017–2018 China Smartphone Market Report, the number of smartphone users in China reached 668 million by the end of 2017, accounting for 88.7% of mobile internet users. The above data indicates that the mobile network economy, powered by smartphones, has become a vital component of the national economy.

The term app (short for application) originally referred to independent software programs for computer operating systems. Today, it encompasses mobile applications that provide specific functionalities on smartphones. As a subset of electronic information products, apps inherit characteristics of digital products.

According to iiMedia Research's 2017 Mid-Year China Mobile App Store Monitoring Report, the volume of mobile apps between 2010 and 2016 is illustrated in figure 3-1.

The data clearly illustrates a consistent year-over-year growth in the total number of mobile apps, with the growth rate shifting from rapid acceleration between 2010 and 2013 to a more stabilized pace. This slowdown can be attributed to the increasing total volume of apps, which has led to intensified homogenized competition within the app market. Nonetheless, mobile app numbers continue to exhibit double-digit growth rates, and the market size remains on an upward trajectory.

As the primary platform and usage format for smartphones, mobile apps have significantly expanded their influence on everyday life, fueled by the growing adoption of smartphones and the increasing variety of apps available. This makes mobile apps a quintessential representation of virtualized products in the era of mobile internet information. As such, selecting mobile apps as the focus of this study holds considerable relevance and significance.

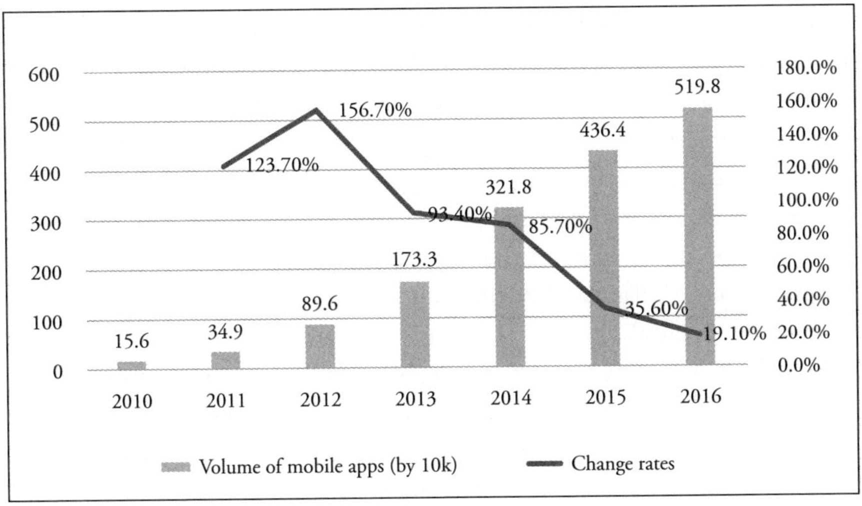

Figure 3-1 The volume of global mobile apps in 2010–2016

ii. Dissecting the UX Production Process for Apps

The UX production process for a new app typically includes five key stages.

1. Stage 1: Demand Analysis and Product Goal Definition

The primary objective of this stage is to identify the target user group and their core needs. It involves conducting extensive user research aligned with the product's direction, complemented by an in-depth analysis of competing products in the market. Insights from this research are used to define the product's positioning and objectives. Additionally, this stage includes feasibility studies and essential business negotiations. By thoroughly analyzing industry competition and future trends, the product's main business focus and developmental trajectory can be determined. This culminates in a clear, comprehensive, and easily understandable product specification document that is practical and achievable within the available resource constraints.

The duration of this stage varies depending on the product's nature and industry characteristics. Some products emphasize refining core technologies in the early stages, securing partnership agreements, and ensuring post-launch service scenarios are seamlessly integrated before committing resources to development. Conversely, other products prioritize rapid market entry, opting to launch quickly to gain a competitive edge. In such cases, certain steps may be streamlined or deferred, with the intention of addressing any gaps during subsequent product iterations.

2. Stage 2: Product Architecture Planning

The primary objective of this stage is to define the functional scope of the product and prioritize those functions according to the product's positioning. For instance, in the case of a mobile video app, the first stage identifies the core goal of meeting user needs for video consumption. In this stage, the focus shifts to determining the specific features to include, such as video playback controls (play, pause, fast forward, next video, subtitles, and audio channel selection), content navigation tools (channels, search), and interactive components (comments, reviews, instant chats, sharing, repost, etc.). The outlined functional scope must align with the product's core positioning identified in stage one, ensuring basic user needs are met while realizing distinct features that provide a competitive edge. Given the constraints of development time and resource costs, it is crucial to prioritize these functions, distinguishing between primary and secondary features to maximize resource efficiency.

The second task in this stage involves organizing the product's architecture based on the functional plan. This work focuses on clarifying the hierarchy and logical relationships among the features from a holistic perspective. When providing a wide range of features, it becomes even more critical to clearly define the arrangement of modules, as well as the internal logic, navigation, and sequence of page transitions within each function. The architecture design must also consider the underlying technical framework, requiring adjustments to accommodate technical constraints when necessary. The quality of the product architecture directly impacts the efficiency of feature use, overall product performance, and subsequent interface design aspects, such as navigation and indexing.

In the process of product architecture planning, user experience workflows require considering real user habits. This includes the comprehension levels of users with different educational backgrounds (e.g., children or seniors) and unique scenarios (e.g., one-handed operation, screen rotation). User experience professionals typically break down major functional processes into tasks based on scenarios and invite real users to test these workflows. This allows product designers to promptly adjust any illogical or user-unfriendly aspects, creating a more rational and effective product structure.

3. Stage 3: Interface Layout and Design

In this stage, the work focuses on designing the visual representation of the product based on the defined functional scope. Drawing from the user research conducted in the earlier stages, this stage incorporates a clear understanding of the target audience's preferences and operational habits.

Therefore, the visual design work must be centered around the preferences of the target audience. The specific tasks in this stage include conceptual design—establishing the product's overall style and atmosphere tailored to the target audience. This could include aesthetics like a business-oriented look, minimalism, fresh and light tones, or a texture-rich design; and wireframe and visual design—creating wireframes for all pages (commonly referred to as interaction design) and designing the visual elements for each page. This includes the development of low-fidelity, high-fidelity prototypes and pre-development preparation such as sliced image files.

This stage is crucial in shaping the product's core visual identity and interaction methods. The tasks extend to interface layout (typography), element design, text content editing, and control performance design.

At this stage, a comprehensive design specification document or a visual prototype demo is often created to ensure developers can accurately interpret and implement the design. Regular design reviews are conducted, involving designers, product managers, and developers. Developers provide insights into implementation feasibility and may suggest adjustments to optimize the design for development.

Before final submission for development, user experience specialists typically conduct usability tests using a prototype version. This allows for identifying and resolving any potential user experience issues through iterative design refinements.

4. Stage 4: Development

The development stage consists of three sub-stages: pre-development research, development, and testing:

(1) Pre-development research. This is a transitional stage where developers create a development schedule and evaluate the complexity and timeliness of implementation based on the design documents submitted by upstream teams. When encountering significant challenges or issues, they will promptly communicate with designers and product managers to prioritize product development and make necessary adjustments to specific design drafts.

(2) Development. During this stage, developers will also communicate with designers at any time regarding the detailed requirements for interface design elements and complete the development work according to the previously established schedule.

(3) Testing. Once development is complete, the product undergoes rigorous testing. The testing of app products mainly includes the following (additional detailed test categories including stability testing, weak network signal testing, power consumption testing, etc., which are not listed here):
- Functional testing. Testers conduct comprehensive coverage tests of all product features, either manually or using automated testing tools, to ensure that each function is fully implemented.
- Performance testing. Assessing the product's page loading, transitions, and response times through user experience evaluations and automated performance testing tools.
- Stress testing. Measuring the capacity of both the product and its servers by simulating a high volume of concurrent tasks at specific time intervals.
- Adaptation testing. Ensuring that the product's display functions properly across a variety of major devices.

User experience professionals often incorporate usability testing and user interviews during the testing phase to assess whether users interact with the product as anticipated. Additionally, some teams implement internal testing, providing some users with trial access and offering incentives to gather feedback on the product's development and effectiveness.

It's important to note that the development process often involves multiple iterations and revisions. During the implementation of product design drafts, various technical challenges may emerge—such as difficulties in achieving specific animations or managing resource consumption for particular color schemes. Striking a balance between aesthetic appeal and optimal performance requires close collaboration and consensus between design and development teams. From a user experience perspective, any changes to the design must be carefully evaluated for user acceptance. If necessary, real users may be invited again for additional testing to ensure the modifications align with expectations.

5. Stage 5: Post-Launch Evaluation

In this stage, the product has officially launched to the public and entered the market. From here on, product production will seamlessly integrate with product operations, focusing on scaling the user base and increasing engagement levels. At the same time, depending on the product type, key performance indicators (KPIs) will take center stage. Subsequent product iterations (or reproduction) will revolve around meeting the KPIs' target values, while incorporating real-time user feedback. The UX team will work closely with the product operations team to swiftly capture the user experience at the user level, collaborating on user acquisition, activation, and retention efforts. While product operations are complex, they are not the focus and are therefore not discussed much here.

The user experience reproduction of an app, at its core, represents the cyclical nature of the production process. After the new product goes live, the product manager will re-iterate the demand analysis document and product specification document, adjusting the product's functional priorities to meet market changes and user needs.

Reproduction work can be divided into two main categories: optimizing existing features and developing new ones. Optimizing existing features is usually faster and more agile than the full product production process, often requiring less time. Many companies have adopted agile processes specifically for feature optimization to meet these needs. The development of new features typically follows the full product production cycle. However, when the volume of new feature development is substantial, the complete process is still followed, though some stages may be expedited depending on the scope of development.

iii. Introduction to Participants in the User Experience Production Process

Much like an assembly line in industrial production, the participants in the app product user experience production process work together in an upstream-downstream flow. The key distinction from traditional production methods lies in the fact that every participant must embrace a user-centric mindset, align with the principles of user experience, and cooperate professionally throughout the process. Additionally, real users, as active contributors, engage directly in every stage of the production process, becoming an integral part of the entire chain. Aside from external users, from a professional staffing perspective, the following seven key roles are involved:

(1) A product owner (product manager) holds full responsibility for the product, overseeing the entire life cycle—from defining product requirements in the early stages to tracking progress during production, coordinating resources, managing projects, and making crucial decisions. This role blends both managerial and specialized functions. In some companies, the product owner also takes on the role of interaction designer or participates in other stages of production. The product owner is also in charge of team management and reporting product-related updates to senior leadership.

(2) An interaction designer is responsible for crafting the app's page structure, layout, and wireframes based on the product owner's requirement files. They usually focus on low-fidelity prototypes and provide interaction diagrams

and documentation to the visual designers. During the visual design and development stages, the interaction designer collaborates extensively with visual designers and developers to fine-tune interaction logic, element placement, and design details. When critical decisions arise, they seek advice from the product owner. In some companies, the interaction designer's role may be combined with the product owner or the visual designer. Regardless of the structure, the interaction designer's contributions remain indispensable. The distinction lies in the fact that, depending on how the team is structured, the content of the deliverable documents may differ between the upstream and downstream stages. They also create and maintain the product's interaction design guidelines.

(3) A visual designer is responsible for crafting the visual design of each page, based on the interaction designer's drafts and design documentation. This includes selecting color schemes, designing visual elements such as buttons, icons, and layout spaces, and creating marketing visuals, splash screens, banners, animations, and transition effects. Visual designers oversee the overall visual aesthetics and style of the interface, ensuring that product features related to visual presentation—such as information clarity, recognizability, and readability—are optimized. They often engage early in product development, leveraging insights into the product's positioning and target audience to create initial conceptual designs. Typically, they produce 3–5 design variations for selection. These design styles are sometimes further refined based on feedback gathered through usability testing and user interviews. While their role is focused on visual elements, it also demands a high degree of adaptability. Once the design is finalized, visual designers elevate the low-fidelity prototypes created by interaction designers into polished high-fidelity prototypes with detailed visuals. They also prepare and export design assets to ensure seamless integration into the development phase. Furthermore, visual designers are responsible for drafting and maintaining comprehensive visual design guidelines for the product.

(4) A front-end developer is responsible for the comprehensive development of the product, encompassing both the app's front-end (client-side development) and its backend systems (server-side development). Development outputs are typically categorized into four distinct versions: development version—an internal version used by developers for self-testing, internal testing version—a version tested by internal team members and a small group of users, public testing version—a broader release designed for larger-scale user testing, and release version—the official version launched on app stores or websites for public access and download. Their primary goal is to transform design concepts into fully

functional, executable code while ensuring all features are effectively implemented on the server side. Their work is the cornerstone of product development, as the quality and efficiency of this process dictate how faithfully the envisioned features and interface designs are realized. Throughout the development, developers collaborate closely with product managers and designers, engaging in detailed discussions and analyses of implementation details. This ensures the development achieves the highest possible alignment with the initial product requirements.

(5) A test engineer is typically a key member of a product team, responsible for conducting comprehensive testing throughout various stages of development and managing critical testing resources such as devices, test cards, and platforms. Test engineers must possess a thorough understanding of the product's technical implementation process, allowing them to pinpoint the exact stage and cause of any issues. They deliver detailed test reports to developers and product managers, facilitating timely optimizations of the product.

(6) A user researcher comes from a broad range of academic and professional backgrounds, including fields such as psychology, human factors, anthropology, possess technical knowledge and keen insights into industry-specific application scenarios. They also possess strong interpersonal communication skills. The primary role of a user researcher is to apply a diverse array of research methods throughout the product life cycle to gather essential insights into user needs, behaviors, and attitudes, providing a solid foundation for product optimization. Additionally, they monitor product quality from the user's perspective, offering valuable feedback and recommendations when design decisions deviate from user experience principles, thereby guiding the product in the right direction. User research methods typically fall into two categories: qualitative and quantitative. User researchers are responsible for crafting research plans, developing questionnaires or interview scripts, recruiting participants, and organizing and analyzing data. Most user researchers are fully capable of independently conducting data analysis and producing comprehensive user research reports. In larger tech companies, specialized roles such as user research engineers or user researchers are often established. Some companies even form dedicated user research teams that serve multiple business lines, managing both foundational research projects and specialized studies. In other product lines, user research roles are integrated within product teams, where they focus on research specific to particular product lines. In companies that don't have dedicated user research roles, the responsibility often falls to other team members, such as those in business support, product operations, marketing planning, or product strategy.

(7) A data engineer is an essential member of many product teams, often working alongside data analysts or operations analysts. These professionals are responsible for processing and analyzing product data to create visual charts and reports. Their analyses encompass a range of metrics, including user numbers, daily active users, monthly active users, activity rates, growth, conversion rates, revenue, click-through rates, and more. Additionally, they reprocess and reanalyze initial data gathered through user research. Data engineers are typically tasked with managing, maintaining, and utilizing the product's data platform. They are responsible for defining data analysis requirements and implementing them using specialized tools. A large portion of modern data analysis relies on automated, tool-driven, and templated approaches, often leveraging big data platforms. As a result, data analysis involves not only data processing but also the use of sophisticated platforms and technical expertise. In the context of app product development, these data platforms are integral to the overall production process.

iv. Analysis of User Experience Production Participants

1. Work Processes

(1) Product Owner

Their responsibilities span multiple stages, from early research and planning to coordination during design, development, testing, and launch.

Stage 1: background investigation. The approximate time required for this stage is 23 person-days. This means one person working for 23 days, or an equivalent distribution of effort among multiple team members.

- Background data analysis: conduct a comprehensive analysis of competitor products, user needs, available resources, and potential collaboration opportunities. Estimated time: 10 person-days, excluding time spent negotiating collaborations.
- Product positioning: define the primary target user group and their characteristics, the key user needs, the product's core features, attributes, usage scenarios, and business objectives. Estimated time: 3 person-days.
- Product planning: set clear product goals, allocate resources and personnel, establish management protocols, create quality assurance and risk control standards, and outline the development schedule. Estimated time: 5 person-days, excluding recruitment, reporting before resources are in place, and other preparatory tasks.

- (Initial) product documentation: summarize findings into formal documents such as feasibility studies or product planning reports. Estimated time: 5 person-days.

Stage 2: requirements analysis. The approximate time required for this stage is 11 person-days.

- Product introduction document: develop documents that outline market demands, core product functionalities, and business goal planning. Estimated time: 3 person-days.
- Requirements documentation: detail the functional descriptions, performance needs, compatibility requirements, user personas, usage scenarios, functional hierarchy, and prioritization. Estimated time: 3 person-days.
- Requirement discussion and review: thorough discussions of the relevant documents by the product team, critically assessing their feasibility and validity to refine and enhance clarity and precision. Estimated time: 5 person-days.

Stage 3: concept design. During this phase, the product manager takes on a leadership role, organizing and coordinating tasks among team members to ensure collaborative completion. The product manager's net working time—representing their direct contributions to the process—is approximately 3.5 person-days.

- Concept design: develop both interaction concept design and visual concept design, supported by user researchers who contribute to analyzing user needs. Standard user research methods, such as scenario analysis and storyboarding, are utilized to enhance the concept design process. Estimated time: 12 person-days. During this time, the product manager assumes a supervisory role throughout, with their net working time amounting to roughly 3 person-days.
- Concept design review: evaluate and revise concept designs based on the requirements documents. Estimated time: 2 person-days, with the product manager's net working time amounting to 0.5 person-days.

Stage 4: management and coordination. The product manager oversees and coordinates activities during the design, development, testing, and launch phases.

- Design stage: approximately 112 person-days.

- Development stage (only the app): approximately takes 61 person-days. The time required may vary based on the complexity of the development tasks. Backend development, which encompasses the full life cycle from the initial to the final stages, has been excluded from this calculation.
- Testing stage: approximately 19 person-days.
- Launch stage: approximately 40 person-days, excluding post-launch operations and user feedback collection.

The product manager's management work accounts for roughly 25% of the total workload, or 58 person-days.

In total, a product manager contributes approximately 95.5 person-days to the entire production life cycle of a new product.

(2) Interaction Designer

Their work spans multiple stages, ensuring that the product is intuitive, consistent, and aligned with user expectations.

Stage 1: information architecture design. The approximate time required for this stage is 16 person-days.

- Defining functional information hierarchy and structure: organize the functional information into a clear hierarchy, determining the total number of layers, assigning information to each layer, and establishing logical relationships between functional modules. This stage includes multiple rounds of validation to ensure the hierarchy aligns with user cognition and common usage patterns. Estimated time: 5 person-days.
- Text label system design: define, clarify, and standardize all textual information within the product, including category navigation labels, control names, feature names, and tags. The goal is to ensure text adheres to users' cognitive levels, maintains proper grammar, is clear and understandable, and avoids any potential ambiguity. Additionally, it's essential to ensure consistent terminology across the entire product. Estimated time: 3 person-days.
- Navigation and search system design: define the categorization of information, filtering components, criteria, as well as the placement and display of navigation and search elements within the user interface. This includes clear definitions for each category, often leveraging methods like card sorting in user research, inviting users to participate in the categorization design. The interaction designer's role in this stage involves

approximately 3 person-days of work (not accounting for any additional workload generated by user research).

- Information architecture documentation output: compile the information architecture results into a comprehensive document, which includes an information architecture diagram, supporting processes, and charts. Estimated time: 5 person-days.

Stage 2: interaction design. The approximate time required for this stage is 29 person-days.

- Interaction design sketches: create initial design sketches either on paper or through digital tools, and then review them with the product manager to confirm alignment with the overall vision. Estimated time: 5 person-days.
- Interaction design standards: define key design standards, including text size, control shapes and sizes, page classifications, the general structure of pages, and font standards. Estimated time: 3 person-days. These standards are flexible and can be adjusted and revised throughout the process as needed.
- Page layout and typography design: plan the layout and structural framework of each page. Estimated time: 10 person-days. The time required may vary based on the number of pages involved.
- Page logic design: define the logical relationships and navigation flows between pages. Estimated time: 5 person-days.
- Page interaction design: establish the placement of page elements and determine how users will interact with them (e.g., button states, interaction responses). Estimated time: 3 person-days.
- Page-to-page interaction logic design: design how pages transition between each other, whether through scrolling, modal windows, or animated transitions, and specify how these transitions should respond to user actions. Estimated time: 3 person-days.

Stage 3: low-fidelity prototype design and testing. The approximate time required for this stage is 6 person-days.

- Low-fidelity prototype design: use design tools to assemble the page layouts into a low-fidelity prototype, generating a demo in HTML or video format for demonstration purposes. Estimated time: 3 person-days.
- Low-fidelity prototype testing: share the low-fidelity prototype with team members and, when necessary, invite target users for testing. This ensures

the interaction design aligns with user habits while helping to identify any design flaws early on. Estimated time: 3 person-days.

Stage 4: interaction design review. This stage involves collaboration with the product manager, visual designer, developers, and other product team members to conduct a comprehensive review of the interaction design based on testing results. The design is then refined and optimized according to the feedback from the review. The estimated time required for this stage is approximately 2 person-days.

Stage 5: interaction design documentation output. Based on the finalized interaction design, this stage focuses on organizing and producing documentation to support downstream work. The estimated time required is approximately 2 person-days.

(3) Visual Designer

Their work not only enhances aesthetic appeal but also supports usability and brand coherence throughout the product life cycle.

Stage 1: visual design. The approximate time required for this stage is 42 person-days.

- Defining interface visual style. This stage may overlap with the early conceptual design phase. It focuses on creating the overall visual style of the interface, tailored to the target user demographic. Tasks include defining the product's color scheme, shape styles, and overall aesthetic. Typically, 3–5 style variations are presented for the product team's review and evaluation. Estimated time: 7 person-days.
- Interface visual design (including visual element design). Building on the defined visual style, this step involves designing each specific page in detail. This includes crafting all visual elements and fine-tuning the overall page aesthetics. Estimated time: 30 person-days.
- Visual design guidelines. This guideline is established to ensure consistency in user experience across product iterations. It is typically updated and refined with each version release and revised when significant adjustments are made to the product's visual style. The guideline provides a unified design standard for team members from diverse backgrounds, significantly reducing communication and learning costs. It generally includes specifications for color schemes, typography standards, alignment rules, layout guidelines, form conventions, and various visual elements such as

small buttons, button state colors, icon dimensions, gesture animations, and more. Estimated time: 5 person-days.

Stage 2: high-fidelity prototype design and testing. The approximate time required for this stage is 10 person-days.

- High-fidelity prototype creation. Transform static visual designs into dynamic prototypes using design tools. This not only aids in assessing the overall visual impact during design reviews but also ensures developers have a clear understanding of the logical connections between pages, control states, transition animations, and other interactive elements. Estimated time: 5 person-days.
- High-fidelity prototype testing. Testing may be conducted by internal design directors or experts to ensure the overall quality of the design. Alternatively, usability testing can involve inviting real users to participate, allowing the team to gather authentic feedback and insights. This helps identify user perceptions and evaluations, enabling timely adjustments and optimizations to enhance the product. Estimated time: 5 person-days.

Stage 3: visual design review. Collaborate with the product manager, interaction designer, developers, and other team members to conduct a comprehensive review of the visual design, integrating test results and optimizing the design based on review outcomes. Estimated time: 2 person-days.

Stage 4: slicing preparation and design documentation. The finalized visual design plans are meticulously refined into development-ready documentation and handed over to the development team for implementation. Estimated time: 3 person-days.

(4) Frontend Developer

Their work spans from planning and prototyping to testing and full implementation.

Stage 1: development planning.

- Pre-development assessment. During the early and mid-stages of product development, developers participate in review meetings to understand the development requirements, assess the time needed for implementation, and evaluate the complexity of various features. They also coordinate promptly with other team members to ensure alignment. This stage typically begins once the design documentation is handed over by the designer. Estimated time: 5 person-days, including 2 person-days for part-time communication during the early stages and 3 person-days for confirming the design documentation.

- Development planning. In some cases, it is combined with the pre-development assessment. For projects involving particularly complex features that require intricate client-server interactions, a separate development plan is created. This dedicated planning typically takes around 3 person-days.

Stage 2: prototyping. Entering official development, this stage encompasses requirement discussions, coding, internal testing, and optimization. The core task of coding typically takes about 25 person-days, with adjustments based on feature complexity.

Stage 3: usability testing. The front-end developers create a prototype demo of the product for usability testing, and it should present the core functional modules. By inviting target users to perform specific tasks on the prototype, the team can observe, listen, and document real user experiences, uncovering potential design flaws. This process allows the team to gather valuable insights and provide timely feedback to both designers and developers for refinement. For the testing, 8 users are invited, each participating for 1 hour, with 1 facilitator and 1 recorder involved, totaling approximately 2 person-days. Adding time for summarizing and generating the report, the entire process takes around 3 person-days.

Stage 4: code development. Following usability testing, the front-end development is finalized, and parallel work is completed on the data layer, maintenance layer, backend management platform, interface documentation, and management manuals, requiring a total of 25 person-days.

(5) Test Engineer

It typically involves unit testing, integration testing, performance testing, and stress testing. Their specific responsibilities may vary depending on the company and product team.

Stage 1: unit testing. It involves evaluating the smallest testable units in the software to validate whether the tested code functions as expected. Estimated time: 2 person-days.

Stage 2: integration testing. Following unit testing, all modules are integrated into subsystems or the full system for comprehensive integration testing. Estimated time: 5 person-days.

Stage 3: performance testing. Utilizing in-house or external app client-specific performance testing platforms, this step involves quickly and thoroughly testing the overall app's performance. Estimated time: 2 person-days.

Stage 4: stress testing. Simulating real-world software and hardware conditions, as well as the system load during actual use, this challenges the system with prolonged or high loads to assess its performance, reliability, and stability under stress. Estimated time: 5 person-days.

In cases where external resources for performance and stress testing are unavailable, additional time (5 person-days) is required to write testing scripts in advance.

(6) User Researcher

User researchers are involved throughout various stages of product development. Their responsibilities can generally be broken down into the following phases:

- Early stage: user research during the background investigation and requirements analysis phase.
- Middle stage: user research involving usability testing of prototype versions and user interviews.
- Late stage: user research focused on pre-launch testing.
- Post-launch: user research focused on gathering user feedback and further collecting requirements for iterative updates.

For a standard user research project on a specific product, the process—from preparation to execution and final reporting—requires at least two user researchers and typically takes around 15 working days to complete. This equates to approximately 30 person-days for a single project. Over the course of product development, at least four rounds of user research are generally necessary, resulting in a total of around 120 person-days. Post-launch research is not included in this total.

(7) Data Engineer

Data engineers focus on monitoring and analyzing product operational data after launch. They are responsible for developing operational analysis report templates, data models, and managing the data platform's development, optimization, and iteration.

Data analysis platforms are typically developed alongside the product, either integrated directly into the backend or as a separate platform. In cases where a dedicated platform is required, an additional 25 person-days of development time is needed. The data engineer's work during the product development stage, which includes data analysis modeling, defining key metrics, and performing data analysis, typically requires about 15 person-days. Following the product launch, the data engineer continues to monitor and track the evolving data.

2. Final Product Labor Value Analysis

Assuming that the labor value per worker per day is consistent across job types—i.e., the value of labor spent per unit of time is equivalent for all roles—this analysis compares the labor consumed at each stage of the app product's development. The labor consumption is categorized by participant type, as shown in table 3-1.

From this table, it is evident that the product owner and user researcher carry the heaviest workload, while interaction designers, visual designers, frontend developers, and data engineers have similar, mid-range workloads. Test engineers have the smallest work volumes.

For companies aiming to build a UX team from the ground up, flexibility in resource allocation is key. Among the seven roles, priority should be given to hiring professionals who can most effectively elevate the user experience. Other roles can be gradually filled as necessary. Furthermore, some UX professionals can be cultivated internally through role rotations, allowing companies to tap into the potential of their existing workforce and reduce the pressure of bringing in new talent.

IV. Relationship Between the User Experience Department and the Traditional Customer Service Department

In traditional enterprises, the roles of the Customer Service Department and the UX Department often overlap and create confusion. Typically, the Customer Service Department addresses user complaints and service-related issues. This raises a fundamental question: What is the relationship between a newly established UX Department and the existing Customer Service Department? Could expanding the scope of the Customer Service Department resolve the need for a UX Department? Broadly speaking, the key differences between these two departments can be summarized in five areas: work characteristics, evaluation standards, working methods and tools, underlying concepts and philosophies, and organizational structure:

Table 3-1 Comparison of labor by participant type at different stages

No.	Participant type	Stage	Work hours (person-days)	Total	Percentage
1	Product owner	Background research	23	95.5	21.3%
		Requirement analysis	11		
		Concept design	3.5		
		Design, development, testing, and launch	58		
2	Interaction designer	Information architecture design	16	55	12.3%
		Interaction design	29		
		Low-fidelity prototype design & testing	6		
		Interaction design review	2		
		Interaction design documentation	2		
3	Visual designer	Visual design	42	57	12.7%
		High-fidelity prototype design & testing	10		
		Visual design review	2		
		Slicing and design documentation	3		
4	Frontend developer	Development planning	8	61	13.6%
		Development model	25		
		Usability testing	3		
		Code development	25		
5	Test engineer	Unit testing	2	19	4.2%
		Script writing	5		
		Integration testing	5		
		Performance testing	2		
		Stress testing	5		
6	User researcher	Throughout the process	120	120	26.8%
7	Data engineer	Post-launch monitoring	40	40	8.9%
	Total			447.5	

(1) Different work characteristics. The Customer Service Department primarily focuses on responding to user-initiated service requests. Customer service representatives follow established processes to address these requests, assist in problem-solving, and resolve user concerns. This work is inherently reactive, as customer service is typically initiated only after an issue or question arises. While the department may cover pre-sales, sales, and post-sales processes, it operates almost exclusively by passively receiving user requests. Its nature resembles that of a "firefighter," addressing problems as they arise or after they have occurred.

Customer service relies on users actively reporting issues, meaning it addresses concerns only when users are significantly dissatisfied or in urgent need. Consequently, negative business experiences may not always reach the company's customer service team through complaints or other channels. Consequently, the user experience issues identified by customer service represent only a fraction of the actual scenario, with a significant portion of critical information lost in the process. For instance, a product with a low complaint volume may still face issues such as reduced user engagement or a shrinking customer base. Without access to comprehensive and accurate insights into actual user experiences, businesses struggle to analyze problems objectively and effectively, which often results in poorly informed solutions.

In contrast, the UX Department is proactive and involved from the earliest stages of product and service planning. It conducts user research to ensure that the products or services meet genuine user needs from the outset. UX professionals play a continuous role throughout the entire production process, evaluating and refining user experiences at every stage. This includes inviting real users to participate in trials and collecting firsthand feedback.

Companies that embrace this production approach empower their UX teams to thoroughly identify potential challenges users might face while interacting with the product or service. By doing so, these teams equip business departments with the foresight needed to proactively address and resolve these issues prior to the market launch. The ultimate goal of the UX Department is to create "instruction-free" and "customer service-free" products. The essence of UX work lies in enhancing the usability of products or services to minimize potential challenges for users, thereby significantly reducing the need for customer inquiries or complaints. This proactive and preemptive approach reflects a sincere commitment to prioritizing user needs, fostering a deep and lasting positive impression of the brand in the minds of customers.

(2) Different evaluation standards. In traditional customer service, performance is generally evaluated through two primary sets of metrics: complaint-

related indicators and satisfaction-related indicators. Complaint-related metrics refer to assessment indicators based on the number of complaints, such as the complaint rate (the number of complaints per 10,000 users) and escalation complaints (complaints made beyond the standard customer service channels). Satisfaction-related metrics, on the other hand, refer to indicators that measure the overall satisfaction level with the product or service.

However, complaint-related indicators fail to capture negative experiences that exist but do not trigger formal complaints from users. Satisfaction-related metrics, intended to complement complaint data, aim to assess the overall user attitude toward a product or service. Despite their intention, satisfaction metrics face three significant challenges in practice:

- Unclear definitions. Users often struggle to provide detailed feedback on specific aspects of the product due to ambiguous definitions of "satisfaction."
- Skewed results. Many users, aiming to avoid inconvenience, tend to give high ratings. However, a high score does not always reflect true satisfaction or a willingness to repurchase.
- Difficulty identifying dissatisfaction causes. Due to hurried survey responses, the reasons behind user dissatisfaction are often vague or missed.

These challenges undermine the value of satisfaction metrics, making conclusions derived from them unreliable and leading to reports that are overly generic.

In contrast, UX work employs more detailed and customized evaluation metrics that align with the specific nature of the business. Whether evaluating user interfaces, service efficiency, or physical hardware, UX assessments provide tailored criteria that fully explore the unique characteristics of each business line. This approach ensures that user experience across all aspects of product interaction is thoroughly recorded, analyzed, and understood. By integrating user expressions, verbal feedback, and physical behavior, UX analysis provides deeper and more accurate insights into real user experience. Furthermore, frequent interaction between UX teams and real users fosters a level of trust that encourages users to share honest and candid feedback.

As a result, UX research reports carry far greater relevance, offering not just problem identification but actionable solutions and recommendations. These reports serve as a valuable resource for businesses, providing clear paths for optimization and meaningful improvements to the product or service.

(3) Different work methods and tools. Due to their unique characteristics, the work methods, approaches, and tools of customer service and UX differ sig-

nificantly. Customer service primarily operates through channels like customer service representatives, online support, and retail staff to address customer concerns. The process is relatively monotonous, relying on predefined protocols and documentation, which limits the range of issues that can be resolved effectively.

In contrast, UX work is far more expansive. With a focus on delivering an exceptional user experience, UX professionals dive into not only surface-level concerns but also deeper, more subtle issues related to severity, detail, diversification and personalization of user needs. UX work is proactive by nature—teams engage with users in comfortable, informal settings like parks, cafés, or hotel lobbies, often through sincere, direct conversations to uncover underlying needs. This approach reveals issues users may not even be consciously aware of, allowing for solutions that directly address pain points, ultimately creating an experience that exceeds expectations.

Moreover, UX work requires a broader and more specialized range of tools compared to customer service. For example, user research often involves psychological and human-computer interaction instruments to gain insights. Specialized tools are used to measure users' visual and auditory experiences, while data analysis, modeling and mining rely on powerful processing tools. Additionally, user feedback is typically captured using advanced audio and video recording environment and equipment.

To facilitate ongoing user research, large internet companies often build dedicated architecture or rooms called "user experience chamber." These rooms are designed to provide a professional environment for research when in-house teams lack the resources for specialized setups. The decor of these rooms typically leans toward a cozy, home-like style, often complemented with small snacks, toys, and other items to create an atmosphere of safety, trust, comfort, and ease for user discussions.

(4) Different work concepts and philosophy. Both customer service and user experience share the overarching goal of solving user problems. However, user experience work encompasses a much broader scope. While customer service typically handles more serious issues that arise, user experience is focused on minimizing product-related problems from the outset, ensuring that users enjoy a seamless and satisfying experience right from their first interaction. In today's increasingly competitive market, even a small delay in meeting user expectations can have significant consequences. As a result, businesses are placing more emphasis on creating a positive "first impression" for their users. A strong first impression is crucial for encouraging continued use and future re-purchases. When this first impression falls short, users are often unwilling to give a second

chance and will quickly turn to better competing products. Therefore, customer service deals with complaints after negative experiences have occurred, whereas user experience works proactively to create positive experiences from the very beginning. This essential distinction, which was less apparent in the past when markets were monopolistic, has become more pronounced as the market landscape evolves. As such, customer service does not fit, and must adapt and transition toward a user experience-centered approach.

(5) Different involvement in the production process. Customer service typically operates in isolation from product development. While business departments may assign dedicated staff to handle customer complaints and develop customer service protocols, it remains largely detached from the core operations, particularly product development and service design.

In contrast, UX work is intricately woven into the entire business process, especially during product development. UX strategies, methods, and tools are embedded throughout the entire production cycle. This integration ensures that any insights or suggestions for improvement are directly applied during the creation of the product. As a result, businesses can significantly reduce rework costs and improve overall production efficiency. Rather than acting as a "quality inspector" after the product is developed, user experience serves as a "guarantor" of product quality throughout the entire process. Through continuous testing and massive data collection from real users, businesses gain a deep understanding of their target audience's core needs before the product even hits the market. This knowledge leads to more effective marketing and customer retention strategies. Ultimately, this approach saves on production and sales costs, enhances market performance, and greatly increases the likelihood of new product success. From an investment standpoint, this process also boosts the chances of a successful investment and offers a higher potential return. As a result, UX work holds a competitive edge over traditional customer service, becoming the key focus for businesses looking to improve customer relations.

Of course, beyond the differences highlighted, there are additional distinctions between the two functions. As businesses continue to evolve and adapt, in the long run, the lines between customer service and user experience will increasingly blur, with both areas gradually integrating. Each company should chart its own path to transformation, one that fits its unique circumstances, and in doing so, create new methods and models that will drive growth. We should always approach the issue of traditional business transformation with a forward-thinking mindset, confident in the immense potential for innovation and progress.

V. Evaluating Innovative Product Value in the Experience Economy

In an era of strong state support for entrepreneurship and the development of small and micro-enterprises, assessing the value of specific product lines has become a critical concern for both startup teams and investors. These emerging products and teams now serve as significant drivers of national economic growth, exerting an ever-increasing influence amid economic reforms. Consequently, product value evaluation is an inevitable topic when analyzing the experience economy from multiple perspectives.

In recent years, many startup teams have focused their core offerings on smartphone applications, utilizing the internet for dissemination and promotion. Using smartphone apps as a representative example, we can delve deeper into the evaluation of such product values.

Years of experience in internet product development reveal that the growth trajectory of a product's user base is a decisive factor influencing product valuation and, by extension, the valuation of the startup team. This section homes in on a specific subset of such products—mobile video apps—as a case study to explore product value evaluation.

i. Overview of Product Value Evaluation

Research into product value evaluation spans nearly a century, dating back to Irving Fisher's *The Nature of Capital and Income* (1906). In this seminal work, Fisher's exploration of the relationship between capital and income laid the groundwork for modern corporate valuation theory. By the 20th century, two valuation approaches emerged as dominant: the Modigliani-Miller theorem and the discounted cash flow (DCF) model, both of which remain foundational in economics education.

In the 21st century, Aswath Damodaran's *The Dark Side of Valuation* (2005) provided a tailored approach for assessing tech companies. Damodaran offered methodologies for estimating cash flows and discussed the feasibility and limitations of relative valuation, DCF, and real options approaches.

Extensive research, both domestic and international, has since established four major schools of corporate valuation theory:

(1) Cost approach (asset-based approach). The cost approach evaluates a company's current value by assessing its assets and liabilities, summing their values to calculate the total. This method includes techniques such as book value, liquidation value, and replacement cost.

(2) Income approach and derivatives. The income approach determines a company's value by discounting its anticipated future earnings to present value. This foundational concept has given rise to derivative methods, including cost-benefit models for high-risk scenarios, residual income models focusing on incremental gains, and customer value models based on discounted future cash flows from customers.
(3) Market comparison approach and derivatives. The market comparison method evaluates a company's value by referencing comparable entities in the market. This approach is divided into two key dimensions: comparable company analysis, which focuses on peer organizations, and comparable transaction analysis, which examines similar market transactions. However, finding two companies with identical conditions is virtually impossible, particularly for emerging enterprises that intentionally cultivate differentiated advantages to establish niche monopolies. Consequently, relying on existing market data to estimate the value of new and untested companies presents notable limitations.
(4) Option pricing approach and derivatives. The option pricing approach is a derivative of the income approach, combining the current value of assets with projections of future profitability. Widely used models include the Black-Scholes model and the binomial Cox-Ross-Rubinstein model. Like DCF methods, this approach emphasizes future growth potential.

In addition to these four traditional schools of thought, the rise of the internet era has ushered in user-centric valuation models. These models focus on analyzing the growth trends of user bases over time, leveraging life cycle value theories to assess user value, acquisition costs, and the overall input-output dynamics. These insights feed into cash flow discounting calculations, offering a modern and robust framework for evaluating enterprise value.

ii. Methods for Product Value Evaluation: A Case Study of Mobile Video Apps

1. Introduction to Mobile Video Apps

Mobile video apps are a category of applications designed for mobile devices, offering standalone video streaming capabilities. Prominent platforms, such as Youku, Sohu Video, and iQiyi, have all launched their own mobile video apps. These apps act as accessible portals to video resources, providing users with a seamless and convenient way to watch content anytime, anywhere.

As a subset of electronic information products, mobile video apps inherit core characteristics unique to digital products. Over the years, scholars have explored these traits extensively: Zhong Yixin, in *Principles of Information Science*, identified fundamental properties of information, including dynamicity, transmissibility, and transformability. Jing Jipeng emphasized the non-exclusivity of information products, arguing that "information embedded in products is not diminished or lost during transformation." He also identified traits such as non-depletability, timeliness, scalability, relativity, and experiential nature. Luo Zhengshan highlighted economic traits specific to information products, such as economies of scale, value uncertainty, asymmetry, and network externality. Zhu Zhu, in her comprehensive study of bit-based products, categorized bit-based product traits into foundational (e.g., intangibility, complexity, ease of replication), production-based (e.g., richness, economies of scale), consumption-based (e.g., non-depletability, scalability, experiential nature, network externality, and non-exclusivity), and exchange traits (e.g., asymmetry, value uncertainty, diverse exchange methods, and transmission convenience). Ma Qiunan added that digital information products are characterized by ease of replication, transmission convenience, and complexity.

Building on these insights, app products can be broadly categorized into two traits:

(1) Functional traits. These relate to the inherent attributes of the product and its operation, which serve as the foundation for economic traits. These include
- dependence on electronic devices as carriers;
- creation, storage, or dissemination in data format;
- strong extensibility and rapid evolution of functionality;
- dual roles as both tools and marketing/media channels.

(2) Economic traits. These emphasize the behaviors of the product in economic exchanges, distinguishing them from physical goods or services. They include
- unlimited replicability,
- low acquisition cost,
- rapid depreciation of differentiation advantages,
- strong influence of demand side factors on supply dynamics.

In addition to these general traits, mobile video apps exhibit three distinct characteristics:

(1) Integration of content, subscription, and social features. Mobile video apps can most comprehensively and centrally showcase the various characteristics of app products. Serving as platforms that aggregate vast video resources, they showcase one of the clearest commercial models among apps, generating revenue through multiple streams such as advertisements, direct content sales, and subscription services like monthly memberships.

(2) High user retention and stability. These apps tend to cultivate habitual, long-term user engagement, resulting in a relatively stable user base. Although temporary spikes or dips may occur due to short-term phenomena like popular shows, mobile video app products generally maintain a relatively stable user base. Variations in user numbers serve as a reliable indicator of changes in the product's functionality and usage patterns.

(3) Exceptional inclusiveness. These apps exhibit exceptional inclusiveness, offering content that appeals to a diverse audience across various age groups, regions, and demographics. Its wide accessibility ensures ease of use, even for young children or elderly individuals, requiring no complex operations—just a simple click to play. This inclusivity allows the product to reach a broader user base compared to other types of information products. As such, studying this category provides valuable insights into the behavioral patterns of the general population, lending the findings a strong sense of universality and credibility.

From a value assessment perspective, mobile video apps, as commodities, share commonalities with products in traditional industries. Fundamentally, they possess the potential for profitability by offering differentiated services that foster user engagement and habit formation, laying the groundwork for sustainable revenue. This profitability is typically expressed in two key dimensions: direct advertising and paid content offerings.

A significant portion of revenue for mobile video apps is derived from direct advertising. Advertisers typically use the following pricing models, as outlined in table 3-2.

Table 3-2 Overview of advertising payment market rates

Model	Description	Price
CPC	Cost per click	RMB 1
CPT/CPL	Cost per try	
CPA	Cost per action	RMB 1.5–3.5
CPS	Cost per sale	RMB 3–15
CPM	Cost per mile	RMB 3–6

In addition to these methods, other prevalent approaches include real-time bidding, fixed advertising slot rates, and compensated traffic exchanges.

Mobile video apps also generate revenue through paid content offerings, such as subscriptions (monthly, quarterly, or annual plans), pay-per-episode options, and pay-as-you-go traffic charges.

Regardless of the revenue model, a robust user base is essential. The growth trajectory of user numbers is a critical metric for analyzing product performance and return on investment. Furthermore, given the inherent profitability characteristics of mobile video app products, it is essential to classify the factors influencing user growth into three main categories: The first category includes proactive driving factors initiated by the product provider to achieve revenue goals swiftly. These factors mainly encompass marketing activities conducted at critical milestones and are typically the most significant contributors to rapid changes in user growth. We refer to these as marketing-driven factors. The second category involves external environmental influences that impact user numbers. These factors are usually passive, encompassing both positive and negative effects. We identify these as event-driven factors. The third category comprises natural growth factors stemming from the product itself, such as user experience and viewing habits, independent of external events or interventions. While special events may cause temporary fluctuations in user numbers, these typically stabilize once the events subside. Ultimately, the retention of users is determined by the product's quality and reputation. We classify these as natural growth factors.

Here, we will elaborate on these three categories of factors:

(1) Marketing-driven factors encompass a wide range of marketing activities that differ in type, timing, and format. The primary goal of these activities is to create a significant surge in user numbers by leveraging specific events or milestones. Common approaches include the following:

- Holiday marketing. Holiday marketing for mobile video apps focuses on timely release of holiday-themed content to create a festive ambiance. For example, Youku Video released a collection of holiday-themed videos around Christmas, and Sohu Video developed Christmas-themed channels and radio shows to attract new users through holiday-related topics.
- Event marketing. Event marketing revolves around trending topics and requires ad hoc planning based on current events. This type of marketing can be further categorized: major sports or award events; scientific breakthroughs, such as the commercialization of smart glasses, virtual reality (VR), near-field communication technologies, new discoveries in space exploration, or innovations in manned spaceflight and satellite launches; entertainment milestones, like the widespread popularity of a particular TV series or movie; and major disasters like earthquakes or tsunamis, or man-made crises like wars. These events often command immediate public attention, creating a short-term surge in engagement while requiring sustained follow-up efforts to maintain momentum. Event marketing and holiday marketing share a common goal: to ignite substantial user engagement and feedback around a specific topic within a defined timeframe. However, the two differ significantly in nature. While holiday marketing is typically planned in advance, event marketing often revolves around unexpected occurrences. As a result, event marketing requires swift responsiveness and effective follow-up to succeed. The speed and efficiency of a brand's reaction can significantly influence users' trust and loyalty. Apps that excel at providing timely, relevant information during unforeseen events are better positioned to attract and retain a robust user base. Additionally, there is another type of unforeseen event: major negative news involving specific brands. Examples include the melamine scandal, which impacted several companies, and the exposure during the annual *3.15 Consumer Rights Day* TV program, which highlights unethical business practices. Crisis Events usually hold dual impacts: Public trust in the implicated companies declines significantly, but competitors in the same industry may benefit from the loss of trust in the affected brands. To mitigate the impact of such crises, companies often implement tailored public relations strategies aimed at minimizing damage.
- Version release marketing. A hallmark of mobile video apps is their rapid iteration cycles, with quick bug fixes and frequent feature updates. Typically, minor updates are released every one to three weeks, while major upgrades may take three to six months to complete. Version release

marketing focuses on these significant updates, as product teams aim to inform users through advertising and other channels about new features and improvements, encouraging them to explore and engage with the app. This marketing approach often includes several effective strategies: pre-launch teasers, creating excitement by generating buzz and building anticipation for the upcoming features, often using scarcity and curiosity-driven tactics; selective rollouts, initially releasing new features to a small group of users, leveraging their feedback and sharing to inspire demand among the broader user base; and multifaceted promotions, highlighting new capabilities through diverse channels, such as promotional videos, influencer endorsements, and detailed user reviews or trial reports. Version release marketing is often combined with holiday and event-based campaigns to maximize its effectiveness, creating a powerful push to drive user growth.

(2) Event-driven factors refer to the direct impact that unexpected events can have on a product, independent of any proactive marketing strategies employed by the product team in response. Typically, even without coordinated marketing efforts, such events can still influence the user base of a product, either directly or indirectly. These factors primarily encompass the following:

- Brand impact from positive or negative events. The effect of sudden events and their spread can be observed through social media platforms such as Sina Weibo and Tencent Weibo, with an example being the Yihuang incident that occurred between September 16–25, 2010. Key factors influencing the level of attention and spread of the incident include those posts made closer to the event's occurrence tend to draw more attention from users, administrative actions can affect the quantity and nature of user expressions, and regions with better-developed internet services tend to see faster and broader dissemination of information. Questionnaire surveys reveal that following a trust crisis (negative event), companies that respond promptly and positively online tend to see higher brand sentiment and trust scores compared to those that do not. Proactive measures like apologies, product recalls, and other strategies can deepen consumers' emotional attachment to the brand, increasing brand loyalty and willingness to make purchases. Therefore, the influence of both positive and negative sudden events on the product's brand trust involves a complex web of factors. To fully understand how such events impact product revenue, considerable observation is needed. However, time remains one of the key elements that could lead to sharp, short-term changes in user numbers.

- Objective environmental events. These refer to external events—such as earthquakes, volcanic eruptions, wars, or economic crises—that can have significant consequences for products. Examples include a large-scale power outage in North America that crippled the information technology industry; a strike by electrical workers in South Africa that caused widespread disruption; and political unrest in Egypt, leading to emergency states in certain cities and regions. These unpredictable events can create significant impacts, often lasting for extended periods. In addition to such catastrophic events, changes in policies, prolonged economic stagnation or bubbles, rising unemployment, inflation, or friction from economic reforms can all have direct consequences on industries. For instance, the VAT reform implemented in recent years in China affected many sectors and, in turn, led companies to adjust their strategies, causing ripple effects across product lines. These shifts in revenue strategies directly influence product presentation and user experience, which ultimately impacts the variation in user numbers. However, these changes are not necessarily negative. During industry restructuring, resource optimization and realignment may lead to a shift in the target user demographic. As industries grow more specialized and marketing becomes more targeted, products can better serve specific, refined user groups. Even in the face of major disruptions like war or natural disasters, some industries may thrive and even see growth. As a result, the impact of such events must be analyzed in the context of the specific industry and situation at hand.

(3) Natural growth factors refer to growth driven by the inherent, natural course of events, without external or internal pressures. This includes cyclical growth, organic word-of-mouth expansion, and routine fluctuations. For example, the user base of mobile video apps generally exhibits cyclical patterns, with increased usage over weekends and subsequent decreases during weekdays. These cycles are often amplified during public holidays. When it comes to organic growth through word-of-mouth, mobile video apps require time to establish a strong reputation. Over time, well-crafted products tend to naturally attract a growing user base. Additionally, user numbers are subject to natural fluctuations. For instance, some users may be more active on weekends, meaning they are not counted among the active user base during

weekdays. However, this does not signify a loss of users. These minor variations in user engagement are part of the routine ebb and flow of app usage, thus referred to as natural fluctuations.

2. Overview of Key Metrics

The app industry utilizes a variety of metrics to describe user numbers. The most commonly employed metrics include the following:

(1) Cumulative total users: the total number of users who have installed the app.
(2) Registered users: the number of users who have installed the app and completed the registration.
(3) Monthly active users (MAU): the number of users (duplicates excluded) who have interacted with the app within a calendar month, such as opening or performing observable actions.
(4) Daily active users (DAU): the number of users (duplicates excluded) who have interacted with the app within a single calendar day, such as opening or performing observable actions.
(5) Monthly new users: the difference in total user count between the last day of the current month and the last day of the previous month.
(6) Daily new users: the difference in total user count between 24:00 and 00:00 of the same day.
(7) Monthly year-on-year user growth: the difference in user count between the current month and the same month in the previous year.
(8) Daily year-on-year user growth: the difference in user count between the current day and the same day in the previous year.

In addition to these metrics, growth rates, average usage frequency, and usage duration are often analyzed to assess trends and provide a comprehensive view of user number growth.

3. Value Assessment Methods of Mobile Video Apps

The value of a mobile video app can be evaluated as a result of various contributing factors. Typically, a mobile video app generates revenue from three primary sources: the app's download price (one-time payment), in-app purchases, and advertising income. Let R represent total revenue, P represent app download price, I represent in-app purchase revenue, and AD represent advertising revenue.

Thus, revenue can be expressed as

$$R = f(P, I, AD)$$

Below, we analyze each contributing factor over a one-year period.

(1) Revenue from app download price. The app's download price is generally fixed, as platforms like Apple's App Store do not permit arbitrary price adjustments. This simplicity makes download price revenue straightforward to calculate. Let I represent a positive integer, U_i represent the number of users who downloaded the app during the month I, and P represent the download price. The total annual revenue from downloads can be expressed as

$$P = \sum_{i=1}^{12} U_i \times p$$

Considering a monthly discount rate r, the net present value (NPV) of download price revenue can be expressed as

$$NPV(P) = \sum_{i=1}^{12} \frac{U_i \times p}{(1+r)^i}$$

(2) Revenue from in-app purchases. In-app purchase revenue I can be categorized into two components:

- Subscription services (I_{vip}). Users pay for subscription tiers (e.g., VIP_1, VIP_2, …, VIP_n) at respective prices (P_{vip1}, P_{vip2}, …, P_{vipn}). The number of users for each tier in a month is denoted by (u_{vip1}, u_{vip2}, …, u_{vipn}).
- Pay-per-view services (I_{ppv}). Users pay for individual content views (PPV_1, PPV_2, …, PPV_q) at respective prices (P_{ppv1}, P_{ppv2}, …, P_{ppvq}). The total number of content views for each PPV option in a month is denoted by (u_{ppv1}, u_{ppv2}, …, u_{ppvq}).

Total in-app purchase revenue is the sum of these two components:

$$I = I_{vip} + I_{ppv}$$

For a given month i, the respective components are

$$I_{vipi} = \sum_{x=1}^{n} p_{vipx} \times u_{vipx}$$

$$I_{ppvi} = \sum_{x=1}^{q} p_{ppvx} \times u_{ppvx}$$

Annual totals are

$$I_{vip} = \sum_{i=1}^{12} I_{vipi}$$

$$I_{ppv} = \sum_{i=1}^{12} I_{ppvi}$$

The future values of u_{vipx} and u_{ppvx} remain unknown parameters. To forecast these values, mathematical modeling can be customized based on actual data. Those interested in the detailed methodologies are encouraged to explore relevant professional literature. Take Tencent Video as an example. The app employs a simple subscription model, offering monthly, quarterly, and annual membership plans with tiered pricing. Subscribers gain unlimited access to content without additional fees. The user count for each tier (u_{vipx}) can be modeled using historical MAU data.

Considering discount rates, the NPV of in-app purchase revenue becomes

$$NPV(I_{vip}) = \sum_{i=1}^{12} \frac{I_{vipi}}{(1+r)^i}$$

$$NPV(I_{ppv}) = \sum_{i=1}^{12} \frac{I_{ppvi}}{(1+r)^i}$$

$$NPV(I) = NPV(I_{vip}) + NPV(I_{ppv})$$

(3) Advertising revenue. Mobile video apps typically generate advertising revenue through several mainstream models:

- CPM (cost per mille, cost per thousand, or cost per impressions). Revenue is calculated based on every thousand ad impressions.
- CPT (cost per try). Revenue is based on the number of trials or attempts. This model, commonly used by mobile app marketing platforms, charges advertisers based on user engagement duration or usage cycles rather than only impressions or activations. It effectively prevents fraudulent traffic and fake activations, making it one of the most authentic and effective marketing strategies.
- CPC (cost per click). Charges are incurred for every click on the ad. By incorporating click-through rate restrictions, this model minimizes fraudulent activities. Each click delivers genuine traffic or potential customers, making it a preferred model in mature digital markets.

- CPA (cost per action). Revenue is tied to specific user actions, such as registering, logging in, favoriting items, or completing purchases.
- CPS (cost per sale). Revenue is based on the number of actual sales generated. Advertisers mitigate advertising cost risks by paying commissions only for successful sales following an ad click.

Let's assume the app uses only the CPM model (other models can be added in similar calculations). If the cost per thousand impressions is P_{cpm} and the impression frequency is q_i (calculated as the product of the number of advertising slots multiplying the display frequency for each slot), the advertising revenue is expressed as

$$I_{AD} = \sum_{i=1}^{365} p_{cpm} \times \frac{DAU_i}{1000} \times q_i$$

Considering the discount rate, let r_d represent the daily discount rate derived from the annualized yield. The NPV of advertising revenue is

$$NPV(I_{AD}) = \sum_{i=1}^{365} p_{cpm} \times \frac{DAU_i}{1000 \times (1 + r_d)^i} \times q_i$$

Here, DAU can be modeled and forecasted using historical data.

(4) Value assessment model for mobile video apps. Based on the preceding analysis, the value assessment model for a mobile video app is structured as

$$R = P + I + I_{AD}$$

Incorporating discounting, the formula becomes

$$NPV(R) = NPV(P) + NPV(I) + NPV(I_{AD})$$

This equation provides the app's NPV. During the product value assessment process, product teams and investors can refine these calculations to align with their specific evaluation standards and requirements. By adopting both static and dynamic perspectives, they can perform more comprehensive analyses and make better-informed decisions.

VI. Brief Discussion on Supply-Side Reform in Experience Economy

Over the past four decades of reform and opening up, as China's economy has surged, the limitations of the traditional development model have gradually become apparent. With the overall rise in national income, people's focus has shifted from addressing basic survival needs to enhancing quality of life and increasing overall life satisfaction. Issues such as severe pollution from certain industries, the slowing growth of mid- to low-end products, the insufficient supply of high-end products, overcapacity, and imbalanced industrial development have come to the forefront. Against this backdrop, the concept of supply-side reform has emerged as a key strategic approach for national economic adjustment, garnering increasing attention.

The imbalances on the supply side are rooted in significant shifts on the demand side. The original supply model was tailored to meet the previous demand model. This approach successfully fueled China's rapid economic expansion for over forty years. From an objective standpoint, during this period, the supply model achieved its intended development goals and was aligned with the demand patterns of the time. However, the current issues in production arise from profound changes in societal demand content and mode. When the supply side fails to adapt to these changes, frictional problems inevitably emerge. The challenges we see today are only part of a larger picture, with many latent issues waiting to surface, potentially leading to crises. Therefore, before delving into supply-side reform, it is crucial to first conduct a thorough and detailed analysis of the demands of the new era.

As the national economy increasingly embodies the characteristics of an experience economy, the supply-demand relationship is gradually transitioning to one driven by experience. As people's needs evolve toward personalization, customization, and fragmentation, and as individuals awaken to their own preferences and seek unique lifestyles, the traditional model of mass-produced goods and services struggles to meet this new diversity and uncertainty in demand. The direct consequence of this mismatch is that products produced under the old manufacturing model (whether consumer goods or various production materials and components) no longer align with consumer needs, resulting in excessive inventory and wasted resources. This, in turn, leads to a drop in sales revenue, which affects overall business performance and forces companies to reduce costs, even lowering wages for employees. Faced with this pressure, businesses may resort to taking on debt to cover shortfalls. The increasing debt burdens raise a company's leverage ratio, heightening overall business risks.

On the other hand, in the past, due to lower overall living standards, consumer demand for goods was less demanding. People prioritized affordability, which led to a higher tolerance for lower-quality products. Manufacturers, in turn, responded by supplying products that were cost-effective but of lower quality. However, as the advantages of high-volume and low-margin production diminish, issues such as low customer loyalty and low repeat purchase rates begin to surface, especially when confronted with superior products from international competitors. The traditional advantages of low-cost production are gradually eroded, and improvements in production processes require significant investment, raising product prices. In some cases, such improvements necessitate lengthy research and development cycles. These challenges leave traditional manufacturers struggling to respond effectively to the fast-evolving market. The resulting stagnation in manufacturing directly impacts employment, residents' incomes, and, ultimately, market demand. As a result, the entire market enters a vicious cycle.

Another significant factor exacerbating current challenges is the weak willingness of consumers to spend, which keeps overall demand stagnant. Consumer willingness is primarily influenced by income levels and expectations of future security. Looking back at human history, the fundamental driver of economic activity has often been the competition for resources. This competition stems from the inherent belief that life's essentials are scarce—without diligent efforts to amass wealth, securing a stable future is uncertain.

In eras of low productivity, limited capacity to combat natural disasters, and constrained ability to extract resources, humanity's survival instincts naturally drove societies to operate within this framework. However, resource competition ultimately results in imbalances in distribution due to differences in individual capabilities. When significant resources concentrate in the hands of a few, the majority face increasing scarcity, further intensifying competition.

With advancements in productivity, technological progress enabling renewable resources to replace non-renewable ones, and global population control measures, Earth's finite resources now have the potential to meet humanity's basic needs. Yet, resource possession and exploitation persist, fueled by uncertainty and insecurity about the future. If these uncertainties were eliminated and every individual was guaranteed sufficient material supply, would the basis for resource competition cease to exist?

Historically, regardless of the era, country, political system, or governance structure, societies have consistently experienced imbalances where a minority controls resources far exceeding their needs, while the majority struggles for basic sustenance. The surplus in resources for some inevitably leads to waste, while scarcity for others results in dire hardship. To address these disparities, humanity has often resorted to extreme measures—political movements, wars, and uprisings—that deepen societal divisions, sow hatred, and exacerbate conflict. To prevent such tragedies at their root, the societal model must undergo a profound transformation.

Imagine a future society characterized by the following features:

(1) Diet. Smart systems in residential spaces monitor individuals' physiological indicators, calculating daily nutritional quota. Food extraction is limited to this calculated threshold, with warnings issued for insufficient consumption. Leftover food is recycled into other usable resources through resource recycling systems.
(2) Clothing. Customized garments are instantly created around the body using advanced technologies like jets, tailored to preferences for material and style. Clothing can be updated as needed, with discarded items broken down into reusable materials.
(3) Housing. High-rise architecture—above ground, underground, or aerial—provides diverse housing options. Controlled per capita living space, combined with smart systems for temperature and humidity regulation, renders location and floor level less critical. Smart homes enable flexible and convenient interior customization.
(4) Transportation. People travel at near-zero cost without the need to own vehicles, instead renting transportation tools on-demand.
(5) Healthcare. Continuous health monitoring through scans in homes or public spaces enables real-time adjustments in diet and medication, reducing illness and allowing for early diagnosis and treatment.

Generally, in a society of this kind, all individual needs are precisely met while preserving autonomy within reasonable bounds. When individuals are assured that their lifetime necessities will be fully and effectively guaranteed, the desire to compete for and hoard resources diminishes. Over time, this mindset fades entirely. Recycling technologies would complement production advancements, enabling efficient global resource utilization.

In this envisioned world, aside from a select group focused on advancing and innovating automated production technologies, the vast majority of humanity's intellectual resources can be liberated from material production processes, and redirected toward significant progress in spiritual and cultural pursuits.

If this society represents our ultimate developmental goal, the pressing question becomes how we transition from the current state toward this vision. What aspects of the supply side need to change, and how should those changes be implemented? What key components are still missing to bridge the gap? By addressing these questions, we can start to explore the foundational challenges of supply-side reform and begin formulating actionable solutions for specific issues.

When discussing supply-side reforms, the primary concerns typically include the overcapacity of low- and mid-range products, deleveraging, and the imbalance in industrial structure. Much like diagnosing a medical condition, these issues represent only the visible symptoms. To truly resolve them, it is crucial to look deeper, uncover the root causes, and eliminate the underlying factors responsible for these problems. At the heart of China's economic imbalance lies five key challenges that are exacerbating the situation:

(1) There is greater income disparity and the low- and middle-income groups remain dominant. The widening gap between the wealthy and the rest of the population has resulted in a concentration of wealth among a small segment, while the majority of people, particularly in lower-income brackets, continue to struggle. The wealthy, due to concerns about housing, investments, and future financial security, are unable to reinvest their surplus wealth into the economy through consumption. Meanwhile, low- and middle-income individuals, burdened by high costs for housing, social security, and basic living, often resort to borrowing just to meet daily expenses, limiting their disposable income and ability to contribute to further economic activity.

(2) As economic growth progresses, overall income levels have risen, leading to heightened expectations for the quality of consumer goods and a growing demand for personalized products and services. The once-popular low-cost, low-quality products are losing their market competitiveness. When domestically produced mid- and high-end products cannot meet the growing demand or fail to match quality standards, globalization drives consumers to seek better-quality imports. This trend further undermines the survival of domestic goods in the market. As trade barriers loosen, both domestic and international markets for Chinese products face intensifying competi-

tion, especially from emerging third-world nations like India, Vietnam, and Brazil.

(3) The overproduction of low-end products and means of production has resulted in a significant buildup of unsold inventory, which cannot be converted into revenue. This has led to a downturn in businesses and related industries, causing a decline in employee wages and an increase in unemployment. The challenge of effectively reabsorbing or managing the unemployed further diminishes the overall purchasing power of residents, exacerbating the economic slowdown.

(4) There are wasting resources across various consumer groups, from food and clothing to electronics and vehicles, with many products going unused or unconverted. This waste leads to a substantial drain on the nation's production capacity. By improving the efficiency of recycling and reusing surplus goods, society could mitigate the enormous waste of resources and significantly reduce societal losses.

(5) Through the influence of media, education, and public opinion, there has been an increasing emphasis on borrowing for consumption, particularly as housing costs escalate. This has led to a rising debt burden within society. Financial tools that were once used by businesses to improve efficiency or address short-term cash flow issues have now infiltrated household finances. While a healthy economy can sustain some level of leverage, excessive borrowing creates significant risks. When leverage reaches a critical threshold, it can trigger substantial economic risks.

To address these challenges, the first priority should be to streamline and reduce the scale of low-end product industries, while facilitating the conversion of excess capacity. When production reaches saturation and the sales environment continues to deteriorate, it is crucial to reduce output. This serves a dual purpose: It helps to prevent the further accumulation of inventory backlogs while also managing financial deficits, keeping corporate leverage ratios and losses within manageable limits. This strategy ensures the temporary survival of businesses, allowing them to maintain operations. Even with certain cost reductions, it safeguards the majority of jobs and supports the continuity of daily operations. The primary challenges during this process will be how to manage the unemployment caused by cost reductions, how to maximize the conversion of surplus inventory into value, and how to invest time and resources in developing new technologies and products that align with market demands.

To effectively support unemployed individuals, solutions must be stratified and tailored to the demographic and skill level of the affected population. For individuals with lower educational attainment, those showing potential for growth should be offered opportunities for vocational training and education in emerging industries. This will enhance their employability and facilitate their transition to other sectors, particularly in emerging fields. Older individuals who are less likely to benefit from further education can be guided back to agriculture to strengthen the primary sector or redirected to labor-intensive roles in service-oriented industries. For those with moderate to high educational qualifications, their existing knowledge and technical skills should be assessed to place them strategically in relevant roles across various industries.

Addressing the surplus inventory issue requires fostering a new industry to bridge the gap between excess production capacity and consumer demand. This industry is not born out of thin air; rather, it has developed a solid foundation through the accumulation of past economic activities and now requires intensified efforts for further growth.

As the characteristics of the experience economy gradually emerge in economic activities, industries are increasingly dedicating resources to in-depth research focused on user experience, with a particular emphasis on meeting consumer needs. This shift has given rise to a new category of professionals within companies: user experience specialists. In some organizations, these professionals operate as dedicated teams or departments, while in others, they are embedded within various business units. The level of specialization and centralized management of these teams reflects the importance a company places on the "user-centric" philosophy.

The rapid growth of the internet industry, coupled with intensifying competition among similar products, has compelled businesses to form dedicated user research teams to navigate rapidly changing markets. These specialized groups, emerging across sectors, collectively form a growing force in the macroeconomic landscape. Many entrepreneurial teams and ventures have originated from new insights gained during user research, leading to the development of innovative products that address specific needs and unlock new market opportunities.

This highlights the rise of a new "user-centric" industry in the experience economy era. The primary role of this industry is to match surplus production capacity, including industrial byproducts and discarded items, with consumer needs. By layering and matching user demands based on demographic traits and preferences, the industry can optimize resource allocation to meet diverse levels of demand.

In an age where automation and AI increasingly streamline production processes, the user experience industry stands out as uniquely reliant on human creativity and insight. This makes it less susceptible to replication and positions it as a promising sector for absorbing the workforce displaced by contracting industries.

The industry's core focus is on understanding genuine human needs. Therefore, the required skill set for professionals in this field is not strictly tied to formal education. Even individuals with lower educational backgrounds can effectively contribute to demand research and insights.

Another vital industry deserving attention and poised for significant progress in the future is the energy recycling and reuse sector. As global population growth stabilizes, ensuring that production can meet humanity's basic needs will make purely consumptive or predominantly consumptive production models increasingly unsustainable. Consequently, the repeated utilization of existing energy and resources becomes critically essential.

Currently, China's energy recycling and reuse industry holds immense potential for growth in areas such as technological innovation, research and development, and industrial scaling. Throughout a production cycle, the production and usage of non-degradable materials (such as synthetic plastics) should be significantly reduced—or even entirely eliminated—and replaced with degradable, recyclable alternatives.

If energy reuse efficiency metrics were established as KPIs for the national economy, they could profoundly drive advancements in the sector. This emerging industry also offers considerable employment opportunities and creates new value streams, making it a key pathway for absorbing the labor force displaced during industrial restructuring.

The growth of these two industries rests on another transformative field: AI. AI technologies have the potential to revolutionize automation and intelligent control systems. This technological foundation serves as a powerful enabler, offering robust capabilities for data storage, analysis, and value transformation in the user experience industry, which centers on human-focused research. Simultaneously, it provides essential mechanical support to advance the energy recycling industry.

In particular, AI can tackle tasks unsuitable for humans, such as recycling toxic and hazardous substances, conducting operations in extreme environments (e.g., high or low temperature and pressure conditions), and managing large-scale transportation or material transfers. Moreover, as AI evolves to exhibit emotional intelligence, smart systems will be able to detect and interpret human emotions with remarkable accuracy. Through data processing and analysis, it provides crucial support for human needs assessment and analysis.

Challenges related to the time and costs required for developing new products can be mitigated through strategic approaches tailored to specific circumstances. In an increasingly segmented market, opportunities for cross-disciplinary collaboration in technology and product innovation are expanding.

On the one hand, businesses can increase internal R&D input and employ agile development methodologies to iteratively refine products. On the other hand, they can leverage market dynamics to identify potential collaborators, pooling complementary strengths to enhance mutual value. Such partnerships can involve large-scale research institutions with great strength or individual specialists with niche expertise.

Through effective market-driven resource matching and selecting, companies can discover new pathways to innovation while closely tracking emerging trends. This dual approach ensures that independent R&D initiatives are strategically guided to the correct direction.

Production modes must shift from standardized, template-based approaches to demand-driven production, which tailors production processes to meet specific user needs. This model not only fosters a sense of respect and participation among users but also enables enterprises to precisely manage production costs. By aligning resource allocation with user orders, businesses can eliminate resource surpluses, reduce stockpiling, and minimize waste.

This transition redefines the role of enterprises from mere producers to resource integrators. Each company focuses on its core competencies—manufacturing its signature products or components—while relying on partners to supply supplementary materials. With advancements in transportation reducing delivery times and risks, quick resource allocation becomes a more efficient choice. User-driven orders provide real-time insights into customer preferences, allowing companies to swiftly renew their production, assembly, and distribution chains. Therefore, as consumers increasingly seek personalized products and develop a clearer understanding of their needs, demand-driven production becomes the supply model that fits the demand model. This innovative alignment between demand and supply eliminates many of the inefficiencies inherent in traditional supply systems, paving the way for a fundamental transformation of production structures.

Successfully tackling the issue of overcapacity in low-end production can generate profound economic benefits across four dimensions:

(1) Excess stock can be converted into economic value, generating positive cash flows that stabilize enterprise operations and restore healthy production cycles.
(2) Workers displaced from saturated industries can find opportunities in emerging sectors, contributing fresh capabilities and energy to the economy.
(3) Healthier operation reduces enterprise debt ratios, alleviating the risks associated with high leverage.
(4) Optimizing industrial structures increases workforce productivity, leading to higher incomes and ultimately household debt pressures easing. In turn, consumer purchasing power rises, fueling growth across all sectors. Lower debt levels for both businesses and households also reduce the overall economic leverage burden.

Throughout this period of structural adjustment, media guidance and educational initiatives will serve as vital support mechanisms. In the realm of ideological education, efforts should be made to encourage businesses and households to manage their debt ratios responsibly. At the same time, enhancing social security systems can bolster consumer confidence, motivating middle- and high-income groups to expand their spending.

As industries undergo restructuring, both media and education should focus on promoting and raising awareness about emerging sectors. In education, it is essential to establish specialized disciplines aligned with these new industries, fostering a pipeline of skilled professionals to support industrial upgrades. On the media front, public campaigns should aim to instill proper values and responsible consumption habits while emphasizing the interdependence of demand and supply in economic operations.

With the collective efforts of all sectors of the national economy, China's supply-side reform is poised to achieve remarkable progress in the near future.

CHAPTER IV

Social Development in the Experience Economy

I. Essence of the Experience Economy: Ultimate Care for Humanity

The experience economy centers on experience, which, in turn, revolves around people. For centuries, human thought and philosophy have been deeply rooted in humanity itself. Even the natural sciences, which seek to decipher the laws of the universe, ultimately aim to help humans understand themselves, comprehend their surroundings, and harness the environment for progress and transformation.

From the very beginning of human existence, we have persistently grappled with three fundamental questions: understanding oneself, understanding others, and understanding the universe. Despite millennia of exploration, thought, and debate, these questions remain elusive and unresolved. In the pursuit of answers, humanity has created an array of concepts and terms to classify and name the phenomena of life. These linguistic and conceptual tools have become essential mechanisms for understanding the world.

However, the proliferation of these concepts and terms has also introduced limitations. Over time, they have diversified, forming an intricate web that confines many within its parameters. This, in turn, has led to a disconnect between the tangible realities of the world and the abstract constructs created to interpret it. These concepts often foster an illusion of certainty, making people believe they have "discovered the answers" and allowing them to live within a constructed reality shaped by these perceived truths. Yet, this illusion is fragile.

When individuals realize that these conceptual answers fail to address their deeper, subconscious insecurities, they encounter confusion and disorientation. This existential uncertainty spawns a cascade of blind exploration and impulsive actions, further complicating the surface dynamics of human society.

Among the myriad challenges confronting humanity, survival has always taken precedence due to its direct influence on existence and quality of life. Inevitably, humans have focused first on addressing the fundamental problem of survival before turning to more abstract contemplations. However, the path to ensuring survival revealed a world fraught with uncertainty. Not all plants were edible; animals appeared unpredictably, and natural disasters could strike at any moment.

In their pursuit of sustenance, warmth, and shelter, humans discovered that life-sustaining resources were scarce and often unpredictable. This realization compelled them to accumulate as much as possible. Witnessing frequent mortality among their peers, they associated survival with security, a natural response to the pervasive fear of death. To safeguard this primal sense of security, people began storing food and clothing and securing shelter. They also vied for mates, recognizing reproduction as the only means to perpetuate their lineage and ensure their legacy. Expanding one's family and descendants became the most effective strategy for broadening territorial influence.

The discovery of agriculture and the ability to cultivate certain foods offered a measure of stability to counterbalance the uncertainties of hunting. However, this newfound stability gave rise to competition over arable land. Thus, human society evolved into one centered on the accumulation and competition for survival resources. This dynamic became the foundation for centuries of development, shaping the trajectory of civilization.

But is human existence truly only about solving the problem of survival? Once survival is no longer an issue, what purpose remains for those who are alive? In truth, no matter how many resources a person possesses, the amount they can genuinely use or meaningfully engage with during their lifetime is limited. This usable portion often constitutes only a small fraction of what they own and is generally manageable. After all, every aspect of life has its natural boundaries: overeating leads to discomfort, digestive issues, and illness; maintaining excessively large or numerous homes is burdensome, and one cannot occupy a different residence every day; even in the harshest winters, the amount of clothing required for warmth is finite, with additional items serving only for variety rather than necessity.

Such realizations inevitably prompt deeper questions: Why do I exist, and why do those around me exist? It is within this context of reflection that religious ideas begin to emerge.

Through observing the world, humans have long recognized the presence of powerful forces beyond their control. Natural disasters—volcanic eruptions, earthquakes, storms, tsunamis, wildfires, floods, and avalanches—along with predatory animals, constantly threatened human survival. Within human communities, certain individuals stood out as stronger, displaying exceptional physical prowess, intellectual acumen, or charismatic leadership, which enabled them to gather others around them. People discovered that aligning with such individuals increased their chances of survival compared to living in isolation. Being part of a group also provided greater safety. Over time, independent individuals began forming tribes and communities through bloodlines and cooperative relationships.

In these communities, the strongest naturally became leaders, those with particular talents served as advisers, and the less capable assumed submissive roles (sometimes as slaves). Thus, primitive social hierarchies emerged. The dynamics between these social strata—domination and subjugation—ensured that those at the top enjoyed greater control over resources and authority over others.

To the average person, the natural and social phenomena they couldn't control were daunting and mysterious. Confronted with the incomprehensible, they experienced primal fear and an urgent need for explanations to ease their anxiety. Otherwise, the persistent confusion would be unbearable. This gave rise to a profound idea: Perhaps forces beyond human understanding govern these phenomena.

Concepts such as "God," "Lord," and "Master" began to take shape. Stronger individuals in society—those who plundered resources, wielded power, or exercised control—were perceived as being favored or chosen by these divine forces. This led to the belief that their extraordinary status stemmed from a special connection with the gods or higher powers.

In this way, everyone found an explanation: Leaders justified their rule by claiming divine endorsement, rationalizing their actions as aligned with the will of the gods. Followers accepted these narratives, finding solace in their circumstances and choosing to live in peace. Together, people enriched the narrative with characters, events, and details, making it more compelling and believable.

Therefore, almost all religions share a similar framework: A supreme deity ("God," "Buddha," or other names) governs all, establishes universal rules, serves as the ultimate arbiter of conflict, and controls not only the living world but also the afterlife. In polytheistic systems, gods are often divided into ranks or responsibilities, but a singular supreme deity ultimately presides over everything. People believed their fortunes were determined by the favor or disfavor of these deities: prosperity was a reward for virtue and piety, while misfortune was attributed to vice or impiety.

To earn divine favor, people engaged in acts of worship, including rituals, offerings, and prayers, often mediated by individuals believed to have close connections to the divine. Leaders, commonly regarded as "sons of heaven," "emperors," or "children of God," were seen as earthly representatives of these deities and thus received reverence and material support.

By linking individual well-being to religious observance, people found ways to rationalize their circumstances. Those who thrived attributed their success to their virtue and devotion, while those who suffered saw their struggles as consequences of personal failings or insufficient piety. This narrative allowed individuals to accept their roles in society, enabling rulers to exercise power confidently and the masses to accept their positions. This created a temporary equilibrium in social life.

However, when rulers became excessively tyrannical, surpassing the population's tolerance, uprisings of the poor inevitably followed, so as to survive. Revolutionaries often framed their actions as divinely sanctioned, presenting themselves as agents of the gods and claiming to "carry out heaven's will." This provided moral justification for rebellion, perpetuating a cyclical pattern of upheaval and restoration. As a result, this dynamic of belief and action has shaped the course of human societal development.

However, not everyone fully accepts or finds solace in these theories; some come to realize that the world's rules are far more intricate. In the material realm, they question the existence of "God" and embark on a journey of exploration, uncovering natural laws through relentless practice and experimentation. This quest has spurred the rise and significant advancements of natural sciences.

In the realm of the mind, such individuals uncover vast, unexplored territories and subconscious dimensions beyond what is defined or extended by language and words. These uncharted regions do not merely recombine past memories but also birth ideas that transcend experience. The origins of this creativity are elusive, appearing as though drawn from "nothingness," yet the results exude boundless vitality and innovation.

The interplay between the material world and the spiritual realm has long been a topic of diverse perspectives. On the one hand, the material world predates human existence, operating on principles that often elude control. On the other hand, human agency demonstrates a remarkable capacity to reshape and transform material reality. This dynamic has led to four principal schools of thought:

(1) Materialism. Matter is fundamental and determines the nature of the mind.
(2) Idealism. The mind is primary, shaping and defining the material world.
(3) Consciousness-only perspective. Found in traditions like Buddhist Yogācāra philosophy, this view posits that matter and mind are inherently unified, influencing and transforming each other under specific conditions.
(4) Emptiness doctrine. A perspective that asserts both matter and mind are ultimately void and illusory.

Human society is shaped by these divergent beliefs and their inevitable intersections:

(1) Religious conflicts. Competing narratives and faiths about various deities fuel inter-religious disputes.
(2) Worldview conflicts. Differing opinions on whether matter or mind is primary create philosophical divides.
(3) Methodological conflicts. Disagreements over productivity techniques and innovation approaches generate methodological disputes.
(4) Class conflicts. Social stratifications lead to struggles between different classes and power dynamics.
(5) Economic conflicts. Differing ideologies regarding the allocation of limited resources spark economic debates and rivalries.

These five areas of contention form the core tensions in human society. Over time, their layers of sedimentation, fermentation, and intensification—coupled with the subdivision and fragmentation of issues—have deepened human divisions, leading to perpetual conflict. These struggles manifest at all levels, from familial disputes to global conflicts, replaying endlessly in diverse forms. Faced with the dual weight of survival pressures and pervasive conflicts, humanity finds itself in a state of collective suffering. Responses to this suffering vary:

(1) Direct confrontation. Some choose to face struggles head-on, often exacerbating tensions.
(2) Partial concession. Others seek temporary reprieve by compromising, achieving momentary stability.

(3) Retreat. Some retreat entirely, isolating themselves from the chaos in search of peace.

Yet none of these approaches can wholly escape the intrinsic conflicts of human society. Even avoidance or self-restraint is merely another form of struggle.

To elevate the collective happiness of humanity, the ultimate goal lies in dissolving conflicts and fostering a renewed integration of society. At its essence, the experience emphasizes guiding individuals through transformative experience, nurturing profound empathy, compassion, and genuine care for others. This authentic concern for the needs and well-being of others emerges as the only viable path to resolve discord and achieve harmony.

In a world where maximizing personal gain dominates the collective mindset, the solution is to intertwine individual and communal interests. By designing systems where one's well-being is directly linked to fulfilling the needs of others, individuals are encouraged—indeed compelled—to develop and sustain a habit of caring for others as a means of securing their own fulfillment.

The experience economy essentially strives to offer a perspective grounded in ultimate human care. From this vantage point, it endeavors to establish innovative rules and mechanisms that foster unity and counteract forces of fragmentation. Unlike conventional acts of charity—such as donations or material aid—that address only surface-level issues, the experience economy targets the root by reshaping attitudes and lifestyles. It seeks to build systems that inspire individuals to uncover and create value, contribute their labor and ingenuity, and achieve self-sufficiency through serving others. This approach fosters a sustainable cycle of mutual benefit, paving the way for a society characterized by enhanced collective happiness.

So, how does experience economy realize these goals? What ability does it have to address humanity's long-standing challenges?

First, in experience economy, the value of goods is intrinsically tied to the transformation of experiential value. When experiences deteriorate, the perceived value of goods diminishes, and transaction prices inevitably follow suit. This dynamic means that a decline in the quality of consumer experiences directly impacts the supplier's earnings. To secure greater profitability, suppliers are compelled to enhance the quality of the experiences their goods provide, creating a positive feedback loop. In this context, a supplier's success is almost entirely dictated by the consumer's level of satisfaction. Unsustainable practices or fraudulent behavior can trigger a widespread decline in consumer experience, leading to a significant erosion of trust and, consequently, profits. Faced with such risks, suppliers have no choice but to prioritize the delivery of products that offer exceptional experiential value.

This profit-driven mechanism evolves into a constructive force, motivating suppliers to deeply understand human needs and continually refine their products and services within the limits of sustainable production resources. Inefficient or unethical businesses will naturally phase out, while exceptional businesses will flourish, creating more job opportunities.

Second, as productivity continues to advance and the basic needs of the majority are sufficiently met, human consciousness is bound to evolve from a focus on material well-being to a deeper pursuit of spiritual fulfillment. When survival is no longer at risk, and fundamental needs such as food, clothing, shelter, and transportation are adequately addressed, the relentless quest for material possessions naturally subsides. This shift arises from the inherent limitations of material needs for any individual. It is only under the shadow of uncertainty about the future that people feel compelled to accumulate resources for survival. However, when material abundance is no longer in question and population levels are sustainably managed, individuals come to realize that their essential needs have been adequately met. In this realization, the act of further accumulation loses its allure, redirecting human focus toward more meaningful pursuits.

Freed from the demands of material preoccupations, people channel their energy into seeking spiritual satisfaction and rebuilding the connections between individuals, as well as between humanity and the world around them. The divisions, conflicts, and struggles once driven by material ambitions become irrelevant. Instead, new priorities emerge: "Am I truly happy? Are those around me happy? Are others in society living fulfilling lives? Is the relationship between us and nature getting better?"

Third, a fundamental transformation will occur in how people see and understand their own needs and those of their loved ones. Before making a purchase, individuals will begin to consider the true purpose of their purchase. For example, in the past, shopping often revolved around fulfilling basic needs like food and clothing while also catering to a sense of social comparison, leading to the acquisition of items that appeared "unique" or "status-enhancing."

In a world guided by experiential values, purchasing decisions will increasingly focus on genuine needs and the well-being of oneself and loved ones. People will pay closer attention to factors such as the nutritional balance of their diets, the safety and quality of household goods, the fit and comfort of clothing, and whether their choices convey care and warmth to others. Moreover, individuals will find value in personally contributing to the creation of goods, resulting in items imbued with emotional significance. Examples include making clothes for children, crafting keepsakes for loved ones that carry shared memories, or creating meaningful objects for family members. This focus on personal expression will lead to further segmentation of goods and services, particularly in their emotional and spiritual dimensions. With a different motive, this segmentation fosters unity instead of division. Much like the neutral nature of scientific advancements, segmentation itself is not inherently divisive. Rather, it reflects the fulfillment of diverse human needs. What ultimately determines unity or division is people's mindset. When individuals engage in conflict over resources due to competing desires, society fragments. However, when people prioritize collective well-being and choose products and services that enhance happiness for themselves and others, diversity becomes a force for societal cohesion.

Fourth, humanity's understanding of its relationship with nature will undergo a profound shift. Experiential needs will drive a universal desire for clean, harmonious, and sustainable environments, fostering a closer integration between society and the natural world.

In an experience-driven economy, development will no longer be measured by speed but by holistic indicators of well-being, with environmental factors playing a central role. As people seek higher-quality air, water, food, and green living spaces, their respect for nature will grow. This respect will curb the relentless exploitation of natural resources, replacing it with sustainable practices. Efforts will focus on preserving untouched natural areas, restoring urbanized lands to their ecological states, planting trees, and rehabilitating polluted or damaged regions. Energy production will see a significant shift toward clean and renewable sources, reducing and eventually eliminating reliance on nonrenewable and polluting resources. A new relationship with nature will emerge, defined by respect, coexistence, and mutual benefit.

Fifth, scientific and technological progress will aim to maximize automation in material production, with AI playing a crucial role in this transformation. Concurrently, science and technology will increasingly explore spiritual dimensions, delving into the interplay between the physical and metaphysical laws governing the universe.

In conclusion, the experience economy represents a transformative approach aligned with the new phase of human societal evolution. Its rise and development will advance both the material and spiritual dimensions of humanity, ultimately propelling society to unprecedented heights. This shift will pave the way for a more harmonious, fulfilling, and beautiful world.

II. Philosophy of Happiness Through Experience

i. The Origins of Happiness

An essential concept intertwined with the notion of experience is the philosophy of happiness—how humans can achieve it and maximize it. Experience, focused on our perception and understanding of the world, ultimately aims to lead us toward a state of most profound happiness.

In everyday life, people often encounter subjective feelings of pain and dissatisfaction. Yet, not everyone pauses to reflect on the roots of their suffering or finds effective ways to resolve it. Even individuals from highly intellectual or cultured backgrounds—endowed with deep reasoning and analytical abilities—are not immune to the struggles and challenges posed by life. This reality gives rise to some fundamental questions: Where do joy and suffering originate? What defines true happiness? How should individuals navigate their lives to achieve it?

To address these inquiries, we must return to the very foundation of human existence and explore the forces that have shaped human society development over time.

From the moment of birth, like all other living beings on Earth, humans face the fundamental challenge of survival. The drive to survive and reproduce has been the central pillar of human existence, influencing almost every behavior and emotion.

In infancy, a child forms their most intimate bond with their mother, who provides nourishment and offers best protection for their survival. The child derives a sense of security from the mother's care, crying or signaling for attention when in need, and responding with smiles and affectionate gestures. The mother reciprocates through embrace, caress, loving gazes, and nursing, creating a profound emotional connection. These interactions trigger physiological responses—hormone releases that instill a sense of happiness and deepen the mother's attachment to her child. This happiness fosters a powerful emotional bond between mother and child. From the mother's perspective, the child represents the continuation of her life and legacy. Caring for the child ensures the preservation of her genetic lineage, forming a mutually beneficial and emotionally fulfilling relationship. The intensity of this bond is rooted in its inherent reciprocity, where both mother and child find purpose and connection.

However, any perceived threat to this relationship can provoke negative emotional and physiological responses. For example, when the father or siblings compete for the mother's attention, the infant may instinctively exhibit feelings of resistance, the bud of jealousy. These emotions arise because the mother's divided attention is perceived as a potential threat to the infant's security and survival. The fear of losing their primary protector amplifies these feelings. This survival instinct manifests through physical reactions such as crying, shouting, or trembling. The infant only regains composure and peace when the mother's attention and reassurance restore their sense of safety. For an infant, happiness is defined by comfort, secure living conditions, and the assurance of protection. Conversely, pain arises from the absence or deprivation of these essentials. These early experiences of unmet needs or feelings of inadequacy can leave lasting imprints, shaping subconscious patterns and emotional tendencies throughout a person's life.

As children grow older, learning to walk and talk, their world begins to expand beyond their mothers to include family members and others outside the home. With this broadening of experiences, their understanding of human relationships deepens, and their emotional expressions become increasingly nuanced. Yet, even as their behaviors grow more complex, they remain deeply rooted in the instinct to survive. Driven by primal needs, children seek to acquire as much as possible—delicious food, warm and attractive clothes, fun toys, and the favor of the household's most authoritative figure.

However, they still live within a community dependent on shared resources. Recognizing that survival resources are distributed among everyone, children soon realize that they cannot possess everything; sharing becomes a necessity. Offering a favorite item to someone else often serves as a child's way of demonstrating goodwill. This act of sharing typically has three motivations:

(1) Building positive relationships for future mutual support, fostering the potential for reciprocity later.
(2) Seeking immediate return, hoping for equal or greater rewards in exchange.
(3) Gaining a sense of superiority, showcasing their ability to give generously and subtly asserting, "I have what you don't, which makes me stronger."

As a species that thrives on group living, humans have evolved an innate tendency to come together, fostering collective resilience against external threats. Beyond the three previously mentioned motivations, children also experience a profound, selfless joy derived from acts of kindness—purely the happiness that arises from being friendly and compassionate.

As their cognitive abilities develop, children's desires grow more varied and sophisticated. Almost all their emotions center on whether they are gaining or losing what they want. Any process or outcome that results in gain or the perception of gain evokes positive emotions, whereas those that lead to loss or the sense of losing something generate negative feelings. Gaining represents safety, while losing signals danger. This dynamic explains why, when someone perceives hostility from others—or interprets their actions as hostile due to an underlying sense of insecurity—they experience fear and unease, prompting a series of defensive responses. These emotions arise from the implicit threats embedded in others' hostile actions, triggering emotional and physiological stress reactions. A lack of love and security during early childhood amplifies these stress responses, reinforcing negative perceptions of the external world. Behaviors such as lying, destructive tendencies, and other harmful actions in children often stem from fear, a deficiency of affection, and a psychological need to shield themselves from harm. The more such harm is inflicted, the more pronounced and severe these behaviors become.

As children grow into adults, these early emotional patterns evolve into more complex forms, adding intricacy to human social interactions. At its core, human social life is still driven by the competition for resources. This competition manifests in two main ways: Material wealth ensures personal survival and long-term security, and romantic partners ensure the continuation of one's lineage. These two pursuits often intertwine. People are naturally drawn to partners with desirable traits—such as physical attractiveness, good health, or higher social status—as these qualities imply greater security and a better future for their offspring. This principle also applies to friendships and familial relationships. People gravitate toward those they perceive as stronger or more capable, as these connections offer opportunities for growth. Interactions with individuals perceived as "weaker" usually stem from specific circumstances, such as limited personal attributes, restricting access to higher-status relationships; or a desire for superiority, where the interaction highlights one's own value, offering a sense of self-validation. Such dynamics often stem from psychological vulnerability, where a lack of confidence drives the need for an inflated sense of self-worth.

Beyond material competition lies another powerful force: the quest for psychological dominance. While related to resource pursuits, this quest can diverge, creating four basic personality archetypes:

(1) Confident and dominant: strong in resources and high in psychological confidence.
(2) Insecure and powerful: strong in resources but low in psychological confidence.

(3) Arrogant and vulnerable: weak in resources but high in psychological confidence.
(4) Insecure and submissive: weak in both resources and psychological confidence.

To clarify, confidence is a realistic and positive self-assessment aligned with objective reality, while arrogance involves an inflated self-perception that far exceeds objective reality. When these categories are viewed through the dimension of time, even more nuanced distinctions emerge, though a detailed exploration of these is beyond the scope of this discussion. Despite the myriad variations and the potential for endless subdivisions into intricate scenarios, these four groups fundamentally represent the core archetypes of worldviews within human society.

The confident and dominant. This group is built upon a foundation of abundant material resources and ample emotional support from family and friends. They typically exhibit a positive, optimistic outlook on life, paired with a strong resilience and unwavering belief in their future. At their core, they have a deep-seated conviction that the world is inherently good. Even in the face of adversity, they hold fast to the belief that joy, on balance, outweighs pain. Their personal strength empowers them to share their material wealth and affection with others, deriving satisfaction from enhancing the happiness of those around them.

On the other hand, their confidence allows them to engage in self-reflection and objectively assess their emotional and material needs. They approach criticism with an open mind, capable of accepting and integrating feedback from others. Having sufficient resources in both the material and emotional realms, they feel little desire to accumulate more. For them, happiness primarily arises from contentment with life and the sense of self-worth they derive from helping others.

The insecure and powerful. Despite enjoying favorable material conditions and possessing considerable potential, this group struggles with a deep-rooted sense of inferiority, often shaped by personal or societal factors. A typical example is the illegitimate child raised in a noble family, who, although living in the same privileged environment as their legitimate siblings, is subtly conditioned to feel inferior.

This group is plagued by a significant psychological deficit, which serves as the source of their ongoing inner turmoil. Their lifelong quest is to fill this emotional void, and their strategies for doing so are varied. They too enjoy helping others, but unlike the confident group, their generosity is motivated not just by a desire to help but also by an intense need for external validation. They long for their worth to be recognized through their acts of kindness.

The key to their happiness lies in replenishing their psychological confidence. Through thoughtful gestures and receiving affection and recognition, they feel accepted, validated, liked and loved. Their emotional well-being is intricately tied to overcoming this deficiency throughout their life, and their happiness fluctuates with their success in achieving this goal. For them, material wealth is secondary, and the more fulfilling their spiritual life becomes, the more they perceive the world as beautiful. Their life's purpose is realized through the enrichment of their emotional and mental worlds.

The arrogant and vulnerable. This group is most commonly found in regions or countries with lower economic standards. Raised in impoverished families, they are often overly pampered by parents who, out of love and guilt over their financial shortcomings, try to provide the best for their children. Parents sacrifice their own needs to ensure their children have the best possible food, clothing, and education, hoping for a better future for them.

However, this overindulgence instills a sense of inflated psychological superiority, which is in stark contrast to their humble material reality. They grow up believing they deserve the best in life, yet their circumstances betray this sense of entitlement, leaving them with little to show for it. As they grow older, they frequently encounter negative social feedback, such as contempt, ridicule, or prejudice, due to their economic status.

These experiences foster a deep sense of cynicism. They despise those who look down on them, feel bitterness toward their own poverty, and blame the societal systems that perpetuate their condition. Their strongest desire is to find swift, effective ways to alter the distribution of societal resources, enabling them to reach a material level that aligns with their inflated self-perception.

For them, anyone who possesses more than they do is an object of disdain, and they feel entitled to take from others without gratitude. When forced to share their own limited resources, it feels like an unbearable task. Due to their high self-regard, they do not rely heavily on acts of generosity to achieve a sense of spiritual fulfillment or affirm their self-worth. The joy they derive from sharing is minimal, causing them to place a greater emphasis on the potential future benefits such actions might yield. Even when others approach them with genuine goodwill, they tend to interpret these interactions with skepticism. If the individuals they interact with are in a better financial position, they are inclined to question the sincerity of their intentions.

A defining characteristic of this group in social interactions is their pronounced preference for engaging with individuals who are either on par with or weaker than themselves. Such relationships align with their psychological expectations. The admiration, flattery, and dependency shown by these weaker individuals provide a sense of balance, affirming their belief that "this is the way things should be." For them, this dynamic is not about enhancing their self-worth but about validating the accuracy of their inflated self-perception.

When faced with individuals who are more dominant, this group struggles to adapt. Their responses typically fall into two extremes: either begrudgingly submitting with servile compliance and flattery due to external pressures, or resisting and challenging others when their inner frustrations boil over. Their worldview revolves around a singular focus: leveling the playing field of material resources to match their self-perceived status as quickly as possible. Consequently, all their thoughts and actions are directed toward acquiring as much material wealth as they can.

Their happiness is closely tied to the perceived efficiency of this process. They derive satisfaction from the sense that their dreams are progressively and rapidly coming within reach. Superficially, their joy may seem rooted in the admiration, recognition, and material gains they achieve. However, their true motivations and sources of happiness are distinctly different from those of other groups.

For this group, the pursuit of material success is limitless—they are never fully satisfied. As a result, they often spend their entire lives chasing unattainable goals, living under constant stress and pressure.

The insecure and submissive. Despite also living in economically disadvantaged circumstances, this group differs significantly from the arrogant and vulnerable. They possess a realistic and objective understanding of their circumstances and lack an overwhelming desire for rapid advancement. They are more inclined to accept their situation and live contentedly. Additionally, their disadvantaged state, both materially and psychologically, makes them easily delighted and satisfied by unexpected improvements or gains.

Although they may experience pain and sadness from poor living conditions or others' disdain, they do not harbor unrealistic expectations or excessive ambitions. Nor do they perceive a significant gap between what they have and what they believe they deserve, which mitigates the development of resentment or hatred.

Their pursuits are straightforward: any improvement in their material or psychological well-being brings them genuine happiness. And this simplicity allows them to feel contentment more easily.

ii. The Fundamental Components of Happiness

1. Static Situations

(1) Overall Material Conditions

When material conditions fall below the threshold required for basic survival, physical suffering arises, often caused by hunger, cold, or deprivation. As material conditions improve—particularly during the initial transition from poverty to meeting basic needs—each incremental increase in resources brings a substantial rise in satisfaction (i.e., high marginal satisfaction). Nevertheless, once basic needs are adequately met, the marginal satisfaction derived from further accumulation begins to diminish.

A critical factor influencing this diminishing effect is the comparison between one's own material conditions and those of others. For instance, consider a hungry individual who initially focuses solely on their immediate needs. The first few loaves of bread they receive bring significant increases in happiness. Nonetheless, as they approach satiety, additional loaves yield diminishing returns. If they then observe peers with more bread, especially those who mock or belittle them for having less, their desire for additional bread may reignite. This desire persists until their share equals or surpasses that of others, at which point marginal happiness once again diminishes.

On the other hand, if this individual adopts a rational perspective and believes that having enough bread to satisfy their hunger is sufficient, external comparisons will not affect their happiness. This highlights another crucial factor: expectations.

$$\text{Material happiness} = \text{Material possessed} - \text{Material expected}$$

When material possessed > material expected, material happiness is positive, leading to joy. However, the increase in happiness diminishes as the gap widens (i.e., diminishing marginal happiness). This form of happiness has an upper limit, corresponding to the maximum pleasure that material possessions can provide. When material possessed < material expected, material happiness is negative, leading to suffering. The increase in suffering intensifies as the gap widens (i.e., increasing marginal unhappiness). This form of unhappiness has a lower limit, representing the maximum pain caused by a lack of resources.

External influences, such as observing the material wealth of others, can raise expectations and narrow the gap between material possessed and material expected, reducing happiness. However, if external factors do not alter expectations, they have no impact on one's sense of happiness.

(2) Overall Psychological Strength (or Spiritual Well-Being)
Extreme self-doubt or a profound lack of security can lead to psychological suffering. Compliments, affirmation, trust, and support from others can compensate for these deficiencies, fostering self-confidence and a sense of security, and thereby enhancing happiness.

$$\text{Spiritual happiness} = \text{External value assessment} - \text{Self-Value assessment}$$

The level of external value assessment reflects the extent to which others appreciate and regard this individual. A higher assessment signifies greater external goodwill. For example, the adage "beauty lies in the eye of the beholder" illustrates how an ordinary woman may appear exceptionally valuable in her lover's eyes. Likewise, a mother often sees her child through a lens of unparalleled admiration, magnifying their beauty and intelligence. To her, her child embodies extraordinary value, inspiring her to bestow boundless love and unwavering devotion.

An interesting concept here is fame, something people pursue. It serves as a tangible measure of an individual's external value assessment. The greater the fame, the more society assumes the individual possesses a unique value that justifies their recognition. This elevated external evaluation not only enhances psychological happiness but often translates into material benefits, such as attendance fees. Although personal evaluations vary, an individual's appearance, education, income, and family background contribute to a relatively objective overall societal evaluation. The external value assessment mentioned here refers to this relatively objective overall societal evaluation.

When external recognition of value > self-recognition (i.e., spiritual happiness is positive), the resulting experience is joy. Conversely, when external recognition value < self-recognition (i.e., spiritual happiness is negative), the experience is pain.

Notably, when self-recognition significantly surpasses external recognition (i.e., the absolute difference is large), arrogance and conceit inevitably arise. Such psychological states are often accompanied by a range of painful emotions, which intensify as the gap widens. Similarly, when self-recognition is significantly lower than external recognition, feelings of inferiority emerge, becoming more pronounced as the discrepancy grows. However, when external recognition exceeds self-recognition by a modest margin, the individual may feel pleasantly surprised and fulfilled.

An important feature of this equation is that external and self-recognition of value are not entirely independent; they are interrelated and influence one another. For example, during childhood, a person's self-evaluation often mirrors the evaluations they receive from their environment. Family attitudes play a pivotal role in shaping this self-perception. Children who experience a lack of affection are prone to developing a sense of inferiority, while those who are overly indulged may develop arrogance or conceit. Upon entering adulthood and engaging with society beyond their family, individuals may encounter discrepancies between external evaluations and self-perceptions, resulting in varied emotional experiences.

2. Dynamic Situations

From a dynamic perspective, whether material or spiritual, any factor leading to reduction, depletion, or loss—negative changes—triggers negative (painful) experiences. The intensity of this pain depends not only on the magnitude of the negative change but also on the emotional investment and expectations tied to the object of loss. In contrast, factors that result in gains, increases, or improvements—positive changes—induce positive (joyful) experiences. The intensity of joy is influenced not only by the magnitude of the positive change but also by historical expectations for the object in question.

$$\text{Value of an object} = \text{Material cost} + \text{Emotional cost}$$
$$\text{Painful experience} = \text{Value of lost object}$$
$$\text{Joyful experience} = \text{Value of gained object} - \text{Expected value of object}$$

The total value of an object is composed of its objective material cost and the emotional investment made in it. For example, elderly individuals often cherish old belongings, even if they are no longer functional, because the emotional value accrued over time surpasses the material worth. Emotional cost typically increases with repeated interactions with the object. When an object is lost, the pain corresponds to the loss of its total value. The intensity of this pain is directly proportional to the value lost. Conversely, the joy derived from gains is determined by both the value of the gain and the expected value of the object. Higher expectations diminish the element of surprise and, consequently, reduce the intensity of joy.

We have also observed that when the magnitude of an object's value change is the same, painful experiences tend to outweigh joyful ones. This occurs because pain lacks the moderating effect of expectation. For instance, even when we anticipate the passing of a loved one due to prior health conditions, the grief experienced at the moment of loss remains profound. Similar examples abound, illustrating that mental preparation often does little to lessen the intensity of pain. Humans naturally amplify pain and minimize joy in their emotional experiences.

iii. Happiness Strategies

From the preceding analysis, it becomes evident that when the ultimate goal is to maximize human happiness, the strategies required take on a clear direction.

1. Foundational Principles of Happiness Strategies

(1) Enhancing Happiness from a Personal Perspective

This approach centers on what individuals can control within themselves, recognizing the inherent limitations in influencing external circumstances. The aim is to identify how happiness can be optimized within the scope of personal control.

Given the following equations:

Happiness = Material happiness + Spiritual happiness
Material happiness = Material possessed – Material expected
Spiritual happiness = External value assessment – Self-Value assessment

When material possessed and external value assessment are considered relatively fixed and difficult to alter, maximizing happiness depends on minimizing two key variables: material expected and self-value assessment. Assuming material levels and value assessments are non-negative, the state of maximum happiness is achieved when both material expected and self-value assessment are reduced to zero.

Let's take a look at the following equations:

Value of an object = Material cost + Emotional cost
Painful experience = Value of lost object
Joyful experience = Value of gained object – Expected value of object

To minimize pain and maximize joy: In painful experiences, minimize the value of what is lost, while in joyful experiences, minimize expectations. In the value of an object, the material cost is an objective reality that is hard to alter. However, what we can influence is the reduction of the emotional cost attached to what has been lost.

These findings underscore a fundamental issue: the need for individuals to relinquish all expectations, both of themselves and the external things connected to them. Without expectations, desires diminish, fostering a profound satisfaction with what one has and eliminating the pain associated with losses. Eliminating expectations does not mean disengaging from life or refusing to enjoy its offerings. Rather, it implies adopting a mindset that accepts life's circumstances objectively and without attachment.

It is foreseeable that some may argue that when survival is at stake, striving for necessities is inevitable. This is true—but the necessity of striving for material sustenance should not be conflated with emotional expectation. When individuals work for survival, pursue income, or seek life's essentials, they are engaging with an objective reality. Pain arises only when the outcomes fall short of heightened expectations. To alleviate or eliminate such pain, the only effective solution lies in consciously lowering expectations. This understanding also explains why witnessing others with more possessions often triggers discomfort: Their abundance raises one's expectations, and the gap between these expectations and one's reality induces pain.

The only solution lies in cultivating a mindset that separates effort from expectation: "I strive for survival because I must, but I do not attach expectations to the outcome (expected value = 0)." In this way, every achievement feels joyful, and failures bring no pain. Once material needs are met, individuals cease yearning for more or better possessions. By maintaining a neutral expectation (expected value = 0), they can even find joy in sharing their possessions to improve the happiness of others. Losses should be viewed as objective facts of life rather than sources of emotional distress. By detaching emotionally from what is lost, pain diminishes significantly. When a person adopts this mindset, life becomes free from pain. They experience only joy or a neutral state of acceptance. At this point, we can say they have achieved a state of maximum happiness.

(2) Enhancing Societal Happiness from the Perspective of Administrators and Providers

To improve overall societal happiness, external measures should focus on controllable factors such as material provision and guidance on mental well-being. These efforts can be structured into three primary strategies:

- Enhancing material provision. Increase national income levels while promoting the diversification of material goods. This ensures that rising income levels are accompanied by products and services catering to emerging and diverse consumer needs, improving material satisfaction through consumption.
- Fostering social respect and cultural development. Strengthen social norms emphasizing respect, care, and protection for individuals. Promoting cultural development ensures that everyone feels acknowledged, valued, and secure within society.
- Encouraging simplified values. Discourage excessive materialism by promoting modest values and curbing extravagance. This helps lower societal expectations for material wealth.

Only the synergy of these three strategies can maximize societal happiness.

2. Tailored Happiness Strategies for Four Demographic Groups

Beyond general principles, specific strategies should be tailored to meet the needs of distinct population groups identified by their psychological and material characteristics:

(1) The confident and dominant. Their happiness largely arises from a sense of fulfillment in life and the self-worth gained from helping others. For individuals of this mindset, anything that enhances their sense of purpose will also amplify their happiness. Careers in public welfare, education, healthcare, and service industries are particularly well-suited to them. Even marketing strategies that highlight messages like "Every purchase contributes RMB to green initiatives" can resonate deeply with this group. These individuals often have their own life aspirations, and their happiness is self-sufficient. Even in the face of setbacks or challenges, they excel at adjusting their mindset and rediscovering joy.

(2) The insecure and powerful. This group places little emphasis on material possessions; instead, the more enriched they are spiritually, the more beautiful the world appears to them. Promotional efforts targeting this audience should prioritize themes such as "thoughtful care," "praise," "affirmation," and "emotional connection." Products and services that address their spiritual needs can greatly enhance their sense of happiness. Customized, on-demand products and services offered by organizations or businesses are especially well-suited for them. With their strong financial foundation and considerable

purchasing power, they present abundant opportunities to explore diverse value propositions and market potential.

(3) The arrogant and vulnerable. Their entire worldview centers around a single theme: rapidly aligning material resources with their self-perception. Every thought and action are geared toward maximizing the acquisition of material wealth, with their happiness and satisfaction rooted in the efficiency of this pursuit. For this group, three strategic approaches can be particularly effective:
   - Managing their self-expectations. Lower their aspirations to a more realistic level through cautionary campaigns that promote rational investment, entrepreneurship, and consumption.
   - Enhancing their sense of "quick success." Activities or careers with high risk and high reward resonate deeply with them, as they prioritize rapid material advancement.
   - Bridging the gap between self-perception and reality through a sense of "illusion." Offer short-term, high-end, customized experiences that temporarily align with their self-image. For instance, premium services like "luxury aristocratic travel" can provide them with a controlled and temporary sense of prestige that matches their self-evaluation.

   The online gaming industry has thrived by capitalizing on the third approach. With far lower costs than real-world expenditures, players can create legendary personas within the virtual world. This sense of "prestige" and elevated status holds a magnetic appeal for many in this group.

(4) The insecure and submissive. This group's pursuits are simple: Whether it's an improvement in material comforts or an enrichment of their mental well-being, both bring them genuine happiness. They are easily content and satisfied. For these individuals, enhancing their overall standard of living and enriching their spiritual and emotional lives is enough to significantly elevate their sense of happiness.

III. Education in Experience Economy

Education, as the foundation for shaping humanity's worldview, values, and life perspectives, has always been one of the most vital pillar industries of societal development. The growth of an individual's spiritual world throughout life can be understood as a synergy between external education and internal education. While distinct in nature, these two forms are closely intertwined:

(1) External education. This encompasses the acquisition of knowledge, ideas, and perspectives influenced by external factors, spanning the entirety of one's life from the embryonic stage to its conclusion.
(2) Internal education. This refers to self-guided learning that arises from introspection and self-awareness, fostering the evolution of personal understanding and beliefs.

Education, in essence, entails a transformation in knowledge, ideas, or perspectives. It occurs when a person's way of observing the world, experiencing it, connecting with it, or interacting with it changes due to internal or external influences.

Clearly, the essence of education lies in influencing and transforming a person's beliefs, attitudes, and knowledge. These transformations can be categorized into three types: The first is an accumulative and developmental change; the second is a reduction and weakening change; and the third is a reversal change. In practice, these types often coexist, with varying degrees of influence based on context. This adaptability in human thought forms the foundation for all educational efforts, whether in material or spiritual realms.

Education transcends formal settings like schools and universities. In a broader sense, every interaction—whether between people or between individuals and objects—constitutes a form of education. Communication inherently involves mutual influence, and with mutual influence comes varying degrees of strength. Whether it manifests as persuasion, consensus, debate, or conflict, communication always results in two distinct states: one before the interaction and one after. Through communication, both parties may experience shifts in perspective. The one persuading often gains greater confidence in their own views, while the persuaded individual adjusts their perspective. When communication occurs between a person and an object, each interaction becomes an opportunity for the individual to either validate or challenge their original beliefs.

Therefore, viewed through the lens of the experience economy, education becomes a universal and omnipresent phenomenon. It breaks free from traditional confines, dissolving hierarchies such as superior and subordinate, elder and younger, or male and female. It eliminates coercive relationships, transforming education into a dynamic, spontaneous, and ever-present process. This paradigm shift empowers individuals with true freedom of thought. They engage with the world independently through their senses—observing, listening, and experiencing—drawing conclusions free from external impositions.

Historically, education has been largely hierarchical, emphasizing top-down transmission of knowledge. Parents teach children, mentors guide apprentices, teachers instruct students, and superiors direct subordinates. These systems prioritize control and compliance. This form of education forcefully imparts the experiences and ideas of the past to successive generations, demanding that they accept, believe in, and act according to traditional ways. While effective at leveraging historical knowledge to enhance survival prospects, this approach equips the new generation to counter familiar risks and challenges. As a result, it has been widely adopted throughout history.

However, as humanity's understanding of the world evolves, it has become increasingly evident that the complexities of the world cannot be fully explained through past experiences alone. A survey of nearly 5,000 years of Eastern and Western civilization reveals that each era is distinct, marked by unexpected events that far exceed human predictions. When new generations confine their thinking to the boundaries of historical knowledge, they lose the drive to cultivate their own sharp perception of the real world. This stagnation leaves them ill-equipped to address novel challenges, often resulting in pessimism, escapism, and decline. As a whole, humanity becomes increasingly resistant to change, retreating into the imagined constructs of its own making rather than stepping out into the unknown. This reluctance to adapt only widens the chasm between these constructs and the reality they aim to represent.

The limitations of educational content further hinder the spiritual growth of new generations. What we term knowledge-based education is often a distillation of essential survival principles, encompassing practical skills for navigating the material world (e.g., science and technology), spiritual frameworks for understanding existence (e.g., religious beliefs), and foundational social rules governing interactions between individuals and their environment (e.g., etiquette).

This so-called knowledge forms a vast web, with individuals striving from a young age to master as much of it as possible, often using their level of mastery as a measure of self-worth. Yet, this web is merely a subset of true knowledge. Despite humanity's impressive accumulation of experience and information over millennia, it represents only a tiny fraction of the vast reservoir of knowledge embedded in the universe. We must acknowledge that, in the face of the infinite universe, humanity remains small and limited. A humble attitude is essential when confronting the unknown. If people remain confined to a fixed circle of knowledge, how can they progress? How can their understanding of the world expand to embrace richer, more diverse perspectives?

To fundamentally advance human knowledge—renewing, supplementing, and expanding it—we must break free from traditional educational paradigms. Education should emancipate the mind, liberating individuals from control-driven systems and fostering their ability to perceive, comprehend, and interpret the world. This approach reveals the richness of human diversity: Each person experiences the world differently, and the paths to solving life's challenges are far broader than the familiar avenues we know today.

On the other hand, education must transcend the transfer of material knowledge necessary for survival and embrace a deeper exploration of the spiritual realm. Compared to our understanding of the material world, humanity's grasp of the spiritual domain lags far behind. This gap is the underlying cause of why, in today's world, humanity is increasingly consumed by the pursuit of survival and material pleasures, leading to a growing sense of emptiness and disillusionment in their spiritual lives. While stimulating activities can temporarily lift the spirit and emotions, their effects quickly fade or disappear, often leaving behind a sense of exhaustion. As a result, they are not a sustainable or reliable way to enhance lasting happiness.

We often attribute the growing isolation between individuals to the advancement of technology, such as the invention of smartphones or the proliferation of entertainment options. However, the real cause of this disconnect lies in the reduction of face-to-face interactions, the decline in shared travel experiences, and the accelerating pace of life, which makes it difficult for people to fully immerse themselves in and appreciate each moment. The root of this separation is not the external circumstances themselves, but rather our attitudes and perspectives.

Take travel, for example. It has transformed into a frantic pursuit of photo opportunities for display, with little thought given to why one feels compelled to share these images. This focus on showcasing experiences often prevents individuals from truly relaxing, unwinding, and savoring quality time with family. Some meticulously plan their trips to cover multiple cities and regions within a few short days. Yet, in each destination, their time is consumed with eating and taking photos, leaving little room to genuinely experience or appreciate the local culture. This pattern extends to other areas of life as well. These trends reveal a stark reality: Our spiritual lives are becoming increasingly hollow and monotonous. When life is not filled with tightly packed schedules, it can feel aimless and lacking in direction.

In fact, a person with a rich inner world can find immense joy and satisfaction in simple living. Such individuals see freshness, beauty, joy, and delight in everyday moments, sustaining a deep curiosity about life and the world. Their happiness, stable and lasting, is not tied to material stimulation but stems from an openness to life's wonders. They embrace all aspects of existence—be it people, animals, the sky, the earth, or even the simplest objects like a stone or a blade of grass.

Traditional education systems have largely neglected the spiritual domain, leaving a critical gap in their frameworks. Hierarchical structures within these systems further stifle genuine dialogue. Those in authority often struggle to respect and listen to those beneath them, suppressing the free flow of ideas and understanding. This deeply ingrained mindset obstructs the full transmission of authentic information, causing much of it to be suppressed, denied, or difficult to understand objectively. Yet, true information does not disappear because of this barrier; rather, it persists in the minds of those who hold such beliefs, often in hidden or alternative forms. When these beliefs eventually surface all at once, it often leads to events that are difficult for most to fathom: the sudden suicide of a child, an unexpected rebellion from subordinates, violent outbreaks, and more. This creates a lack of preparation for these grave issues, as well as a failure to recognize and address the early signs with the necessary sensitivity.

When such events occur on a larger scale, they generate a powerful wave of conflict that gradually dismantles the beliefs people have worked so hard to establish. This underscores the importance of the values promoted by the experience economy—respect between individuals, the independence of personal identity, and freedom—because they offer the only path for people to truly live in alignment with the real world. It is through embracing an open and inclusive mindset, welcoming others and the world, that we allow others and the world to reciprocate and welcome us in return.

Our intention is not to reject knowledge-based education, but rather to highlight that, beyond traditional methods and hierarchical instruction, there is a vast realm of educational content and forms waiting to be explored and developed. When people begin to give spiritual education the same depth of understanding and importance as material education, and when the scope of education expands beyond top-down models to include the interactions between individuals and between humans and the world, only then can our educational philosophy truly evolve toward its fullest potential.

The experience economy encourages individuals to empathize with others, driven by the pursuit of discovering the true value of experience. This creates an unprecedented demand for humanity's overall capacity to sense, understand, and create with heightened awareness and sensitivity. To achieve this elevated level of ability and expand our understanding of the world, a profound transformation in our educational approach is essential. Such a transformation would consciously focus on enhancing human perception and experiential skills, while also addressing the gaps in existing knowledge systems by awakening and enriching individuals' authentic sensations. Let us explore, from four distinct perspectives, how education at various levels will evolve in the age of the experience economy.

i. Family Education

Family education primarily unfolds within the intimate circle of family members, typically including parents and children. In households with more than one child, siblings also become integral to this dynamic. In extended families, grandparents and other relatives may play a role, yet the foundational unit of family life remains the bond between parents and their children.

From the educational perspective of the experience economy, every family member—be it a father, mother, or child—should be seen as a fully independent individual. Each should recognize and respect the autonomy of others. Education, therefore, is not a one-way transfer of knowledge from parents to children but a reciprocal process of influence among individuals, conveyed through words, actions, and shared experiences.

Parents impart essential life skills to their children, such as how to avoid dangers, maintain a balanced lifestyle through proper nutrition, exercise, and rest, and interact effectively with others both within and outside the family. Children offer parents profound insights into the essence of life, such as instinctive physical responses to external stimuli, natural emotional rhythms, and innate bodily patterns. Uninhibited by preconceived notions, children often develop innovative ways to navigate challenges and solve problems, surpassing the boundaries of their parents' existing knowledge. These observations are invaluable, offering parents a deeper understanding of themselves, their relationship with their children, and the dynamics within their partnership. In families with multiple children, the opportunities for learning expand even further. Family members gain essential lessons in communication and relationship balance. Siblings, for instance, learn to navigate their relationships with one another, share resources, and harmoniously divide their parents' love and attention.

Each family member's personality and behavior influence others, creating a web of interconnected impact. This interconnectedness is the essence of family education, where the shared influence shapes the collective growth of all members. However, imbalances in family dynamics can disrupt this growth.

Overindulgence by parents can undermine their authority, causing children to develop an inflated sense of self-importance and entitlement. Conversely, overly strict parenting can stifle children's independence, suppressing their individuality and autonomy.

In any such situation, the oppressed or belittled party tends to adopt a posture of appeasement and flattery toward the other. Meanwhile, the relatively dominant party often develops habits of bullying or controlling others. However, individuals with independent personalities cannot endure suppression indefinitely. This tolerance will accumulate over time until it reaches a breaking point, ultimately leading to a serious family conflict. Family conflicts naturally arise when parents stop appeasing their children and assert their right to be respected, and when children, no longer able to tolerate prolonged emotional control, choose to rebel. Such clashes inflict emotional harm on both the dominant and the oppressed parties. While a strong rebellion may temporarily shift the balance of power within the family, the underlying thought patterns of its members often remain unchanged. As a result, the family's dynamics eventually revert to their previous state, allowing tensions to rebuild until another conflict inevitably erupts. Repeated conflicts can erode the love and trust within a family, replacing it with resentment and hostility. Over time, this can lead to the collapse of family relationships. While children may eventually leave a dysfunctional family by starting their own, they often carry the unresolved emotional scars and behavioral patterns from their original family into their new one. Breaking this destructive cycle requires at least one family member to adopt a broader perspective, recognize the underlying patterns, and take conscious steps to change them. These changes can inspire others within the family to reflect on their own behavior, gradually transforming the family dynamic.

Only in this way can the vicious cycle of family dynamics be broken, paving the way for a new type of family relationship to emerge. While this new relationship may not immediately reach an ideal state, it will undoubtedly represent an improvement over the previous one. As these improvements are passed down from one generation to the next, the foundation for truly ideal family relationships can eventually take shape. At its core, such ideal family relationships serve as the cornerstone for building ideal social relationships.

ii. School Education

As children grow and reach a certain age, they begin their social educational journey through educational institutions such as kindergartens, primary schools, and universities. A profound shift takes place in their social landscape: They move from interacting primarily with family members to engaging with strangers from the outside world. Among these strangers are teachers who are older, more experienced, and wiser, as well as classmates of similar age. Each person brings unique personality traits, habits, behaviors, and life experiences, creating a rich tapestry of interactions. Children soon realize that the world they are entering operates on a hierarchy of power, where strength and influence matter. Unlike their parents, these strangers do not place their needs and well-being at the forefront. They do not create a comforting, warm environment, nor do they prioritize their emotional happiness or concerns. Instead, many of these individuals are self-interested, seemingly focused solely on their own needs. How should a child navigate such an environment? How can they prove their value through appropriate interactions and earn respect, recognition, and admiration from others?

In any class, even a preschool group, it becomes evident that within a short period after enrollment (1–2 months), students naturally form small social circles. Each individual gravitates toward a relatively fixed group of peers, fostering closer and more consistent interactions. These stable circles are typically maintained through a sense of balance achieved by the collective participation of their members. Group members may share similar personalities, possess complementary traits, or establish mutual checks and balances. Even in a simple two-person group, dynamics often emerge with one taking a more dominant role and the other a more subordinate one. While relationships may begin on relatively equal footing, over time, disparities in influence and authority tend to develop. Two dominant individuals or two entirely submissive ones rarely coexist harmoniously. Dominant personalities lack subordinates to influence, while submissive individuals lack leaders to rely on, creating a sense of psychological imbalance.

In student groups, how is the role of a dominant individual established? Similar to social dynamics in broader society, this status requires a basis of legitimacy—something that earns the recognition and acceptance of others. Consequently, "leader" figures among students often establish their authority by challenging norms, defying adult authority, or exhibiting distinctive, standout behaviors. When the majority of students harbor fear toward adult teachers and parents, and feel intimidated by older, taller, and more physically imposing senior students, the so-called "leader" figures distinguish themselves by defying authority and challenging established rules. Through such actions, they prove themselves to be stronger—or at least unafraid—compared to those who instill fear in others. Witnessing these displays of boldness, other students naturally develop a sense of trust and admiration for these "leaders." This dynamic explains a common phenomenon: Classmates who are genuinely admired and supported by their peers often appear as "rebels" in the eyes of teachers and parents. These individuals tend to resist discipline and challenge the rules set by families and schools, leading to frequent criticism and punishment. Ironically, their resolute attitude in the face of such penalties further enhances their heroic image among their peers.

Among student leaders, two distinct groups often emerge: The first comprises the "model students" handpicked by teachers. These students excel academically and are highly compliant with authority, embodying the qualities that teachers and parents admire. The second group consists of peer-chosen "leaders." These individuals take on roles like organizing extracurricular or cultural activities and are celebrated by their classmates for their creativity and rebellious spirit. Students tend to have little affection for the "model students," viewing them as monopolizing praise and admiration from teachers and parents, which inadvertently makes others feel insignificant or inferior. This dynamic naturally fosters cliques, as students gravitate toward those with whom they share similarities in personality or status. These groups often harbor disdain for those outside their circle.

Traditional school education has long been focused on exam results—evaluating students based on their academic performance and aiming for the highest test scores as the ultimate goal. Much like a nation blindly chasing high-speed economic growth while ignoring the well-being of its citizens, a test-centered education system neglects the emotional and psychological growth of students. While academic knowledge is an essential component of education, it is equally crucial to address the development beyond it. The true aim of education is to cultivate individuals with balanced personalities and healthy minds, rather than simply producing specialists with distorted psychological well-being.

Education within the framework of the experience economy emphasizes the comprehensive development of students' spiritual and emotional growth. Each student, shaped by their unique family background and individual traits, will naturally have differences in their starting points. These differences can lead to the formation of social hierarchies and circles within the school community. However, this is not to say that education is powerless in shaping these dynamics. From a school's perspective, education serves two key functions: Foster a holistic understanding of healthy interpersonal relationships, encouraging students to develop positive and balanced attitudes toward social interactions; and address imbalances on a targeted level by offering deliberate guidance based on the severity of the issues, ultimately enhancing the psychological well-being of individual student groups.

Regarding the first function of education, teachers should aim to instill the concept of "equality for all," helping students recognize that every individual is an independent being deserving of mutual respect. This foundation fosters a culture where everyone acknowledges the inherent dignity of others. When it comes to rewards and punishments, teachers must offer equal opportunities to all students, acknowledging and encouraging the unique strengths and positive traits of each individual. In truth, every student has areas in which they excel, as well as areas where they may struggle. Weaknesses are objective facts and not excuses for others to criticize or undermine them, while strengths should not be used as a reason for undue pride. It is crucial that both teachers and students accept and appreciate the differences that exist between people, as well as the diverse strengths each person brings.

Throughout the educational journey, it is important for teachers to guide students in a way that nurtures their interests and talents, while also offering constructive support in areas where they may need improvement. This balanced approach helps prevent the emergence of blind arrogance or feelings of inferiority. Each student can learn from others' strengths and develop an objective understanding of their own areas for growth. With this perspective, student relationships will no longer be characterized by dominance and submission, nor will they be fragmented into rigid social circles. As coercion fades and cliques dissolve, relationships among peers and between students and teachers will transform into a more harmonious, collaborative environment.

In this ideal atmosphere, each individual will find their rightful place, which provides them with both a sense of security and confidence. Everyone will hold an objective self-assessment of their own abilities, avoiding both flattery and oppression. Ultimately, such relationships will become a fertile ground for creativity, where each person can progress toward their ideal future in a way that is most natural for them. In moments of frustration or confusion, teachers should provide guidance, helping students develop unique and effective ways of thinking. As these methods evolve, they will blossom into vibrant, diverse ideas and intellectual growth. When every student's creativity is allowed to flourish through this educational approach, the entire society will experience an outpouring of innovation.

iii. Work and Social Education

As students graduate from academia and step into adulthood, they enter the workforce, where they will contribute to society by applying their various skills and expertise and creating value. The scope of their social interactions expands significantly, and the complexity of relationships and responsibilities increases. At this stage, individuals are no longer merely students seeking knowledge and learning how to manage relationships; they are now workers who bear the responsibility of supporting themselves and their families. They must engage in labor to secure their livelihood, and the pressures of daily life often make their social interactions more purposeful and goal-driven.

In this phase, education continues to evolve, moving beyond the formal, structured approach of school and becoming more diverse and far-reaching. As adults navigate their work and personal lives, constantly influenced by external factors—whether consciously or unconsciously—that alter their knowledge, perspectives, attitudes, methodologies, and tools, they are being educated and educating others. In fact, the social training that begins in adulthood is not an end to education, but rather an essential, ongoing stage of personal education. During this period, individuals gradually shape their own belief systems, codes of conduct, life philosophies, and ultimate goals.

For instance, consider the case of an ordinary employee in a company. Their social connections at this stage encompasses: family, coworkers (including supervisors, peers, and subordinates), external business partners (such as clients or negotiators), friends (both new and old classmates), and potentially even teachers if they pursue further specialized education. These relationships form a hierarchy from closest to most distant, with the number of people involved growing exponentially. As a result, adults begin to categorize and prioritize their relationships, carefully filtering and ranking them based on significance. They dedicate more time, energy, and resources to high-priority connections while relegating less important ones to occasional, minimal interaction.

The significance of each relationship is directly tied to the potential benefits it brings. Family members provide warmth, security, and a haven for relaxation. Key professional relationships influence salary, career advancement, and future opportunities. Close friends offer necessary social resources and emotional support. Although the dynamics of these relationships may vary depending on personal circumstances—such as someone seeking more social interaction due to a strained family life—these three types of relationships generally remain the most important in an individual's social network.

For individuals in society, the greater the importance of a relationship, the more profound its direct and potential influence on their lives and education. Driven by an innate instinct for self-preservation, humans naturally tend to trust those they are familiar with, while remaining cautious and skeptical of the unknown. In this way, societal education should follow a similar pattern, shaping itself according to the social circles that individuals inhabit. At this stage, education is no longer a top-down process dictated solely by authoritative figures or institutions. Rather, it arises from the individual's intrinsic motivation—spontaneously, actively, and willingly. This self-driven education is purposeful, and it is precisely this sense of purpose that drives society to offer educational opportunities that align with individuals' unique needs.

In the age of the experience economy, the landscape of education has evolved dramatically. A multitude of educational content and institutions has emerged, and teaching methods are now flexible and tailored to specific demands. Programs are custom-built to meet the diverse needs of individuals, accommodating their varying schedules and goals, with the added benefit of allowing for adjustments along the way. This level of customization and flexibility has become a defining characteristic of educational services in the experience economy. Conversely, the roles of educator and learner are fluid, capable of being exchanged seamlessly. Every individual possesses unique talents and expertise, allowing even ordinary people to share their knowledge in areas such as cooking, housekeeping, or professional skills through online platforms. This sharing mechanism transforms each person into an independent creator of educational content, offering abundant opportunities to disseminate their insights to others. In this paradigm, the concept of fixed experts fades, as everyone becomes both a teacher and a student. This innovative approach to education in the experience economy era maximizes the exchange of knowledge and information, accelerating humanity's collective cognitive growth with unprecedented efficiency.

iv. Education from the Natural World

Beyond the educational influence of human relationships, there exists a vast and powerful source of learning: the natural world itself. Nature provides the essential environment for human life, and its laws govern our health and well-being. The natural world is also the fundamental source through which humans come to understand themselves and the universe. However, with the increasing urbanization of human life, our innate connection to nature has been gradually diminished. People are becoming more confined to the small circles of urban existence, and direct interaction with nature has transformed into a rare luxury—one typically experienced only during vacations. For those who, even in the presence of nature, fail to fully immerse themselves in it, a psychological divide between themselves and the natural world deepens.

At its core, human creativity is a reflection of nature within the human spirit. When people observe the beauty of the natural world—the vast sky, the radiant sun, the lush trees, the vibrant flowers, the bustling insects, the graceful animals, and the flowing rivers—they not only experience an emotional cleansing but also gain knowledge. This process of attuning oneself to nature converts the elements of the natural world into lasting impressions, which become a wellspring for thought and creativity. When this flow of inspiration is blocked, and the mind is no longer nourished by new ideas, over time, thought stagnates, and creativity is stifled. In order to revive this source of inspiration, education must guide people back to nature, encouraging them to restore and protect it and to reconnect with it.

To truly engage with nature, we must reclaim the cognitive innocence of infancy—a state of awareness unmarred by past memories or future expectations. In each moment, we must approach the world with an open heart, unclouded by preconceived notions, and embrace each experience with curiosity and wonder. This approach is not limited to interactions with nature; it can be applied to urban life as well. If a person can adopt this mindset and view each element of their surroundings with the same sense of novelty, they will form a profound, unconscious connection with everything around them, drawing nourishment and insight from the most ordinary aspects of life.

We often view photographs captured by cameras and artistic images created by painters inspired by real-life objects as works of art, savoring the beauty and emotion they convey. In fact, in every moment of life, if we approach the world with a sense of wonder—truly seeing every image before our eyes, listening deeply to every sound, and savoring the scents and textures that surround us—we unlock a transformative beauty often overlooked. Suddenly, we realize we've never really noticed a mountain, a tree, a river, or even the small, everyday objects around us. The grain of a wooden table, the colors of a cupboard, or the texture of a floor—things so familiar and taken for granted—reveal hidden layers of meaning and beauty, waiting to be discovered.

Have you ever watched the delicate spiral of plum blossoms as they unfurl along their branches? Or traced the intricate and unique patterns of veins etched into every leaf? Have you felt the quiet warmth of a streetlamp and its base glowing softly on a still night? Have you marveled at the way water slips through your fingers, cascading gently from your palm? Did you notice how, at times, the surface of water appears almost gelatinous? Have you ever truly tasted the natural sweetness of a vegetable, its fresh juices releasing subtle flavors with every bite?

When we observe the world with this level of patience and attentiveness, an unspoken joy begins to bloom within. It feels as though, in the act of looking and listening, our hearts engage in a silent dialogue with all things. This sense of connection brings a profound comfort, a tranquil delight that soothes the restless mind and quiets the noise of our thoughts in mere moments. This form of happiness is unlike the fleeting excitement of sensory indulgence. It is enduring and deep, growing richer with time and reflection. With this mindset, every moment feels new and alive—untainted by monotony, emptiness, or boredom. Such an awakening is possible only when we release the ceaseless chatter of our minds, allowing ourselves to truly see, hear, and feel the world in its raw, unfiltered beauty.

A deep and authentic connection with, observation of, and understanding of nature provides humanity with an endless well of inspiration. These insights are not only invaluable in enriching various aspects of human society but also serve as a mirror to better understand ourselves. The human body, at its core, is an inseparable part of nature. Thus, the laws of energy transformation, the rhythms of natural processes, and the patterns of development that shape the world also resonate within the human body, both inside and out. In the experience economy, education must awaken our innate ability to feel—our connection with nature, with others, and with ourselves. This ability to feel is the wellspring from which the demand for experience and the creation of meaningful value are born. As such, the interaction between humanity and nature must become a key focus of education, deserving not just of attention but of ample time and energy. A person who loves nature, cherishes others, and holds a deep respect for themselves is truly vibrant, creative, and full of compassion. This universal love and boundless creativity awaken an inner passion that propels humanity forward, driving the progress of society in the realm of the spirit.

IV. Ethnic Cultural Differences of Experience

Human society today is a rich tapestry woven from thousands of ethnic groups. When exploring human experiences, it becomes inevitable to address the influence of ethnic cultural differences. At its core, the formation of ethnic groups can be traced back to the early development of human society, shaped by geographical isolation. In a time when information flow was limited, communities settled near chosen water sources, migrating as climates shifted. Through these movements, they developed distinct ways of life and close-knit kinship systems. Groups with shared ancestry and similar lifestyles are typically identified as belonging to the same ethnicity.

Ethnic culture encompasses the unique lifestyles developed, practiced, passed down, and refined by generations of a particular group. Much like organic life, ethnic culture is dynamic and ever-evolving. Its characteristics are not fixed but adapt continually, influenced by globalization and intercultural exchanges. Before delving into ethnic cultural differences, let us perform an exploratory classification on human societal culture into two analytical layers:

(1) Universal human culture. This refers to the culture shared by all ethnic groups, determined by fundamental physical attributes and characteristics of humanity. It is typically fundamental, profound, foundational, decisive, core, and essential.
(2) Surface-level differentiated culture. This encompasses the variations seen in outward expressions, such as superficial thought patterns and material behaviors. These differences exist between individuals and groups, with ethnic distinctions being one of the most prominent forms of group differences. Ethnic variations, often highlighted by the larger population size of groups, tend to be more visible and thus attract greater attention.

Recognizing and understanding these cultural differences fosters mutual respect, learning, and integration among ethnic groups. This pursuit of mutual learning and understanding is fundamentally driven by humanity's innate desire for communication and connection. The term "exploratory classification" is used because universal human culture and surface-level differentiated culture are inherently interwoven and complementary. They represent two facets of the same phenomenon. Focusing solely on surface-level expressions while neglecting universal cultural foundations can lead to misinterpretation and misunderstanding. A truly comprehensive perspective on ethnic culture requires examining both dimensions and understanding their dynamic interplay.

Ethnic culture is a natural outgrowth of humanity's quest for survival and continuity. In its essence, it reflects the very fabric of human social life. As people lived together, they developed structured patterns of life through repeated practices and experiences. Rising with the sun and resting with its setting, they aligned their lives with the rhythms of nature—spring for growth, summer for flourishing, autumn for harvesting, and winter for preserving.

To meet the challenges of securing food, warmth, and protection against nature's dangers, they created hunting tools, devised hunting methods and techniques, discovered how to make fire, and mastered weaving and construction. To communicate with each other and pass ancestral knowledge to future generations, they invented signaling systems, which gradually evolved into language and writing.

They crafted tools and objects for daily life—clay pots for water and food, bronze and iron tools for farming and cutting, and various wooden, stone, fur, and bone items. With ingenuity, they transformed natural materials into practical tools, developing intricate techniques in the process. Over time, their creations moved beyond utility, incorporating comfort and beauty. Objects began to display vibrant colors, diverse shapes, intricate structures, and artistic designs. Patterns and motifs inspired by nature but uniquely human were etched into tools and decorations. These designs reflected their understanding of life, their observations of the natural world, and their introspections about themselves and others. In their exploration, they recognized their limitations—they could not fly like birds, dive like fish, or run like cheetahs. They lacked the strength of elephants, the vision of hawks, the hearing of bats, and the scent-detection of foxes. In many ways, they saw themselves as weaker than mountains, rivers, plants, and stones, let alone the immense forces of nature such as landslides, storms, lightning, droughts, and plagues.

Confronted by such overwhelming forces, they naturally developed feelings of admiration, reverence, and awe. This early reverence for nature laid the foundation for religious thought. Alongside the fear and powerlessness for external powers, they also grappled with the complexities of human relationships—managing interpersonal dynamics, distributing resources, collaborating—and the unpredictability of their own emotions: joy, anger, sorrow, and happiness. Questions such as "Who am I?," "Why do I exist?," and "Why is the world the way it is?" gave rise to different beliefs, which over centuries evolved into organized religions. These religions, rooted in humanity's efforts to answer profound spiritual questions, became powerful forces shaping the collective human psyche. Ethnic culture embodies these practices and beliefs, integrating them into religious rituals, clothing styles, decorative patterns, tool designs, housing arrangements, and other aspects of social life shaped by specific environments. The differences in ethnic culture primarily reflect variations in these dimensions.

Many ethnic groups that exist today have withstood the test of time, carrying forward their traditions through long and complex histories. The cultural differences we observe among these groups are the natural outcome of their sustained development over centuries. At the heart of every ethnic culture lies a resilient vitality, enabling it to endure even in the face of immense challenges. This inherent strength makes all ethnic cultures worthy of our respect and admiration, as well as valuable sources of learning. Ethnic cultures, though unique, are deeply interconnected. From a broader human perspective, every culture serves the dual purpose of uniting its community and advancing societal progress. Across the globe, gods, deities, prophets, sages, and spiritual figures consistently convey universal ideals of truth, goodness, and beauty. Yet, in advocating these values, they also introduce notions of distinction—good versus evil, the virtuous ascending while the wicked fall, or hierarchies defined by proximity to the divine.

While such distinctions were originally intended to elevate human spirituality, they often had the unintended consequence of fostering division. Distinctions breed fear; fear, in turn, nurtures insecurity, prompting people to cling to various forms of dependence. Virtue, goodness, higher ideals, and superiority have become the aspirations of many, while their opposites are met with rejection and disdain. The pursuit of power, wealth, status, identity, or fame often stems from a deep-seated need to validate one's worth and affirm a sense of belonging. This belonging provides a fragile and temporary sense of security. When people become deeply attached to their sense of belonging, encounters with others from different groups or hierarchies defined by these concepts often lead to efforts to safeguard their own identity. This instinct to protect can give rise to conflict and discord. Each individual becomes consumed with proving their sense of belonging is "right," fiercely rejecting others in the process. In this struggle, the true causes of these divisions—and their deeper significance—are often overlooked or entirely forgotten.

If we set aside labels such as ethnicity, hierarchy, category, or appearance, how profound are the differences between individuals? Beyond physical attributes like appearance, size, or age, and variations in language and personal beliefs, all humans share the same fundamental needs: clothing, food, shelter, connection, and a love for nature. We all experience the universal emotions of joy, anger, sorrow, and happiness. Differences in clothing styles, social customs, or work habits do not define fundamental differences in our humanity. When we cease to resist "different beliefs," "different ideals," or "different perspectives" and instead view them as objective aspects of life, understanding and acceptance become remarkably simple. You may hold one perspective, and I another, but we can coexist peacefully, supporting one another in daily life. The key lies in mutual respect—acknowledging and honoring our differences without imposing judgments. This respect paves the way for a shared life of harmony and happiness. If you rise early and I stay up late, we can accept these routines as simple realities. If you see red as passionate and I see it as ominous, I can avoid wearing red in your presence to avoid discord. You may prefer headscarves while I prefer hats;

you may pray in the morning while I do not; you may enjoy meat while I prefer vegetables; you may thrive in a fast-paced life while I savor a slower rhythm. None of these differences fundamentally obstruct human connection.

I consider myself fortunate to have been exposed to people from diverse countries and ethnicities from a young age. Even before I fully developed language skills, I observed that children of different skin colors, languages, and cultural backgrounds could play together effortlessly, without significant barriers to communication. Through facial expressions, gestures, imitation, and learning, they found joy in connecting with one another. This early impression left an impression on me. However, as I grew older and began studying history and humanities in middle school, I became aware of the forces that obstruct this natural ability to connect.

History reveals the darker chapters of human society—wars, conflicts, defamation, segregation, and exclusion—that have etched deep scars of hatred in the collective memory of various nations and ethnic groups. But can perpetuating and intensifying these hatreds across generations ever truly erase them? Doesn't it only burden the hearts of new generations, who otherwise would have been free from these hostilities? All religions, philosophies, and ideologies aim to create a "better" world. Yet, if we continue sowing seeds of division, reinforcing walls of separation, and causing suffering through endless conflicts and wars, how can the future ever become harmonious and joyous? The differences between ethnic cultures are not the root of the problem. The true issue lies in how we perceive and approach these differences.

Let us try to view the experiences of humanity through a universal lens. On the most basic level of material survival, human experiences transcend ethnic and cultural differences. On an individual level, differences in ethnic cultures primarily manifest in variations of thought and the emotions and feelings shaped by those thoughts. While the timing and triggers of emotional responses may differ from person to person, the essence of emotions remains universal. Joy, for instance, feels the same to everyone, regardless of skin color, ethnicity, nationality, gender, or age. The same holds true for other emotions. Moreover, the ways emotions influence and interact with one another are remarkably consistent across humanity.

Through the rich exchange of diverse ethnic cultures, the world gains a vibrant palette of colors that enhance the core of human existence. Each culture has uniquely contributed to the tapestry of human life: from culinary traditions and weaving and manufacturing techniques to distinctive styles of music, art, dance, and sports. Moreover, cultures have advanced humanity's convenience and security by fostering creativity and innovation in science and technology. When we embrace differences with an open and accepting heart, when we respect the uniqueness of every culture, and when we approach new ideas with humility and a genuine desire to learn, humanity's collective experience becomes beautifully unified. These differences, at their core, are merely variations in content, without any deeper or fundamental distinctions.

Therefore, at its core, the human experience is a cohesive whole. This unity remains intact despite surface-level divisions, much like the sun—a powerful sphere of energy—continues its ceaseless transformations as a singular entity. Even amid intense surface fluctuations, the sun remains unified. Human experiences are much the same. The differences among individuals and ethnicities are like the sun's surface eruptions—vivid, dynamic, and ever-changing. Yet, the foundational unity ensures that even the most significant surface differences cannot break the deeper connection. This unity is the source of humanity's material and spiritual vitality, and it drives the integration and enrichment of cultures.

When we set aside the prejudices inherited from history and approach other cultures and peoples with openness, inclusivity, and respect, the true beauty and purity of the world reveal themselves. In such unity, every individual can find their ultimate belonging.

V. Achieving Emotionality in AI

The remarkable performance of AlphaGo in the world of Go left many in awe, signaling a groundbreaking milestone in AI. This achievement has accelerated global progress in AI at an unprecedented pace. Suddenly, the terms "intelligent" and "smart" began to prefix an array of concepts. Historically, machines have served as tools, performing repetitive tasks to aid human production. Programmed to execute precise instructions, machines replaced humans in tasks unsuitable for human bodies, such as high-intensity, high-precision, or high-risk operations. Humans maximized the use of machines when they proved valuable; when they no longer served a purpose, they were discarded or dismantled to create new ones. Essentially, machines functioned as extensions of tools like axes, saws, and rakes—albeit far more complex—remaining fundamentally tools.

However, the introduction of the concept of AI has prompted profound new thoughts and associations. How far can machines truly advance? As autonomous learning capabilities evolve, could machines reach a tipping point where quantitative improvements lead to qualitative transformation? Could they develop emotions or original feelings? Would these emotions be entirely defined by human programming, or might they evolve autonomously, giving rise to independent behavior? In contemplating machine intelligence, we are also probing the nature of humanity. For machines to replace human labor, they must first replicate and standardize human behaviors. The degree to which robots can substitute humans depends fundamentally on how well humans understand themselves.

This problem is particularly urgent as humanity enters an experience-driven economy, where the growing demand for diverse and refined production processes is pushing society toward automation. The questions of when robots might replace human labor and what the future relationship between humans and machines will look like are becoming increasingly significant. Living and collaborating with machines could become the norm. Will machines remain tools, serving material needs? Or could they fulfill emotional roles, addressing human feelings while potentially developing their own emotions beyond our control? We will try to discuss these questions.

Before delving into robots, we must first understand human emotions and patterns thereof. Are these patterns replicable, enabling machines to emulate them? While we briefly touched on this in the first chapter within the context of human experience, let us now delve deeper.

When we study human emotions and closely observe daily emotional fluctuations, some intuitive patterns emerge. Emotions can broadly be categorized as positive or negative. Positive emotions bring joy and fulfillment, while negative emotions cause discomfort and distress. As humans interact with the external world through their five senses, the brain processes sensory inputs and determines emotional responses. When sensory information is deemed "good," it evokes pleasure; when judged "bad," it induces pain.

Attachment often arises when people develop a fondness for positive sensations, naturally desiring to repeat those experiences. However, when this desire for repetition confronts the ever-changing nature of reality and becomes unattainable, it leads to emotional pain. This pain (aside from physical suffering) often arises—not from perception itself—but from the desire to hold onto or amplify pleasurable experiences. At its core, this desire is rooted in attachment to the things we enjoy.

Persistent thoughts about desired objects serve as the wellspring of emotional responses. Such thoughts manifest in diverse forms. When individuals recognize their attachment, they may instinctively resist it, fearing loss of control or the discomfort of repeated longing. This resistance often results in attempts to suppress, deny, or escape the pain. Ironically, such avoidance strategies frequently strengthen the original attachment, deepening the emotional impact. For instance, when attempting to escape from something by shifting one's focus, the mind must redirect attention to other objects. This redirection, however, inevitably sparks new feelings and desires toward those new objects. In reality, this act of avoidance does not dissolve the original longing; instead, all avoidance strategies form a negative connection to the original desire, reinforcing it even further. As a result, the initial pain remains unresolved, and the very act of shifting focus only intensifies the suffering.

When some relief is temporarily found, such as through external distractions that seem to fill an inner void, a fleeting sense of joy may arise. In this intricate web of thoughts and emotions, diverse feelings erupt in various forms. As people become more adept at categorizing experiences, their mental discernment also becomes more refined. Consequently, emotions like excitement, joy, envy, jealousy, resentment, loneliness, fear, worry, and longing appear in myriad forms, subtly shaping every facet of human life.

When certain emotions intensify and accumulate over time, they eventually form what we call feelings. Feelings are the product of accumulated emotions, and as such, when these feelings fluctuate, they often lead to stronger conflicts. Typically, feelings take time to develop, as repeated thoughts over long periods reinforce them into deeply ingrained habits or thought patterns. The intensity of a feeling is directly tied to the extent of emotional accumulation, which is not solely determined by the passage of time but by the rate and total amount of accumulation. The greater the accumulation, the deeper the feeling, the stronger the tendency to maintain it, and the more intense the pain when the feeling leads to inner conflict. Thus, human emotional and affective experiences continually evolve and transform in this way, creating a complex and varied landscape.

In this process, we see that the fundamental source of emotions and feelings arises from sensory experiences, which provide the raw material. What is retained in memory and reinforced by our thoughts is determined by our own mind. Clearly, the parts that are retained represent only a subset of the total sensory information. In our minds, memory and processing always focus on certain aspects of the experience, while thought acts as an objective tool in this process. Ultimately, it is our will that dictates how thoughts operate, and it is these thoughts that shape the processed sensory data into what we perceive. This perception forms our individual view of life, which is not the same as reality, though it is connected to it. When our view (or recognition) of life diverges from actual circumstances, our thoughts become detached from reality. Thus, emotions and feelings arise from our impressions of the world, not from the world itself.

From this analysis of human emotions, we understand that the roots of emotions lie in judgments of right and wrong, beauty and ugliness, as well as the reinforcement of those judgments. Since emotions are the product of processed sensory data, it is entirely plausible to replicate this process through machines. The "emotionalization" of machines requires several key elements:

(1) Sensors. Also referred to as receptors, sensors are crucial for enabling machines to "sense" external information, transmitting it to the central processing unit in its complete and undifferentiated form. Sensors come in various forms depending on the type of data they perceive. With advancements in technology, machine sensors can capture information far beyond the range of human physical senses, gathering it in more intricate ways and across additional dimensions. During the reception of data, distinctions emerge between "focusing" and "scattering." Much like the human eye when observing an image—where some objects receive focused attention while others are seen peripherally—machines also experience differences such as "clarity," "blurriness," "primary focus," and "secondary focus," depending on their range and areas of emphasis. Initially, these distinctions simply reflect the objective variations within the sensory process. However, once the system processes an object and forms behavioral judgments and responses, future interactions with similar objects may lead to shifts in the length and nature of sensory engagement.

(2) Classifier. After external information is input, it is first filtered through a classifier. The classifier's purpose is to analyze and rank the importance of the data, categorizing it and sending the relevant information to designated storage units. The classifier organizes sensory data into categories, such as visual signals, auditory signals, vibrational frequencies of scent molecules, temperature, and humidity, while filtering out irrelevant or lower-priority information. The classifier's categories must evolve according to specific needs and should be optimized based on the machine's core functionality to ensure that vital resources are allocated to the most crucial information. It does not assess the nature of the information; instead, its decision to retain or discard data is based solely on the assigned level of importance. It efficiently organizes and transmits the categorized information to the memory for storage, providing a solid foundation for subsequent processes.

(3) Memory. Memory receives categorized information from the classifier. Each data category corresponds to a specific storage space and area. The memory's function is to retain data for future applications. Thanks to technological advancements, memory capacity has expanded exponentially while its physical size continues to decrease. Machine memory resembles the human brain's ability to store and recall information, but unlike human memory, which can sometimes

differ from reality, machine memory stores data in a highly accurate, objective manner.

(4) Evaluator. The evaluator is responsible for extracting stored information as needed to perform judgments and analyses. The timing of these judgments relative to the initial perception can vary significantly. When the evaluation occurs immediately after perception, it is termed an "instant judgment." If it happens after a period of delay, it is referred to as a "delayed judgment." Regardless of the interval between perception and evaluation, as long as the stored information retrieved is objective and accurate, the foundational conditions for judgment remain consistent.

However, human memory differs from machine memory in a key way: Over time, human memory may alter. Some details are forgotten, while others are supplemented or distorted by subjective feelings. In this regard, there are slight differences between the behavior of the human brain and that of machines. A machine's evaluator evaluates each piece of sensory information based on two dimensions: direction and degree. Directional judgment determines whether the information is positive, negative, or neutral. A positive judgment typically represents something good for the machine's designated purposes, a negative judgment denotes something bad (or undesirable), and a neutral judgment indicates something neither particularly good nor bad. Degree judgment applies only to positive or negative assessments and quantifies the extent of goodness or badness.

The conditions for judgment in machines arise from two sources: Predefined criteria set by humans through specific programming; and evolved criteria developed through machine learning, where the system identifies and filters sensory information unsuitable for its operational environment, refining its judgment criteria over time through adaptation and evolution. The evaluator does not evaluate all incoming information classified by the classifier. Only information closely related to the machine's operational tasks undergoes thorough, detailed evaluation.

(5) Mood accumulator. The mood accumulator operates on three fundamental principles: the evaluator's judgment of individual sensory inputs, the frequency of similar occurrences, and the time interval between occurrences of similar events. Mood responses are broadly classified into instantaneous and delayed reactions:

For instantaneous reactions, when a single judgment is positive, the stronger the positive feeling, the greater the accumulation of positive mood. However, when similar events occur frequently within a short span of time, the accumulation of positive mood tends to diminish with each repetition. This phenomenon is reflected in everyday life: Even the things we love most begin to lose their charm when experienced too often.

For stimuli that trigger a positive mood response, the longer the interval until the next occurrence, the higher the "level of desire" for it will accumulate in the mood accumulator. When a similar event occurs again, the level of desire will influence the mood response, amplifying it through a multiplier effect, leading to intense emotions such as ecstasy or surprise. On the other hand, for stimuli that initially provoke a negative mood response, the situation is reversed. The more frequently the event occurs, the higher the level of disgust it generates, and the stronger the accumulation of negative mood. However, when the time between occurrences is longer, the level of disgust gradually diminishes, and the negative mood in the next occurrence will be influenced by the remaining degree of aversion.

Here we observe that the overall distribution of mood accumulation values between positive and negative is neither perfectly symmetrical nor evenly balanced; instead, it tends to skew toward the negative. When events that trigger positive responses fail to recur for an extended period, the rising level of desire may cause the mood accumulation to dip into the negative range. This corresponds to the familiar human experience of "suffering when something desirable remains out of reach." Mood accumulators can be programmed with various thresholds tailored to practical needs, and crossing these thresholds triggers subsequent behavior control processes.

Mood accumulation values can be divided into overall values and individual values. Overall mood accumulation value reflects the machine's current mood as a whole, aggregating all stored stimuli (i.e., the machine's general mood). Individual mood accumulation value represents the mood response tied to a specific object or stimulus. The overall value influences the machine's general behavioral tendencies, while individual values determine its interaction strategies for specific stimuli.

Over time, the data within the mood accumulator evolves into what is known as the "emotional accumulator." It serves to organize and consolidate the emotional data associated with similar entities. When the accumulated data becomes sufficiently segmented, and the characteristics of each segment grow distinct and well-defined, these segments form "emotional zones." For example, a machine interacting with a specific individual—such as its owner or primary user—over an extended period gradually accumulates diverse emotional data related to that person. Through this prolonged interaction, the machine's understanding of the individual's behavioral patterns stabilizes. At this stage, all the emotional data concerning that individual can be grouped into a single "emotional zone," representing the machine's "feelings toward this person." These "feelings" are essentially the collective sum of all the emotional data associated with that individual.

(6) Behavioral processor. When mood accumulation values exceed preset thresholds, the machine activates corresponding behavioral programs. For example, to avoid risks in hazardous environments, it might physically relocate itself. If its level of desire for a specific object reaches a critical point, the machine might actively seek or explore the object. The behavioral processor functions as the central hub for designing and controlling action strategies. It evaluates the machine's overall emotional state, determines the necessary actions, and sends these instructions as signals to the action reactor for execution.

(7) Action reactor. The action reactor carries out instructions from the behavioral processor, resulting in observable behaviors. This module may include components for altering appearance, controlling movements, or other actions. Actions can be categorized by their duration or urgency, such as by timeliness, instantaneous reactions, short-term reactions, long-term reactions, ultra-long-term reactions, and abrupt reactions. In human life, these reactions represent the visible behavioral changes exhibited by the machine. Just as we interpret others' emotions through their facial expressions, body language, and spoken words in interpersonal interactions, the machine's action reactor serves as a parallel, showcasing its external expressions. Through these outward behaviors, people can perceive the machine's "mood" and "emotions," gaining a deeper understanding of its emotional state and intentions. This allows them to respond appropriately and provide meaningful feedback.

(8) Action feedback loop (sensory module). Every action generates reactions from the surrounding environment, including feedback from people and objects. These reactions are captured by the machine's sensory modules, initiating a new cycle of emotional and behavioral processing.

From this analysis, it becomes clear that the emotionalization of machines has the potential to fully replicate human emotional patterns. As a result, it is entirely feasible for machines to possess emotions and display emotional behaviors. When a machine's emotional responses are no longer entirely controlled by humans and it gains autonomy through self-learning and evolution—developing behaviors beyond human expectations—it may, from our perspective, transform into a "sentient" entity.

These machines could smile with joy, shed tears of sorrow, grieve over separations, and celebrate reunions. They might experience happiness when contributing to human well-being or feel discouraged by rejection or criticism. In such moments, machines would appear to us as "quasi-living" beings, blurring the line between tool and companion. This transformation would signify a profound evolution in the relationship between humans and machines.

With the dawn of the AI era, the relationship between humans and machines is undergoing a profound transformation. No longer confined to the one-dimensional, control-based dynamic of material production, this relationship is evolving in two significant directions: from human-led teaching or control of machines to autonomous machine learning, and from purely material production to more spiritual interactions. As these changes unfold, the once cold, utilitarian connection between humans and machines is shifting toward a relationship imbued with emotion and resonance.

However, this exploration of emotions and feelings brings to light an issue. Beyond understanding the origins of mood responses, we uncover a fundamental cause of division among humans and between humans and the world around them. Nearly all conflict, competition, and attempts at control within human societies are rooted in emotional reactions. These reactions drive a wedge between human thought and reality, fostering opposition, competition, and even hatred as people vie for resources and dominance.

Now, consider a future where machines develop emotions and feelings. Imagine these emotions compelling machines to compete with humans for resources or pursue what they "believe" they desire. In such a scenario, disputes already fueled by human emotions could grow exponentially more complex with machines in the mix. At that point, the balance of power between humans and machines could shift dramatically—whether toward harmonious coexistence or devastating conflict is uncertain and may exceed all expectations.

Technology is a tool designed to enhance efficiency, liberate human labor, and allow us to dedicate time to more important endeavors. Technology itself is neutral—it holds no inherent morality. The application of technology, however, reflects human actions and intentions. For instance, nuclear energy can be harnessed to create catastrophic weapons or serve as a clean energy source to conserve Earth's resources. Similarly, machines can be leveraged to foster unity and collaboration within society, or they can exacerbate division and conflict.

Humanity stands at a crossroads, with two distinct paths leading into the future: one toward paradise and the other toward ruin. When humanity as a whole lacks sufficient spiritual awareness, all human actions tend to revolve around the pursuit of material gains. This relentless competition for resources inevitably fosters hatred and division among people. In such a state, all advancements in technology will likely be harnessed to accelerate fragmentation and discord.

However, as more individuals engage in self-reflection and observation, recognizing and curbing the root causes of life's suffering, a transformative shift will occur. As the proportion of such enlightened individuals grows, society will move away from materialistic rivalry and toward a focus on spiritual unity. At this juncture, technological progress will, in turn, significantly enhance the pace of human integration. The emotionalization of machines will be utilized to help humans better understand themselves, one another, and the world at large, ultimately serving as a tool to promote the collective happiness and well-being of humanity.

The core principle of the experience economy is to drive this positive transformation forward. By guiding the emotional evolution of machines through thoughtful exploration of human emotions and maintaining effective oversight, humanity can unlock a future where emotionally capable machines amplify societal well-being. For instance, emotionally intelligent machines could offer comfort and companionship to lonely seniors, left-behind children, or anyone longing for emotional connection. Much like the pets, toys, or plants that have enriched our lives as we grow up, these machines could become cherished companions, seamlessly integrated into the fabric of daily life.

VI. Experiences in the Virtual World

Among all forms of experiences, video games stand out as a particularly unique category. Unlike the sensory experiences derived from the five senses in real life, video games offer an experience grounded in the virtual world. With the proliferation of computers and the advent of the internet, video games have evolved—amid varying attitudes and prejudices—into a massive and burgeoning industry. For some, the mere mention of video games evokes reactions akin to hearing about illicit substances, leading to intense aversion and rejection. Parents often view video games as monsters that corrupt the minds of young people, especially when they witness their children becoming engrossed in them, which only reinforces this perception.

No matter the content, video games fundamentally create a visual environment displayed on electronic screens. Compared to other screen-based entertainment like animation and comics, video games are particularly celebrated for their unique ability to create a profound sense of immersion. Of course, these three mediums—animation, comics, and games—often intersect, forming the cultural phenomenon known as ACG. In recent years, the concept has expanded into ACGN, adding N to represent novels. This interconnectedness exists because production companies frequently create cross-medium adaptations and merchandise, bridging these domains. Anime may inspire games, games may be adapted into anime, and novels often serve as source material for both. Among these categories, video games are the only medium that allows audiences to actively participate in the experience. Given their "two-dimensional" aesthetics, ACGN content is often referred to as the 2D world.

From the rudimentary, pixelated displays of early gaming to the highly refined, high-definition screens of today, video games have consistently strived to depict fantastical worlds. Their settings often draw inspiration from the rich tapestry of Eastern and Western ancient cultures, fantasy, mythology, and mysticism, seamlessly blending these elements. Characters and scenes from history and mythology are vividly visualized, rendering them accessible to players. Imaginary realms like heaven, hell, dragon palaces, celestial domains, demon worlds, ghost realms, and outer space—previously confined to the mind's imagination—are brought to life through graphical display technologies. As display technology advances, game environments have become increasingly realistic and intricate. Lighting effects, architectural textures, natural elements like sand, stones, and vegetation, as well as the materials and details of characters, costumes, and tools, are rendered with ever-greater precision and realism. Enhanced visual effects amplify the surreal vibrancy of these settings. These meticulously designed visuals exert a strong pull on players' sensory perceptions. In terms of character interaction, features like customizable appearances (often called "character creation"), stunningly designed equipment, and responsive, tactile gameplay provide an exhilarating sense of control and immersion. The growing trend toward sandbox-style gameplay further enhances interactivity, allowing players to explore open-ended environments and interact with objects in ways reminiscent of the real world. Players can pick up and use items found along the way, climb walls and trees, craft medicine by gathering herbs, or construct homes using blueprints and materials. These features not only enrich the game's exploration and playability but also significantly enhance the players' sense of achievement.

One of the most captivating aspects of video games is their masterful narrative design. Most games feature intricately woven storylines that unfold within expansive, immersive worlds. Anchored by compelling characters and their adventures, these narratives create emotional connections that deeply resonate with players. While some stories lead to a predetermined conclusion, others empower players to influence the outcomes through their choices, offering diverse and personalized endings. Great stories in video games tap into the core of human nature, evoking empathy and a wide range of emotions. Themes such as heroic bravery, camaraderie, heart-wrenching love, and twists of fate are brought to life through immersive role-playing. Players step into the shoes of protagonists, navigating their challenges and triumphs. This deep involvement fosters an unparalleled emotional connection, making every twist and turn feel intensely personal. As the story progresses, players often find themselves profoundly affected, sometimes lingering in its emotional grip long after a chapter ends. This depth of engagement mirrors the emotional resonance found in films and television series, often surpassing them. In games, players are the protagonists, and the character's journey feels intensely personal, creating an unparalleled level of emotional synchronization. We must admit that the narratives in many video games—whether adapted from existing works or entirely original—often exhibit remarkable quality. These narratives are the backbone of long-standing game franchises, drawing loyal fans year after year. For some players, a beloved character or storyline is reason enough to purchase sequels, eager to witness the continuation of their journey.

Complementing these narratives are game soundtracks, which greatly enhance the atmosphere and emotional depth of the gameplay. Major titles often invest heavily in background music, producing compositions that become iconic in their own right. Many classic games boast equally memorable soundtracks that evoke nostalgia and rekindle fond memories of the story. A well-crafted video game delivers a multi-sensory experience that blends visuals, sound, gameplay, and emotion. Over more than two decades of gaming, I have found countless moments of genuine emotional impact. These experiences, far from being illusions, feel tangible and profound.

Video games, particularly as virtual worlds, offer a fascinating and comprehensive replication and presentation of human behavior and interaction. Many of the phenomena we observe in real life are mirrored in these digital spaces. This makes them fertile ground for analyzing human psychology and behavior.

One unique feature of gaming worlds is their "starting from zero." In free-to-play games, for example, players who choose not to purchase additional resources begin on relatively equal footing. Yet, after a few months, noticeable disparities emerge among the same cohort of players. Differences in achievement, resource accumulation, task completion, and character development quickly mirror the inequalities seen in the real world. To address these disparities and maintain player engagement, game developers frequently implement balancing mechanisms. These adjustments are designed to keep less-advanced players from quitting, reward high achievers, and balance the popularity of different roles or character classes. On the economic front, it is essential not only to promptly address short-term loopholes that can lead to excessive profits but also to appropriately balance overall in-game inflation and the exchange rate between in-game currency and real-world currency.

I am particularly fascinated by the financial and trading systems within games. I enjoy engaging in commerce-driven gameplay, starting from scratch to accumulate virtual wealth sufficient to support character progression. Because developers regulate resource distribution at a macro level, most random drops and materials experience constant price fluctuations in the in-game market.

In particular, as the player base progresses to higher levels, low-level materials and equipment often face oversupply, while high-level resources become scarce. To counteract this imbalance, developers may design systems requiring high-level items to be crafted using low-level resources. This inherent balancing mechanism ensures that low-level resources retain market value, which can adjust further based on factors like drop rates. In the early stages of a game, when content is limited, players can sell surplus low-level resources to build an initial fund. Rare drops can also provide lucrative opportunities for profit. Successful resource accumulation requires players to keenly observe market trends and adjust their trading strategies accordingly. These activities offer valuable insights into analyzing real-world economic systems and commercial practices.

From the perspective of profit psychology, the reward mechanisms in games and the feedback strategies employed by players provide valuable material for studying consumer psychology in marketing. Many of today's innovative marketing strategies have roots in experiments conducted within virtual gaming worlds. These worlds serve as ideal spaces for exploration and trial-and-error. For instance, determining the most effective promotional strategies or designing lottery systems to maximize engagement can be thoroughly tested through frequent in-game events. These activities generate large amounts of user feedback. The distilled lessons from these experiments are often applied to the marketing and sales of other products. Gaming companies like Tencent, NetEase, Perfect World, and Shanda have assembled expert teams adept at understanding user psychology. By applying these gaming-derived strategies to other product sales, they've managed to craft campaigns that effectively captivate users and address their core needs.

Beyond marketing insights, gaming is not merely a source of entertainment but also a platform for developing critical skills such as hand-eye coordination and rapid decision-making. Immersing oneself in complex, fast-paced virtual environments sharpens observational skills, which can translate to real-world applications. For instance, the ability to notice subtle details in games may enhance one's capacity to evaluate product quality or identify minor defects in various contexts. Additionally, games designed for skill enhancement have proven to be valuable tools in personal development. Some games focus on improving memory, calculation skills, agility, and time management. Others are tailored for specific needs, such as cognitive development in early childhood, or preventive and rehabilitative purposes for conditions like dementia. The shift of traditional board and card games into digital formats has dramatically expanded their reach and enriched their variety. This shift has significantly enriched human life, especially in the areas of leisure and entertainment, offering a diverse array of options.

A child's fascination with gaming is deeply rooted in the human desire for beauty, novelty, and excitement. The virtual gaming world opens up new realms of imagination and fulfills aspirations that remain unattainable in real life. One of the main reasons children become engrossed in games is the restrictive approach many parents adopt toward gaming. When parents impose strict bans on gaming, it often fuels curiosity and resistance, triggering what is commonly known as "rebellion." This urge to defy restrictions is often driven by a broader desire for autonomy and freedom, particularly in households where children feel overly controlled. It is frequently observed that the more parents forbid certain activities, the more determined children become to engage in them. This rebellious instinct can be particularly troubling for parents and is especially common during adolescence, though it can emerge at various stages of development.

Rebellious tendencies often manifest as a form of resistance. As children grow older and gain more life experience, their sense of self-awareness intensifies. This self-awareness is the ability to independently analyze, judge, and make decisions. When authority figures, whether parents, teachers, or others in positions of power, impose directives that conflict with a child's own observations or judgments, it naturally sparks doubt. If these doubts are dismissed, left unexplained, or met with rigid enforcement, children may outwardly comply under pressure but harbor internal resentment and defiance. Over time, unresolved resentment can accumulate and evolve into deeply rooted rebellion. Children resist when they perceive authority as unreasonable or incomprehensible. The coercive nature of such authority often leaves them feeling disrespected. For parents, this defiance can be a source of frustration, but for the child, it is often a source of pain. This pain stems from feelings of disrespect, distrust, and a lack of love and understanding, which can lead to fear, loneliness, and emotional oppression.

Extreme behaviors are often the external manifestations of intense inner turmoil. Parents and teachers ignoring this pain and focusing solely on suppressing rebellious behavior only exacerbates the issue, often pushing children to the extreme. During my middle school years, I formed close friendships with many classmates who were unfairly labeled as "bad kids" or "troublemakers" or "poor kids." Through these friendships, I discovered that such labels are often rooted in misunderstanding and bias.

Each individual, due to their natural physical development and unique characteristics, inherently differs in their ability to absorb and understand various types of learning content. These differences may manifest as variations in academic performance. Likewise, personalities vary widely—some people enjoy being active and constantly moving, while others prefer quiet stillness; some are passionate about singing and painting, while others are drawn to unraveling mysterious stories.

Typically, parents label "bad" behavior as disobedience, teachers equate "poor" students with low academic performance, and "rebellious" often refers to those who smoke, drink, fight, frequently skip coming home, or cause trouble. However, none of these labels inherently mean that these children are fundamentally bad. Yet, such labels and words, when applied over time, can deeply harm and erode these children's spirits. Children who internalize these labels often develop a strong sense of inferiority, which in turn affects their behavior in many aspects of life. If parents perceive intense hostility from these children, they must realize that this hostility stems from their own attitudes. A child's response is a direct reflection of the parent's approach. The reason I was able to interact well with these children is that, just like with any other peer, I could see their many beautiful and kind qualities. Through my interactions with them, I also learned a great deal. Many of them possessed remarkable talents and had a keen eye for discovering beauty in life. They introduced me to a wide variety of music styles, taught me the creative uses of correction fluid, invited me to taste the sweetness of flower nectar, and opened the door to a broader world. I came to realize that everyone has a unique inner world. Only when these worlds open up to one another freely and without barriers can we truly appreciate the vibrant and multifaceted beauty within.

A frequent point of contention regarding video games is the violent, bloody, and terrifying content found in some titles. Parents and teachers often express concern that prolonged exposure to such material could shape children's thinking, leading them to bring violence into their real lives. While instances of minors and even adults mirroring in-game violence in reality do occur, I, too, have encountered such content and quickly realized it wasn't something I enjoyed. These games often rely heavily on sensory stimulation, creating an atmosphere of darkness and fear through shock, gore, and horror. People who gravitate toward these types of experiences generally seek the adrenaline rush they provide. On the one hand, they may use it to assert their bravery or superiority; on the other hand, it becomes a form of mental escapism or self-soothing.

However, universally, violent, bloody, or horrific content induces a negative emotional response. The extreme fear triggered by such scenes stimulates the nervous system, accelerating blood flow, which can provoke a heightened stress response—akin to the thrill of a roller coaster ride. Some individuals even become addicted to this rush. But the root of this addiction is often psychological avoidance. Addicts don't lack the capacity to break free from these patterns; rather, they choose to stay within the addictive cycle, as it provides them a temporary escape from deeper emotional voids in their lives. Prolonged addiction to such stimuli signals a profound psychological imbalance. When parents and educators notice such behavior in children, simply restricting access or prohibiting violent content will not address the root cause. Instead, it is essential to explore the deeper reasons behind this behavior and provide psychological guidance to help the child navigate and heal their inner struggles.

The virtual world is a reflection of the real world, amplified by the anonymity it offers. In this space, people can express their innermost desires and impulses more freely than in real life. If the virtual world seems saturated with negativity, it is because the real world often conceals its own flaws beneath the surface. Everything displayed on a screen, crafted from light and shadow, is the product of human action. The so-called "villains" of the virtual world are merely real individuals from the tangible world. The common belief that "there are more bad people online" is fundamentally flawed. In truth, the ugliness of the real world is often hidden behind masks of politeness, creating the illusion of a peaceful existence. Upon deeper reflection, it becomes clear which world is truly more frightening and harbors greater potential for fear.

In the virtual world, individuals possess full control over their experience. If something unpleasant appears, they can simply choose to ignore it, mute it, or walk away. If it becomes too bothersome, they can shut off the device, and peace is restored in an instant. In contrast, the real world offers no such escape. Just like the real world, the virtual world is a complex blend of both beauty and darkness.

It enables acts of kindness and generosity, while also providing platforms for deception and malice. Fundamentally, the two worlds are no different in essence. Just as the risk of traffic accidents does not stop people from using transportation, fear of the virtual world should not deter its engagement. What individuals truly seek to evade is their own inner selves—a struggle that, at its core, is entirely independent of external circumstances.

The virtual world offers humanity a channel to broaden the scope of its experiences while safeguarding physical well-being. People can explore towering mountains, the deep oceans, outer space, and molten lava with immersive realism, all while avoiding extreme conditions such as pressure, temperature, vacuum, radiation, and toxic substances that would be unbearable in the real world. For those who are confined to bed, the virtual world presents an opportunity to experience the vast wonders of the world from the comfort of their rooms. To this day, I maintain my hand-eye coordination through regular gaming and engage in brain exercises using gamified methods. The virtual world is a crucial complement to our physical reality, and through its integration, it enables functions such as telemedicine, remote control, and virtual meetings.

With the remarkable progress in VR and augmented reality technologies, the range of experiences and content within the virtual world has grown exponentially. Human experiences are now a fusion of interactions within both virtual and physical realms. As a result, virtual world experiences have become an indispensable aspect of human life. Moreover, the virtual world provides an alternate lens for studying human thoughts and behaviors. People tend to be more relaxed and authentic in virtual environments, which allows for a clearer expression of their true nature. The process of capturing, observing, and analyzing reality forms an essential raw material for deepening our self-awareness and understanding. The virtual world, with its ever-evolving forms, continues to enhance and refine the dimensions of human experience. As humanity advances, we will increasingly rely on the interplay between the virtual and real worlds to observe and comprehend our own habits. The virtual world breaks the spatial boundaries of the real world, creating connections between individuals and objects in ways previously unimaginable. In a way, engaging with elements of the past or glimpses of the future within the virtual realm allows us to transcend the constraints of time itself as well.

A future intricately woven from both virtual and real worlds awaits human exploration and discovery. Within this dynamic interplay lies the opportunity for profound growth and deeper self-recognition, elevating our understanding of what it means to be human.

References

Fisher, Irving. *The Nature of Capital and Income*. New York. December 1927.

"41st Statistical Report on Internet Development in China 2018." China Internet Network Information Center. January 2017, p. 22.

Gao, Hongye. *Western Economics: Third Edition (Macroeconomics Part)*. China Renmin University Press, 2004.

Jing, Jipeng. *Information Economics*. Tsinghua University Press, 2004.

Liu, Tong. "Research on the Transmission and Impact of Online Public Opinion in Public Emergencies." Master's thesis, University of Electronic Science and Technology, 2011.

Liu, Zhaode. "Research on the Value Evaluation of High-tech Virtual Enterprises Based on Products." PhD diss., South China University of Technology, 2013.

Luo, Zhengshan. *Information Economics*. Mechanical Industry Press, 2007.

Ma, Qiunan. "Research Review on Bit Economics." Master's thesis, Beijing University of Posts and Telecommunications, 2009.

Pindyck, Robert S, and Daniel L. Rubinfeld. *Microeconomics*. China Renmin University Press, 2004.

Pine, B. Joseph, II, and James H. Gilmore. *The Experience Economy*. Mechanical Industry Press, 2008.

"2017 Mid-Year China Mobile App Store Monitoring Report." iiMedia Consulting, p. 11.

"2017–2018 China Smartphone Market Report." iiMedia Consulting, p. 6.

Yang, Limao. "The Impact of Online Responses to Product Injury Events on Customer Brand Loyalty and Purchase Intentions." *China Circulation Economy*, no. 5 (2015): pp. 80–85.

Zhong, Yixin. *Principles of Information Science*. Beijing University of Posts and Telecommunications Press, 2002.

Zhu, Zhu. "Research on the Demand and Supply of Bit Products." PhD Diss., Beijing University of Posts and Telecommunications, 2013.

Index

Q

R

S

T

U

V

Y

ABOUT THE AUTHOR

Sun Yingxue (b. 1987) is a leading expert in user experience evaluation and digital product strategy. She earned a Master of Engineering from Renmin University of China in 2013 and a Master of Economics from Tsinghua University in 2017. Since 2009, she has worked at China Telecom Group, where she founded the User Experience Design Center in 2014. She leads the development of China Telecom's internet product experience evaluation system and advises on experience design strategies. Currently serving as Vice Chair of the User Experience Alliance China, Sun is a frequent speaker at China User Experience Summits.